THE BIG BOOK OF PALEO SLOW COOKING

THE BIG BOOK OF PALEO SLOW COOKING

200 Nourishing Recipes That Cook Carefree, for Everyday Dinners and Weekend Feasts

NATALIE PERRY

HARVARD COMMON PRESS

Brimming with creative inspiration, how-to projects, and useful information to enrich your everyday life, Quarto Knows is a favorite destination for those pursuing their interests and passions. Visit our site and dig deeper with our books into your area of interest: Quarto Creates, Quarto Cooks, Quarto Homes, Quarto Lives, Quarto Drives, Quarto Explores, Quarto Gifts, or Quarto Kids.

© 2017 Quarto Publishing Group USA Inc.
Text © 2017 Natalie Perry

First Published in 2017 by Harvard Common Press, an imprint of The Quarto Group, 100 Cummings Center, Suite 265-D, Beverly, MA 01915, USA.
T (978) 282-9590 F (978) 283-2742 QuartoKnows.com

Harvard Common Press titles are also available at discount for retail, wholesale, promotional, and bulk purchase. For details, contact the Special Sales Manager by email at specialsales@quarto.com or by mail at The Quarto Group, Attn: Special Sales Manager, 401 Second Avenue North, Suite 310, Minneapolis, MN 55401, USA.

21 20 19 18 17   1 2 3 4 5

ISBN: 978-1-55832-879-2
Digital edition published in 2017
eISBN: 978-1-55832-904-1

Library of Congress Cataloging-in-Publication Data

Perry, Natalie, author.
The big book of Paleo slow cooking : 200 nourishing recipes that cook
    carefree, for everyday dinners and weekend feasts / Natalie Perry.
ISBN 9781558328792 (pbk.) | ISBN 9781558329041 (eISBN)
1. Electric cooking, Slow. 2. Natural foods. 3. Nutrition. 4. Cooking.
TX827 .P47 2017 | 641.5/884--dc23
2017010991

Design and page layout: Laura McFadden Design, Inc.
Photography: Natalie Perry

Printed in China

The information in this book is for educational purposes only. Please see your health-care provider before beginning any new health program.

To Steve: my favorite taste tester and the best pot washer in all the land.

CONTENTS

Welcome to
Paleo Slow Cooking

I am a third-generation cookbook hoarder. The women in my family have always loved to cook, share recipes, and give each other cookbooks as gifts. And talk about food. Boy, do we love food. Well-loved family recipes connect us, and some are treasured as much as family heirlooms—particularly the ones in my mom's or my grandma's handwriting (like my grandma's pineapple pie recipe, which is one of my favorite things on earth). In our family, cooking for each other is one of our deepest expressions of love.

My collection of 60-plus cookbooks isn't quite as impressive as my mother's or my grandmother's, but I think of the well-loved books that have stains, damage, and notes jotted in the margins as dear friends. Some of those discolored, wrinkled pages have slow cooker recipes, and some of my favorite meals from my childhood came out of my mom's orange and brown Rival Crock-Pot. Slow cooking is homey, comforting, and a little magical. Tossing ingredients into a pot and returning later to a hot, delicious meal seems too good to be true.

In this book, I have tried to capture a modernized paleo version of slow cooking that is just as comforting and convenient as I remember. I truly hope that this will become one of your well-loved books too, falling open to a worn, stain-covered page of a recipe that your family adores.

On Slow Cookers

Slow cookers have changed a lot over the years. Units that were made before the mid-1990s could simmer away for eight to ten hours and cook your food beautifully. To avoid safety issues, cookers made later were adjusted to cook hotter—approximately twenty degrees hotter for each setting. What does this mean? The old Rival motto, "Cooks all day while the cook's away," doesn't really apply anymore. The only thing you can leave for more than eight hours (on low!) in a modern slow cooker without ruining it is a really large, tough cut of meat.

The good news is that despite the change in the machines themselves, slow cooking can still be a wonderful and time-saving method of preparing food. Personally, with four young children, I find the early-evening hours from four to six o'clock

incredibly hectic. If I put something into my slow cooker earlier in the day, when I enjoy being in the kitchen, it relieves a lot of stress later on. I also love not having to babysit a pot on the stove. Plus, slow cookers are incredibly great energy savers, using as much energy as a 75-watt lightbulb, and won't heat up your house in the summer months as an oven would. And you can leave your house while your dinner simmers away!

I'm guessing that if you are holding this book, you have an interest in paleo cooking or at least in removing from your diet some of the common foods associated with intolerances and allergies (such as gluten and dairy). For many years, traditional slow cooking was all about "dump, stir, and walk away," and used seasoning packets, cream of whatever soups, and other processed, prepackaged items. Slow cooking, like regular cooking, does require some prep if you're trying to move toward a healthier, whole food–based diet. You may have to chop some vegetables. You may have to sear meat or add an extra ingredient or two to boost flavor. It's worth it, though!

Here are a few more tips to ensure that your slow cooking experience goes smoothly.

What Size Cooker?

Using a slow cooker that's the right size makes all the difference. For a small family, you may need only a two- or four-quart (1.9 or 3.8 liter) cooker. If you've got a larger family, you may want to invest in a six-quart (5.7 liter) cooker. I like having all three sizes because I use them for different reasons.

Two- to three-quart (1.9 to 2.8 liter) cookers are great for desserts, appetizers, and making baby food. Yes, baby food. My youngest had just started eating solids when I was working on this book, and he developed a taste for slow-cooked meat and vegetables. Sometimes I throw some chicken and vegetables into my 2.5-quart (2.4 liter) cooker and make a batch of food just for him for the week.

Four-quart (3.8 liter) cookers are good for feeding our family of six with a bit left over, and I use a six-quart (5.7 liter) cooker for large batches of soup or stew for company—and for large cuts of meat to shred and freeze for later.

Fill It Up

You need to fill your slow cooker at least halfway, but not to the brim. If a cooker isn't full enough, it will reach a hotter temperature due to the empty space in the basin. If it is too full, food or hot liquid may splatter out of the top and may require a longer cooking time. A few recipes in this book intentionally call for a cooker that seems large for the amount of food in order to add color and caramelization. Still, I wouldn't recommend a bigger cooker for all recipes.

Old vs. New Cookers

The cooking times in this book are recommended for modern slow cookers. If you happen to use an older, vintage slow cooker (lucky you!) then add an hour or so for the high setting and two to three hours for the low setting. With a modern slow cooker, I would recommend rarely using the high setting because of the increased temperatures set by manufacturers. You'll get more tender meat, less overcooked vegetables, and no scorching in your pot.

If you have a model with a "warm" setting, I would recommend using that setting for no more than 30 minutes. Some cookers are still too hot on this setting and will continue to cook and possibly overcook the food.

Older slow cookers are sometimes easy to find in thrift shops. My grandma has been collecting vintage cookers for years and stockpiles them in her basement. When I bought my first vintage cooker, my husband teased me and told me we didn't have the basement storage to start collecting those. Though I have only a couple of thrift-store finds, they are my absolute favorites.

If you do buy an older, used cooker, take it to an electrician to make sure that the cord and plug are in good shape and are safe to use. Second, test the slow cooker's temperature. To do this, fill the appliance two-thirds full of cool water. Cover it, turn it on, and let it cook for eight hours. The water should heat to 185°F (85°C). If it is cooler, the slow cooker's temperature is too low and it won't be safe to use. If the temperature is significantly higher, watch the cooking time the first couple of times you use it, and adjust recipes accordingly.

Special Ingredients

If you're new to making paleo substitutions, these ingredients might be new or relatively unfamiliar to you. If you plan on jumping head-first into a paleo lifestyle, I recommend adding these to your pantry staples.

COCONUT AMINOS

These appear quite often in this book. Coconut aminos (not to be confused with soy-based liquid aminos) can be used as a substitute for soy sauce (tamari) and boost umami, one of the five taste senses commonly referred to as savory or meaty. They are less potent, so you'll need to use about double the amount that you would with soy sauce. You can find coconut aminos online, at health-focused grocery stores, and even some regular grocery stores.

NUTRITIONAL YEAST

I have learned to love nutritional yeast over the past couple of years. It is simply dried deactivated yeast and it gives recipes a cheesy flavor. I use it often in dips or other recipes that would normally rely on cheese as a main flavor.

TAPIOCA FLOUR AND ARROWROOT STARCH

Tapioca flour is starch extracted from the cassava root; arrowroot is derived from several tropical plants. Both are neutral tasting and they can be used interchangeably. Both are great for thickening, emulsifying, and using in grain-free baking.

GHEE

Ghee is simply butter with the milk solids removed. You can buy ghee at some grocery stores or online, or you can make it yourself. It's easy. (See Homemade Ghee, page 287.) Ghee adds a delicious buttery flavor to sauces or to seared meat—and because the milk solids have been removed, ghee won't burn when heated to higher temperatures.

BLANCHED ALMOND FLOUR

Blanched almond flour is finer than regular almond flour or almond meal, and is made from almonds that have had their skins removed. To get consistently good results from the recipes in this book, I recommend extra fine, blanched almond flour. Almond flour that is too coarse makes baked goods grainy and dense.

WHITE POTATOES AND RICE

Whether or not white potatoes and rice are considered paleo depends on who you ask. The paleo community is divided, but most accept them in small, moderate amounts. We eat both at our house regularly. They are both resistant starches, meaning that after they have been cooked and cooled, they are digestion-resistant, acting as soluble fiber and feeding the good bacteria in your gut.

I used white potatoes, in a few recipes in this book, but you can substitute white or orange sweet potatoes, or even parsnips if you like. None of the recipes in this book call for rice, but if you feel you can tolerate small amounts of rice, feel free to use it when the recipe suggests Cauliflower Rice (pages 249 and 250) as a side dish.

SWEETENERS

Natural sweeteners are a tricky subject. Some paleo purists eat only a minuscule amount of honey. Some say that stevia is fine. Some consider any natural sweetener okay in moderation. In this book, I have used honey, pure maple syrup, coconut sugar, and stevia.

APPETIZERS AND SNACKS

1

No potluck table is complete without a slow cooker full of meatballs, but what about bringing a pot of wings or a hearty dip next time? Whether you're attending a party or entertaining at home, your guests will be pleasantly surprised to find out they can have seconds (or thirds) of your dish without post-party regrets.

Recipes

Easy BBQ Wings

This is such a versatile, adaptable recipe! You can use any combination of barbecue rub and sauce you like. The rub recipe referenced is a great all-purpose blend that would go with any of the barbecue sauce recipes in the Pantry Basics chapter (page 278) or any of your own creations. Making the sauce ahead of time makes these a snap!

Prep time 10 minutes
Serves 6

20 bone-in chicken wings
1½ tablespoons BBQ Dry-Rub Seasoning (page 288)

¼ teaspoon sea salt
2 cups (500 g) BBQ sauce (pages 289–291)

1 Rub the chicken wings with BBQ Dry-Rub Seasoning and salt.

2 Place the wings in a 4-quart (3.8 liter) slow cooker. Pour ½ cup (125 g) BBQ sauce over the wings.

3 Cover and cook on low for 3 to 4 hours.

4 Preheat the oven broiler.

5 Transfer the wings to a rimmed baking sheet lined with aluminum foil. Broil for about 10 minutes on high, until the wings begin to turn golden brown in spots.

6 Warm the remaining BBQ sauce if it is cold, and toss a cup of it with the wings. Add the rest if you like them extra saucy.

7 Serve hot.

Lemon-Garlic Wings with Cracked Pepper Sauce

Can I make a confession? I'm not a fan of chicken skin. It's a texture issue for me, so I never understood the appeal of eating wings. Not eating wing skin means a whole lot of picking through skin, membranes, and bones for a mildly flavorful sliver of meat. The labor and mess involved never seemed worth it to me. My three-year-old daughter, however, will clean off a wing or drumstick bone without flinching. She finished off about a half-dozen wings during one testing session. Don't worry, I did taste them and found the sauces I licked from the skin absolutely delicious with my meat sliver.

Anyway, lemon, garlic, and herbs are my favorite flavor combination for chicken—particularly whole roasted ones. Wings are a little more casual and remind me of game-day food, so I created a peppery sauce to give them a little kick.

Prep time 15 minutes
Makes 20 wings

20 bone-in chicken wings

1 teaspoon sea salt

¼ teaspoon black pepper

1 medium lemon (for zest and juice)

8 cloves garlic, minced

2 sprigs fresh thyme

½ cup (120 ml) Simple Chicken Stock (page 280)

2 teaspoons tapioca flour or arrowroot starch

2 teaspoons whole black peppercorns

2 teaspoons honey

1 Sprinkle the wings with salt, pepper, and 2 teaspoons lemon zest, and rub the seasonings into the wings. Place them in a 4-quart (3.8 liter) slow cooker. Stir in the garlic and add the thyme sprigs on top.

2 Cover and cook for 2 hours on high. When the wings are finished, they should be mostly cooked through, and tender.

3 Preheat the oven broiler and cover a rimmed baking sheet with foil or spray with nonstick cooking spray.

4 Transfer the wings to the prepared baking sheet and broil for 10 to 12 minutes, until the skin has crisped up and is golden brown.

5 Meanwhile, pour the cooking juices from the pot into a large skillet. Whisk the stock and the tapioca flour together in a small measuring cup and pour into the skillet.

6 Place the peppercorns in a small plastic bag or wrap them in a paper towel. Hit them with a wooden spoon to crack them into small pieces. Add the cracked pepper to the skillet with 2 teaspoons (10 ml) of lemon juice and the honey.

7 Heat the sauce on medium-high heat, until bubbly. Reduce heat to medium-low and let it simmer for 2 to 3 minutes, stirring often, until thickened. Taste it, and add a pinch of salt, if necessary.

8 When the wings come out of the oven, transfer them to the skillet and toss them in the sauce. Place the wings on a platter and serve.

Pomegranate-Glazed Wings

I have a slight pomegranate juice fetish. It's the only fruit juice we keep in the house regularly, and though we don't drink it straight, it adds a nice, tart brightness to smoothies. I also love using it in unexpected ways. Cooking off some of the water in the juice leaves an intensely tart-sweet-sticky glaze in the most beautiful wine color—perfect for mustard-marinated chicken wings. Grab some extra napkins!

Prep time 15 minutes
Makes 20 wings

20 bone-in chicken wings

1 teaspoon sea salt

¼ teaspoon black pepper

2 cloves garlic, minced

2 tablespoons (22 g) stone-ground mustard

1 tablespoon avocado oil

2 cups (475 ml) unsweetened pomegranate juice

¼ cup (60 ml) red wine vinegar

2 pinches of crushed red pepper flakes

1 Rub the chicken wings with salt, pepper, garlic, and mustard. Place them in a 4-quart (3.8 liter) slow cooker and drizzle them with avocado oil.

2 Cover and cook the wings on high for about 3 hours or until the meat is just barely cooked through. It will continue to cook under the broiler.

3 Line a rimmed baking sheet with foil or spray it with nonstick spray. Preheat the broiler.

4 Combine the pomegranate juice, vinegar, and pepper flakes in a medium skillet. Heat the mixture over medium-high heat and cook for 10 to 15 minutes, stirring often, until the mixture has thickened to a syrup-like consistency, and has reduced to about ½ cup (306 g).

5 Transfer the wings skin-side up to the baking sheet and broil for 10 to 12 minutes, until the skin is crispy and golden brown.

6 When the wings come out of the oven, toss them around in the glaze to coat them. Serve hot.

Sausage-Stuffed Mini Peppers and Pesto Dip

Talk about an easy appetizer! I love using spicy sausage for these—it's such a nice contrast with the cool pesto dip. If you happen to have any of these left over (I doubt you will, but you never know), chop them up, throw them in a skillet with some eggs, and serve them with the leftover pesto dip. I love leftover breakfast hashes!

Prep time 15 minutes

Makes 24 peppers

24 mini bell peppers

8 to 10 ounces (225 to 280 g) bulk spicy or sweet Italian sausage

¾ cup (175 g) Paleo-Friendly Mayonnaise (page 286)

¼ cup (65 g) Paleo Pesto (page 293)

1 tablespoon (15 ml) freshly squeezed lemon juice

1 Cut the tops off the peppers and remove any large membranes.

2 Using a small spoon, stuff the peppers with sausage and arrange them sausage-side up in a 2-quart (1.9 liter) slow cooker. There should be enough peppers to fill the cooker.

3 Cover and cook on low for 3 to 4 hours, until the sausage is cooked through.

4 Mix the mayonnaise, pesto, and lemon juice together. Taste, and add a pinch of salt, if necessary.

5 Serve the stuffed peppers warm with the pesto dip.

Curried Turkey and Cranberry Meatballs with Clementine Salsa

A platter of these meatballs and salsa would be a beautiful (and tasty!) addition to a holiday potluck and will use up some of those fresh cranberries and clementines you might have around during the season. Or add some Cauliflower Rice (pages 249 and 250) to round it out into a full meal.

Prep time 25 minutes
Makes 18 to 20 meatballs

For the meatballs:

1½ pounds (680 g) ground turkey

1 teaspoon sea salt

1½ teaspoons turmeric

1½ teaspoons ground coriander

½ teaspoon ground cumin

¼ teaspoon black pepper

Pinch of cayenne pepper

2 cloves garlic

⅔ cup (73 g) finely chopped fresh cranberries

2 tablespoons (29 ml) avocado oil

Fresh chopped cilantro and thinly sliced green onions, for garnish

For the salsa:

8 clementine oranges

½ an English cucumber, diced

1 jalapeño pepper, seeded, and minced

1 tablespoon (15 ml) lemon juice

2 green onions, thinly sliced

¼ cup fresh chopped cilantro

1 Combine all of the meatball ingredients (except for the oil and garnishes) in a medium bowl. Toss gently with your hands to combine thoroughly.

2 Form the mixture into 2-inch (5 cm) balls and set them on a large plate.

3 Heat the avocado oil in a large cast-iron or stainless-steel skillet over medium-high heat. In two batches, brown the meatballs on both sides and then transfer them to a 4-quart (3.8 liter) slow cooker. This forms a stiff crust on the outside and helps them to keep their shape in the slow cooker. It also adds a lot of flavor! You don't need to cook them all the way through.

4 Add ⅓ cup (80 ml) of water to the slow cooker. Close and cook for 2 hours on low.

5 Combine the salsa ingredients and chill until ready to serve.

6 Transfer the meatballs to a serving platter and spoon the cooking juices over the top. Sprinkle the cilantro and green onions over the meatballs. Serve the meatballs with the salsa.

Ginger-Scallion Turkey Meatballs with Chili Mayo

If you've never tried sambal oelek—*chili garlic sauce used primarily in southeast Asia— you should! It not only adds heat, but also a wonderfully garlicky kind of flavor. It's easy to find in regular grocery stores in the Asian food section and is just as versatile as hot sauces.*

Prep time 25 minutes

Makes about 26 meatballs

For the meatballs:

2 pounds (905 g) ground turkey

4 scallions, thinly sliced

2-inch (5 cm) knob of ginger, grated finely or minced

2 cloves garlic, minced

1½ teaspoons sea salt

1 teaspoon sambal oelek or other chili garlic sauce

2 to 4 tablespoons (29 to 59 ml) avocado oil

¼ cup (60 ml) chicken broth

For the chili mayo:

1 cup (225 g) Paleo-Friendly Mayonnaise (page 286)

2 tablespoons (30 g) sambal oelek or other chili garlic sauce

3 tablespoons chopped fresh cilantro

2 teaspoons (10 ml) freshly squeezed lime juice

¼ teaspoon sea salt

1 In a large mixing bowl, combine the ground turkey, scallions, ginger, garlic, salt, and chili garlic sauce. Mix everything together gently, using your hands. Roll the mixture into 1½-inch (2.6 cm) balls and set them on a large plate.

2 Heat 2 tablespoons (29 ml) of avocado oil in a large nonstick or cast-iron skillet over medium-high heat. Working in batches, sear the meatballs on two sides until golden brown, adding more oil if necessary. They do not need to be cooked through. Transfer the seared meatballs to a 4-quart (3.8 liter) slow cooker. Pour the chicken broth into the slow cooker.

3 Cover and cook on low for 3 to 4 hours, until the meatballs are cooked through.

4 Combine the ingredients for the chili mayo and stir well. Refrigerate until ready to use.

5 Serve the meatballs with the chili mayo.

BBQ Hotdog Bites

A ubiquitous recipe for little smokies cooked in BBQ sauce and grape jelly is floating around church potlucks. I created a healthier, naturally-sweetened version using grass-fed, uncured hotdog bites, homemade BBQ sauce, and a grape juice reduction. I couldn't keep little fingers (or my own, for that matter) out of the pot, so I think I did the original recipe justice.

Prep time 15 minutes
Serves 10

2 cups (475 ml) unsweetened grape juice
2 pounds (905 g) grass-fed, uncured hotdogs, cut into 1-inch (2.5 cm) pieces

1½ cup (375 g) homemade BBQ sauce
¼ teaspoon liquid smoke

1 Simmer the grape juice in a medium skillet over medium-high heat until it has reduced to about ½ cup (160 g).

2 Put the hotdog bits into a 2- or 3-quart (1.9 or 2.8 liter) slow cooker.

3 Pour the BBQ sauce, liquid smoke, and reduced grape juice on top of the hotdogs and give it a big stir.

4 Cover and cook on high for 2 to 2½ hours.

Note: Try the Balsamic BBQ Sauce (page 290) or Blackberry-Chipotle BBQ Sauce (page 291) with this recipe.

Chicken Sausage and Pineapple Bites

If you're eating strictly paleo and you get invited to a potluck, you'll want to bring something to guarantee that you can eat. These tasty sausage and pineapple bites go beautifully with a green salad—which almost always appears on a party buffet line.

Prep time 15 minutes
Serves 6

1 pound (455 g) chicken-apple sausage, cut into 1-inch (2.5 cm) pieces

3 cups (495 g) fresh pineapple, cut into 1-inch (2.5 cm) pieces

Juice from 1 large orange (about ⅓ cup, or 80 ml)

¼ cup (40 g) minced red onion

Pinch of salt

Pinch of crushed red pepper flakes

1 Spear one piece of sausage and one piece of pineapple on a toothpick. Repeat with all of the sausage and pineapple. Put the sausage-pineapple bites into a 2- or 3-quart (1.9 or 2.8 liter) slow cooker.

2 Combine the orange juice, red onion, salt, and pepper flakes in a small bowl. Mix well, and pour it over the sausage and pineapple in the slow cooker.

3 Close and cook on low heat for 5 to 6 hours, tossing the bites around once during cooking, until the pineapple is heated through and the sausage is browned in places.

4 Transfer the bites to a serving platter and drizzle some of the cooking juices over the top before serving.

Balsamic Herb–Braised Mushrooms

Paleo appetizers in the slow cooker don't have to be made entirely of meat, and these mushrooms would make a light, tangy addition to a party spread. You can also whip up a batch and keep them in the fridge to chop up and throw in your morning eggs during the week.

Prep time 10 minutes
Serves 8

1½ pounds (680 g) baby portobello mushrooms
¼ teaspoon sea salt
¼ teaspoon black pepper
¼ cup (60 ml) balsamic vinegar
2 cloves garlic

2 tablespoons (29 ml) avocado oil
2 teaspoons honey
2 sprigs fresh thyme
2 sprigs fresh rosemary

1 Place the mushrooms in a 4-quart (3.8 liter) slow cooker and sprinkle with salt and pepper.

2 Whisk together the vinegar, garlic, oil, and honey, and pour it over the mushrooms. Place the herbs on top.

3 Cover and cook on low for 2½ to 3 hours, stirring once halfway through.

4 Taste, and add a little salt if necessary.

5 Serve warm.

Note: You can substitute ¼ teaspoon each of dried thyme and rosemary if you can't find fresh herbs.

Caramelized Onion Dip

It's hard to describe how much I love this dip. Make sure to include the nutritional yeast, which gives the dip the cheesy flavor you'd normally get by adding cheese or cream cheese to a creamy dip recipe. Sprinkling some crispy bacon bits on top wouldn't be a bad idea either.

Prep time 15 minutes
Makes about 3 cups (720 g) of dip

2 pounds (905 g) sweet yellow onions, diced

2 tablespoons (30 g) Homemade Ghee (page 287)

2 sprigs fresh rosemary or ½ teaspoon dried

Sea salt

1 recipe Paleo-Friendly Mayonnaise (page 286)

1 clove garlic, minced

2 tablespoons nutritional yeast

1 tablespoon (15 ml) coconut aminos

2 teaspoons onion powder

2 teaspoons Dijon mustard

Hot sauce, to taste

1 Place the onions, ghee, rosemary, and ¼ teaspoon sea salt in a 2- or 3-quart (1.9 or 2.8 liter) slow cooker.

2 Cover and cook on high for 2 hours, stirring halfway through.

3 Transfer the onions to a medium bowl and let them cool completely. Drain any excess juices.

4 Stir in the mayonnaise, garlic, nutritional yeast, coconut aminos, onion powder, mustard, and hot sauce. Taste, and add a pinch or two of salt if necessary.

5 Dip is best served chilled, but can be served at room temperature.

6 Serve with vegetable chips or as a topping for baked potatoes or hamburgers. It's also fantastic on eggs.

Hot Jalapeño Artichoke Dip

We buy this dip once in a while at a big chain store, and it's quite possibly the most addictive dip on earth. I made a cleaned-up version of that smooth, creamy, jalapeño artichoke dip—and it's also hard to eat in moderation!

Prep time 15 minutes
Serves 8 to 10 as an appetizer

1½ cups (340 g) Paleo-Friendly Mayonnaise (page 286)

1 12-ounce (340 g) bottle marinated artichokes, drained and chopped

2 jalapeño peppers, seeded (optional), and diced small

2 egg whites

2 cloves garlic, minced

3 tablespoons (15 g) nutritional yeast

1½ teaspoons Dijon mustard

1½ teaspoons sea salt

¾ teaspoon onion powder

Cut-up vegetables and mini peppers, for serving

1 Stir together all of the dip ingredients in a 1½- or 2-quart (1.4 or 1.9 liter) slow cooker.

2 Cover and cook on low for 2 to 3 hours, until the dip is heated through and the sides are bubbly and begin to turn golden brown.

3 Serve dip with vegetables.

Spicy Crab and Avocado Dip with Jicama Chips

There's a lot going on in this dip—real, flaky crab, creamy avocados, and spicy bites from the jalapeño pepper and hot sauce. Traditional crab dips usually contain cheese or cream cheese, but this one gets its smooth texture from clean (meaning, paleo-friendly) mayonnaise and a bit of nutritional yeast. Nutritional yeast may sound unappealing to some, but it's a popular addition to vegan and dairy-free foods to give it a cheesy type of flavor. Try this warm, spicy dip on cool, thinly sliced jicama "chips" and you may forget that the dairy is missing.

Prep time 15 minutes
Serves 8

1 pound (455 g) lump crabmeat
½ red bell pepper, diced
1 jalapeño, seeded and diced
2 green onions, thinly sliced
1 cup (225 g) Paleo-Friendly Mayonnaise (page 286)
1 garlic clove, minced
¼ cup (60 ml) freshly squeezed lemon juice, divided (about 1 large lemon)

2 tablespoons (30 ml) coconut aminos
1 tablespoon nutritional yeast
1 tablespoon (15 g) hot sauce
½ teaspoon fish sauce
½ teaspoon sea salt
1 avocado, peeled, pitted, and diced
¼ cup fresh chopped cilantro, for garnish
1 large jicama, peeled and quartered, for serving

1 Place the crab, bell pepper, jalapeño, and green onions in a 2- or 3-quart (1.9 or 2.8 liter) slow cooker.

2 In a small bowl, whisk together the mayonnaise, garlic, lemon juice, coconut aminos, nutritional yeast, hot sauce, fish sauce, and salt. Pour into the slow cooker and stir well. Fold in the diced avocado. Use a rubber spatula to scrape the sauce from the sides of the cooker above the dip.

3 Cover and cook on low for 2½ to 3 hours. Stir once halfway through.

4 Stir the rest of the lemon juice into the dip and sprinkle with the cilantro. Taste, and add more salt if necessary.

5 Slice the jicama sections very thinly into "chips," using a mandoline slicer, if possible.

6 Serve the dip warm with the jicama chips.

Note: Nutritional yeast is simply dried, deactivated single-strain yeast, and you can find it at many health food stores or the bulk section of some grocery stores.

Buffalo Chicken Dip

Here's another popular game-day appetizer turned paleo! Finding paleo cayenne pepper sauce (or wing sauce) is fairly easy. Just check the ingredient list to make sure it does not contain sugar, vegetable oil, or other additives. To make this dip even faster, you can use 4 cups (560 g) of cooked, mildly seasoned chicken and start at step 4. Be sure to add a half-hour of cooking time if the chicken is cold.

Prep time 20 minutes
Serves 8

3 pounds (1.4 kg) boneless, skinless chicken thighs (about 10 thighs)

3 cloves garlic

1½ teaspoons all-purpose no-salt seasoning

1 teaspoon sea salt

¼ teaspoon black pepper

1 cup (225 g) Paleo-Friendly Mayonnaise (page 286)

½ cup (120 ml) almond milk

⅓ cup (80 ml) cayenne pepper sauce, plus more for serving

4 teaspoons nutritional yeast

¼ teaspoon chipotle powder

Celery and carrot sticks, for serving

1 Place the chicken in a 2- or 3-quart (1.9 or 2.8 liter) slow cooker. Add the garlic, no-salt seasoning, salt, and pepper. Use your hands to blend the seasonings all over the chicken.

2 Cover and cook on high for 2½ to 3 hours.

3 Transfer the chicken to a large plate and discard the cooking juices. Shred the chicken finely and return it to the slow cooker.

4 In a medium bowl, whisk together the mayonnaise, almond milk, cayenne pepper sauce, nutritional yeast, and chipotle powder. Stir the mayonnaise mixture into the chicken.

5 Cover and cook on high for another 30 to 45 minutes, until thoroughly heated and bubbly.

6 Taste, and add more cayenne pepper sauce for a spicier dip.

7 Serve hot with celery and carrot sticks.

Bacon Chili Dip

This dip is like concentrated chili. It can be used as much more than a dip for vegetable chips—as a topping for burgers, hotdogs, baked potatoes, or sweet potato fries!

Prep time 20 minutes
Serves 10 to 12

1 pound (455 g) ground pork
1 pound (455 g) ground beef
2 cloves garlic, minced
2 tablespoons (15 g) chili powder
1 tablespoon dried minced onion
1 teaspoon ground cumin
1 teaspoon sea salt

½ teaspoon black pepper
½ teaspoon chipotle powder
1 6-ounce (170 gram) can tomato paste
1 bell pepper (any color), diced
2 cups (475 ml) beef or chicken broth, plus more if needed
1 12- or 16-ounce (340 or 455 gram) package of bacon

1 Brown the pork and beef in a large skillet over medium-high heat. Strain out the excess grease if necessary.

2 Add the garlic, chili powder, onion, cumin, salt, black pepper, and chipotle powder to the skillet. Stir it well and cook for about a minute. Stir in the tomato paste, working it into the meat.

3 Transfer the meat mixture to a 2- or 3-quart (1.9 or 2.8 liter) slow cooker. Add the bell pepper and broth. Stir well.

4 Cover and cook on high for 2 to 3 hours.

5 Cut the bacon into small strips and cook in a large skillet until crispy. Remove with a slotted spoon and place on a paper towel to soak up the excess grease. Stir the bacon into the chili dip. If it seems too thick, add a little more broth until it's the consistency you prefer.

6 Serve warm with veggie chips.

Spicy Curried Mango-Pineapple Chutney

Sometimes I get a stubborn idea in my head that won't go away—like creating a chutney recipe before I had ever eaten chutney. After doing some research and brainstorming with my brother, who ate chutney nearly every day when he spent two years in South Africa, I created a winner. I adore this spicy-sweet concoction and threw it on my eggs every day for a week. As an appetizer, this would be fabulous paired with baked sweet potato fries or chips.

Prep time 15 minutes
Makes 1 pint (450 g)

1 cup (170 g) fresh or frozen mango chunks

1 cup (165 g) fresh or frozen pineapple chunks

⅓ cup (50 g) unsweetened golden raisins

1 cup (160 g) chopped sweet yellow onion

3 tablespoons (60 g) honey

3 tablespoons (45 ml) white wine vinegar

1-inch (2.5 cm) knob of fresh ginger, finely grated

2 cloves garlic, minced

1 tablespoon (20 g) pure maple syrup

1 to 3 teaspoons (5 to 15 g) Asian chili garlic sauce, to taste

1 teaspoon sea salt

½ teaspoon ground coriander

½ teaspoon turmeric

1 Combine all of the ingredients into a 2- or 3-quart (1.9 or 2.8 liter) slow cooker.

2 Cover and cook on high for 2 to 3 hours.

3 Pulse a few times, preferably with an immersion blender, until the mixture is the desired smoothness.

Sticky Cinnamon Vanilla-Bean Almonds

To me, the only enjoyable part of a shopping mall during the holidays is the smell of cinnamon almonds wafting through the air. Luckily, you don't have to fight the crowds to have that glorious smell—and you can eat these all year round.

Prep time 10 minutes
Makes 4 cups (380 g) of nuts

4 cups (380 g) whole raw almonds
¼ cup (80 g) pure maple syrup
2 tablespoons (40 g) honey
½ teaspoon cinnamon
1 vanilla bean
Sea salt

1 Place the almonds, maple syrup, honey, and cinnamon in a 2- or 3-quart (1.9 or 2.8 liter) slow cooker.

2 Using the point of a sharp knife, split open the vanilla bean. Scrape out the black specks with the back of the knife and place them in the slow cooker. Give the nuts a good stir so they are evenly coated.

3 Cover and cook on low for 3 hours, stirring once halfway through.

4 Spread the nuts out on a sheet pan to cool, and sprinkle them with a pinch or two of sea salt. When they're cool, transfer them to a serving bowl.

Rosemary Black Pepper Cashews

Without fail, between two and three o'clock every afternoon, I get the munchies and end up hunting in the cupboards for something to eat. When I have a bowl of these peppery, herby cashews on the counter, they always hit the spot.

Prep time 5 minutes
Makes 4 cups (548 g) of nuts

4 cups (572 g) raw cashews,
whole or pieces

1½ teaspoons minced fresh rosemary

¾ teaspoon sea salt

¾ teaspoon coarsely ground
black pepper

2 tablespoons (29 ml) avocado oil

1 Combine all of the ingredients in a 2- or 3-quart (1.9 or 2.8 liter) slow cooker. Stir them together well.

2 Cover and cook on low for 2½ to 3 hours, stirring once halfway through cooking. Some of the nuts should be golden brown.

3 Remove the nuts from the cooker and let them cool for a few minutes before serving.

Sweet and Smoky Mixed Nuts

For years I've made spiced or sweetened nuts to add to a crunchy bite to dinner salads—in lieu of nonnutritious croutons. It occurred to me recently that making a larger batch and keeping it on hand makes a great snack, too. Smoked paprika, maple, and cayenne is one of my favorite combinations. I love how the smoky-hot spices play off the maple and how the nuts soften slightly in the slow cooker.

Prep time 10 minutes

Makes about 8 cups (1.0 kg) of nuts

1½ pounds (680 g) raw nuts (such as almonds, walnuts, pecans, cashews, and hazelnuts)

⅓ cup (107 ml) pure maple syrup

¼ cup (59 ml) avocado oil

2 teaspoons smoked paprika

1 teaspoon sea salt

½ teaspoon cayenne pepper

1 Place the nuts in a 2- or 3-quart (1.9 or 2.8 liter) slow cooker.

2 Stir together the remaining ingredients in a small bowl, then pour it over the nuts. Stir everything together so the nuts are well coated.

3 Cover and cook on low for 3 hours, stirring halfway through.

4 Transfer to a serving dish and serve warm or cold. Store in an airtight container at room temperature.

SOUPS AND CHILIS

2

I absolutely adore soup. If I had my way, most of the recipes in this book would be for soups and chilis. Here you'll find light, pureed soups for warmer weather and chunky vegetable soups, chowders, stews, and chilis for crisp, cool weather. All of these freeze well, so stash the leftovers on ice and your future self will thank you.

Recipes

Pureed Summer Squash Soup with Spicy Ghee

Bright, yellow summer squash transforms this soup into a cheerful color. This soup screams summertime, and it's a great way to use up the squash that spills out of your garden. The spicy, buttery ghee is definitely one to try.

Prep time 15 minutes
Serves 6

For the soup:

2 pounds (905 g) yellow summer squash, seeded and chopped into 1-inch (2.5 cm) pieces

2 large carrots, peeled and chopped into 1-inch (2.5 cm) pieces

1 large celery rib, chopped into 1-inch (2.5 cm) pieces

1 small onion, chopped

2 small red potatoes, chopped

6 cloves garlic

1 teaspoon of sea salt

½ teaspoon black pepper

¼ teaspoon dried thyme

1 teaspoon grated lemon zest (about ½ of a lemon)

Pinch of cayenne pepper

1 quart (946 ml) Simple Chicken Stock (page 280)

2 tablespoons (30 ml) freshly squeezed lemon juice

For the spicy ghee:

8 tablespoons (116 g) Homemade Ghee (page 287) or grass-fed butter

¼ to ½ teaspoon crushed red pepper flakes, or to taste

1 Place the squash, carrots, celery, onion, potatoes, garlic, salt, pepper, thyme, lemon zest, cayenne pepper, and chicken stock in a 4-quart (3.8 liter) slow cooker. Cover and cook on low for 6 to 7 hours (or on high for 3 to 4 hours).

2 Transfer the soup in batches to a blender and process until smooth. You can also use an immersion blender, but you might not get a super smooth consistency. Transfer the soup back to the slow cooker when blended.

3 Melt the ghee in a small skillet. Measure out 2 tablespoons (30 g) and stir it in to the soup. Add the red pepper flakes to the remaining melted ghee and let it simmer for 2 minutes. Remove from heat.

4 Stir the lemon juice into the soup and taste. Add more salt if necessary.

5 Serve the soup with a drizzle of spicy ghee.

Hazelnut Parsnip Soup (Rapunzel's Favorite)

According to Disney's movie Tangled, *hazelnut soup is Rapunzel's favorite. My girls didn't need any convincing to try this, and ate two bowls each at dinner and two more for lunch the next day. If your dinner guests are over the age of six, they may also appreciate this light, sophisticated take on a root-vegetable soup.*

Prep time 45 minutes
Serves 6

1½ cups (203 g) whole hazelnuts
5 tablespoons (71.3 g) Homemade Ghee (page 287) or grass-fed butter
4 medium shallots, chopped
3 leeks (white parts only), chopped
2 large parsnips, peeled and chopped

1½ teaspoons salt
½ teaspoon black pepper
1 tablespoon tapioca flour
6 cups (1.4 liters) vegetable or Simple Chicken Stock (page 280)
1 cup (235 ml) unsweetened almond milk

1 Preheat the oven to 350°F (177°C).

2 Spread the hazelnuts on a rimmed baking sheet and roast them for 10 to 15 minutes, until they are toasted and fragrant.

3 Transfer the nuts to a clean kitchen towel. Fold the towel around the nuts and roughen them up to remove most of the skins. (It's fine if they don't all come off.)

4 In a large, heavy pot, heat the ghee over medium-high heat. Add the shallots, leeks, parsnips, salt, and pepper, and cook for 10 to 12 minutes, until the shallots and leeks have softened. Transfer mixture to a 4-quart (3.8 liter) slow cooker.

5 Whisk the tapioca flour into 1 cup (235 ml) of the stock. Pour into the cooker along with the remaining 5 cups (1.2 liters) of stock and 1 cup (135 g) of the toasted hazelnuts. Cover and cook on low for 6 to 7 hours on low (or 3 to 4 hours on high). The parsnips should be fork tender.

6 Transfer the soup to a high-power blender in batches and blend until smooth. You can also use an immersion blender within the slow cooker, but you may not get a smooth consistency without straining the soup.

7 Return the soup to the cooker and add the almond milk. Taste, and add more salt if necessary. You may need to add more if you use homemade, unsalted stock. If you need to reheat the soup, close the cooker and cook on high for about 15 minutes.

8 Chop the remaining ½ cup (68 g) toasted hazelnuts and sprinkle them over the soup when ready to serve.

Butternut Squash and Apple Soup

This soup is one of the first things I make when fall arrives, and butternut squash and apples are abundant. They are a winning combination here—especially with a sprinkle of salty, crispy bacon on top. (If you use dairy, a sprinkle of grass-fed cheddar raises this soup to another level.)

Prep time 20 minutes
Serves 6

1 medium onion, chopped into large chunks

3 cups peeled, seeded, and chopped butternut squash

2 medium red potatoes, chopped into large chunks

2 large tart apples, cored and chopped into large chunks

2 tablespoons (29 g) Homemade Ghee (page 287) or grass-fed butter

1 tablespoon tapioca flour

1 teaspoon dried sage

1 teaspoon salt

1 quart (946 ml) Simple Chicken Stock (page 280)

½ cup (120 ml) unfiltered, unsweetened apple juice or apple cider

1 cup (235 ml) unsweetened almond milk

1 12- or 16-ounce (340 or 455 gram) package of bacon, cooked and crumbled

1 Place the onion, squash, potatoes, apples, and ghee into a 4-quart (3.8 liter) slow cooker.

2 Sprinkle the tapioca flour, sage, and salt over the vegetables and give it a quick stir.

3 Pour the stock, apple juice, and almond milk into the cooker.

4 Cover and cook for 7 to 8 hours on low (or 3 to 4 hours on high).

5 Transfer the soup to a high-power blender in batches and blend until smooth. You can also use an immersion blender in the slow cooker, but you may not get a smooth consistency.

6 Garnish with crumbled bacon and serve.

Creamy Mushroom Soup with Bacon

According to my kids, this is Creamy Bacon Soup. They still have no idea that a main ingredient is mushrooms, which they despise. I may spill the beans down the road—perhaps when they're packing to leave for college. We love how creamy and filling it is, and you'd never know it was dairy free!

Prep time 20 min

Serves 6

1 pound (455 g) brown mushrooms, quartered

1 medium onion, cut into large chunks

6 cloves garlic, smashed

1 sprig fresh rosemary

3 tablespoons (45 ml) red wine vinegar

2 tablespoons (30 ml) coconut aminos

1 teaspoon sea salt

1 quart (946 ml) Homemade Beef Stock (page 281)

2 cups (475 ml) unsweetened almond milk

1 12- or 16-ounce (340 or 455 gram) package of bacon

1 Place all ingredients except the bacon into a 4-quart (3.8 liter) slow cooker.

2 Cover and cook on low for 6 to 7 hours (or 3 to 4 hours on high).

3 Meanwhile, cook the bacon according to your liking. Crumble it and set it aside.

4 When the soup is finished, blend it with an immersion blender or in batches using a blender.

5 Taste the soup and adjust seasonings if necessary. If you make your own beef stock and do not salt it, you might want to add a teaspoon or so of salt. Adding another tablespoon (15 ml) of vinegar will also help brighten the flavors.

6 Serve the soup topped with crumbled bacon.

Broccoli "Cheese" Soup with Crispy Prosciutto

If you don't have an immersion blender, I'd highly recommend investing in one. They're relatively inexpensive, easy to clean, and you'll be glad you have one for pureeing soups and sauces. This soup buzzes together beautifully, and the crispy, salty prosciutto is better than any cracker you could break over the top.

Prep time 20 minutes

Serves 6

1½ to 2 pounds (680 to 905 g) broccoli crowns

2 leeks, trimmed and chopped

4 cloves garlic, smashed

1 lemon, zested and juiced

2 tablespoons (30 ml) coconut aminos

1 tablespoon Dijon mustard

½ teaspoon sea salt

¼ teaspoon black pepper

6 cups (1.4 liters) chicken broth

¼ cup (20 g) nutritional yeast

1 13.5-ounce (398 ml) can coconut milk, chilled

2 tablespoons (30 g) Homemade Ghee (page 287), plus more for frying

10 slices prosciutto

1 Cut ⅔ of the broccoli into large florets and put them in a 4-quart (3.8 liter) slow cooker. Cut the remaining broccoli into 1-inch (2.5 cm) florets and set aside.

2 Add the leeks, garlic, ½ teaspoon lemon zest, coconut aminos, mustard, salt, pepper, chicken broth, and nutritional yeast.

3 Cover and cook for 5 to 6 hours on low. Place the coconut milk in the refrigerator if it isn't chilled yet.

4 Blend the soup, preferably with an immersion blender. Stir in the ghee and the reserved broccoli florets.

5 Open the coconut-milk can from the bottom and drain the liquid. (You can throw it into a smoothie later.) Scrape out the hardened cream and stir it into the soup.

6 Cover and cook for another 15 minutes.

7 Meanwhile, add a couple of teaspoons ghee to a large skillet. Fry the prosciutto in batches in a large skillet over medium heat, flipping once halfway through cooking. It should take only a few minutes for the strips to become crisp. Crumble them up and put them in a bowl.

8 Taste the soup and add more salt or a squeeze of lemon juice if necessary.

9 Serve with crumbled prosciutto.

Pureed Beet Soup with Apple-Fennel Slaw

When I served this sweet, earthy soup to my three young daughters, they gasped, proclaimed it the color of lipstick, and happily gobbled it up. The bright, creamy fuchsia color really steals the show and is the reason my favorite color is "beet."

Prep time 30 minutes
Serves 8 to 10

For the soup:

2 pounds (905 g) beets, peeled and cut into 1-inch (2.5 cm) chunks

2 fennel bulbs, fronds removed

2 medium shallots, peeled and quartered

3 medium carrots, peeled and cut into 1-inch (2.5 cm) chunks

1 teaspoon dried tarragon

2 cups (475 ml) unsweetened apple juice

¼ cup (60 ml) red wine vinegar

2 teaspoons Dijon mustard

4 cups (946 ml) Simple Chicken Stock (page 280)

½ teaspoon sea salt

2 medium oranges, zested and juiced, divided

1 14-ounce (400 ml) can full-fat coconut milk

For the slaw:

1 large apple

1 lemon, zested and juiced, divided

For the soup

1 Place beets into a 6-quart (5.7 liter) slow cooker.

2 Trim the fennel bulbs, cut in half, and slice thinly. Place half of the slices into the slow cooker. Place the other half in a medium bowl and set it aside.

3 Place the shallots, carrots, tarragon, apple juice, vinegar, mustard, stock, and sea salt into the cooker. Add the zest and juice from one of the oranges to the cooker as well. Cover and cook for 6 to 7 hours on low (or 3 to 4 hours on high), until beets are fork tender.

4 Blend the soup until smooth, preferably with an immersion blender. Stir in the coconut milk. Taste, and add more salt if necessary. Cover and let it cook for another 10 minutes or so while you get the slaw ready.

For the slaw

5 Cut the apple into thin slices (peeling not necessary) and add it to the bowl with the reserved fennel. Add half of the juice from the other orange, half of the juice from the lemon, and a generous pinch of salt to the bowl. Toss to coat.

6 Serve soup with a couple forkfuls of slaw in each bowl.

Roasted Garlic and Cauliflower Soup with Crispy Leeks

If you raise an eyebrow at the anchovies in this ingredient list, let me explain. If they're not your thing (or you think they probably aren't), just use them anyway. They add a deep, salty, umami flavor to the leeks and seem to "melt" away during cooking. No fishy taste whatsoever. Honest.

Prep time 25 minutes
Serves 6

1 large head cauliflower, trimmed and cut into florets

12 cloves garlic, smashed

2 tablespoons (29 ml) avocado oil

½ teaspoon sea salt

¼ teaspoon black pepper

1 medium to large russet potato (about 12 ounces, or 340 g), peeled and chopped into 1-inch (2.5 cm) cubes

1 medium shallot, diced

2 sprigs of fresh thyme

2 dried bay leaves

1½ quarts (1.4 liters) Simple Chicken Stock (page 280)

1 tablespoon (15 ml) red wine vinegar

1 large or 2 small leeks, trimmed, rinsed, and chopped

4 anchovy fillets, minced, or ½ teaspoon anchovy paste

4 tablespoons (60 g) Homemade Ghee (page 287)

Pinch of crushed red pepper flakes

1 Preheat the oven to 450°F (232°C).

2 Place the cauliflower florets and garlic cloves on a rimmed baking sheet. Drizzle the oil over the top and sprinkle with a couple of generous pinches of salt and the pepper. Toss it all with your hands to coat well and spread the mixture out evenly on the pan.

3 Roast for 15 minutes, flipping the vegetables halfway through, until they are golden brown in spots, and soft.

4 Meanwhile, place the potato, shallot, thyme, bay leaves, chicken stock, and 1 teaspoon of sea salt in a 4-quart (3.8 liter) slow cooker. Add the cauliflower and garlic when it comes out of the oven.

5 Cover and cook for 5 to 6 hours on low.

6 Blend the soup using an immersion blender or a countertop blender. Return the soup to the slow cooker if necessary. Stir in the red wine vinegar. Taste, adding more vinegar or salt if desired.

7 Place the leeks, anchovies, ghee, and pepper flakes in a small skillet. Cook over medium-high heat for 6 to 8 minutes, until the leeks have turned golden brown and have started to crisp slightly. Remove from heat. They should crisp up more as they cool.

8 Serve the soup with a spoonful of crispy leeks on top.

Creamy Asparagus Soup with Dill and Crispy Ham

This soup serves up asparagus two ways: First, blended in a smooth, flavorful soup, and second, roasted with ham and used as an add-in. I love the way the ham gets crispy edges in the oven and gives more flavor to the asparagus bits.

Prep time 20 minutes
Serves 6

2½ pounds (1.1 kg) asparagus, trimmed and cut into 1-inch (2.5 cm) pieces

2 leeks, trimmed and chopped (white and pale green parts only)

2 cloves garlic, minced

2 tablespoons (30 ml) freshly squeezed lemon juice

2 teaspoons Dijon mustard

1 teaspoon sea salt

¼ teaspoon black pepper

1 quart (946 ml) chicken broth

5 slices diced ham

1 tablespoon avocado oil

1 cup (235 ml) full-fat coconut milk

⅓ cup chopped fresh dill

2 tablespoons (30 g) Homemade Ghee (page 287)

1 Place 2 pounds (905 g) of the asparagus in a 4-quart (3.8 liter) slow cooker. Set the remaining ½ pound (225 g) aside for later.

2 Add the leeks, garlic, lemon juice, mustard, sea salt, pepper, and broth to the cooker, and give it a good stir.

3 Cover and cook on low for 4 hours.

4 When the soup is nearly finished cooking, preheat the oven to 425°F (218°C).

5 Place the reserved asparagus and diced ham on a rimmed baking sheet. Drizzle with avocado oil and toss to coat evenly. Roast it for 8 to 10 minutes, until the asparagus has dark spots and the ham has crispy edges.

6 Blend the soup, preferably with an immersion blender, until smooth. Stir in the coconut milk, dill, and ghee. Taste, and add more salt if necessary.

7 Serve with a couple spoonfuls of the roasted asparagus and ham mixture.

Roasted Tomato-Basil Soup with Spicy Tuna

My mom made the best tuna melts—toasting them to melty perfection in a skillet with butter—and we usually ate them with chicken noodle soup. It wasn't until I was an adult that I realized that tuna is great with tomato soup, too. Scooping up the bits of tuna in this soup brings me right back to mom's kitchen table. If you'd rather not add a spicy element to your soup, just omit the crushed red pepper flakes.

Prep time 25 minutes
Serves 6

For the soup:

2 pounds (905 g) medium to large ripe tomatoes

1 pound (455 g) cherry tomatoes or other small tomatoes

1 large onion, halved and sliced

6 cloves garlic, smashed

¼ cup (59 ml) avocado oil

¼ cup (60 ml) plus 1 tablespoon (15 ml) balsamic vinegar

1 teaspoon sea salt, divided

6 cups (1.4 liters) Simple Chicken Stock (page 280)

2 bay leaves

1 tablespoon (20 g) honey (if necessary)

1 bunch fresh basil, leaves removed and thinly sliced into a chiffonade

For the spicy tuna:

7 ounces canned (198 g) tuna, drained

1 tablespoon (15 ml) extra-virgin olive oil

1 tablespoon (15 ml) balsamic vinegar

½ garlic clove, minced

1 large sprig fresh basil

¼ teaspoon crushed red pepper flakes, plus more for serving

Pinch of sea salt and black pepper

1 Preheat the oven broiler.

2 Place the tomatoes, onion, and garlic on a rimmed baking sheet. Drizzle the avocado oil and ¼ cup (60 ml) of balsamic vinegar over the vegetables. Sprinkle ½ teaspoon sea salt over the top. Using your hands, toss everything together and spread it out evenly on the pan.

3 Broil the vegetables for 10 to 12 minutes, until the smaller tomatoes begin to split and the onions begin to turn golden brown in spots.

4 Transfer the roasted vegetables to a 4-quart (3.8 liter) slow cooker. Add the stock, bay leaves, and ½ teaspoon sea salt.

5 Cover and cook on low for 5 hours.

6 Blend the soup, preferably using an immersion blender.

7 Add the remaining 1 tablespoon (15 ml) balsamic vinegar, honey, and basil leaves. Blend lightly, leaving small bits of basil. Taste, and add more salt if needed.

8 Place the ingredients for the spicy tuna into small bowl and combine thoroughly.

9 Serve the soup with a spoonful of the tuna and additional pepper flakes.

Note: If your tomatoes are ripe and in season, you may not need the honey.

Un-Tortilla Soup

This recipe is sort of a blank slate—a deeply flavored, spiced (but not too spicy) broth that allows you to make a perfectly customized bowl of tortilla soup. Well, un-tortilla soup, unless you make a batch of Paleo Tortillas (page 256) to accompany it—a fantastic idea, really. You can even make multiple batches and freeze the broth in quart-size (946 ml) containers for instant tortilla-soup base later on. It reheats beautifully.

Using dried chillies is easy, despite their potentially menacing appearance. You can find them in Latin sections of many grocery stores or in Latin food markets.

Prep time   25 minutes
Makes   about 4 quarts (3.8 liters) of stock

4 dried ancho or *guajillo* chillies

1½ large yellow onions, cut into wedges

1 28-ounce (794 g) can diced tomatoes

2 teaspoons whole coriander (or 1 teaspoon ground)

2 teaspoons ground cumin

3 bay leaves

½ teaspoon dried thyme

½ teaspoon dried oregano

2 teaspoons sea salt

3 quarts (5.7 liters) Simple Chicken Stock (page 280)

6 cloves garlic, smashed

Suggested add-ins and sides: grilled/shredded chicken or beef, shredded carrots, Southwest Cabbage Slaw (page 252), diced avocado, diced jicama, chopped cilantro, hot sauce, or Paleo Tortillas (page 256)

1 Break the chillies in half and shake out the seeds. Discard the seeds.

2 Submerge the chillies in boiling water and let them soak for 20 minutes until they are soft and pliable.

3 Meanwhile, add the remaining ingredients to a 6-quart (5.7 liter) slow cooker.

4 When the chillies have softened, remove them from the water, discard the stems and any additional seeds, and place them in a food processor. Process until smooth. (If you don't have a food processor, just chop the chillies very fine.)

5 Add the chili paste to the slow cooker and stir to combine.

6 Cover and cook on low for 4 hours.

7 Strain the stock by removing the large chunks with a large slotted spoon or a spider. Pour the remaining stock through a mesh strainer into a large pot. Return the strained stock to the slow cooker.

8 Place desired soup add-ins into bowls and ladle the stock over the top.

Russia Palace's Borscht

Borscht may not seem romantic to you, but it is to my husband and me. Aside from its gorgeous fuchsia color, which is reminiscent of Valentine's Day, it's a common soup in Russia. Steve and I met in Moscow (long story), and we like to make this soup at least once every winter and reflect on our first few encounters together. If you've never had borscht, this is an excellent recipe to start with. I adapted a vegetarian version that supposedly came from the chef of Czar Nicholas I, and added bits of tender grass-fed beef and rich Homemade Beef Stock (page 281). I once made this for a native Russian, who ate multiple helpings and told me it tasted just like his mother's.

Prep time 45 minutes

Serves 10

3 tablespoons (44 ml) avocado oil

1½ pounds (680 g) beef stew meat, cut into ½-inch (1 cm) chunks

1 tablespoon (18 g) sea salt, plus extra for seasoning

Black pepper

2 quarts (1.9 liters) Homemade Beef Stock (page 281), divided

1 medium onion, diced

2 pounds (905 g) beets, grated

3 large carrots, grated

2 large potatoes, diced

1 green bell pepper, diced

1 small head cabbage, shredded

5 tablespoons (150 g) tomato paste

⅓ cup (80 ml) freshly squeezed lemon juice

2 tablespoons (40 g) honey

1 garlic clove, minced

¼ cup fresh dill, chopped

1 Heat half of the oil in a large cast-iron or stainless steel skillet over medium-high heat.

2 Sprinkle the meat generously with sea salt and black pepper. Place half of the meat into the pan (don't overcrowd the pan) and let it cook for 2 to 3 minutes. Flip the meat around with a spatula, and let it cook for another 2 to 3 minutes until it's golden brown on most sides. Transfer the meat to a 6-quart (5.7 liter) slow cooker and repeat with the remaining stew meat, adding the rest of the oil to the pan if necessary.

3 Once all of the meat is removed from the pan, pour a cup of the beef stock into the pan and scrape the bits from the bottom as it bubbles and steams. Pour the contents of the pan into the slow cooker.

4 Add the onion, beets, carrots, potatoes, bell pepper, and cabbage to the slow cooker. (It will be full!)

5 In a large measuring cup, whisk together the tomato paste, lemon juice, honey, 1 cup (235 ml) of stock, 1 tablespoon (18 g) of salt, and 1 teaspoon of black pepper. Pour the mixture into the slow cooker. Pour in the remaining 1½ quarts (1.4 liters) of beef stock.

6 Cover and cook on low for 6 to 7 hours, stirring halfway through. Beef should be very tender and vegetables fully cooked.

7 Stir in garlic.

8 Serve with a sprinkle of fresh dill. Taste, and add additional salt if needed.

Note: Borscht is traditionally served with sour cream. Try adding a dab of unsweetened Whipped Coconut Cream (page 273) to your bowl—or if you eat some dairy, I suggest using a little organic sour cream or crème fraîche.

Guacamole Bacon Burger Soup

I love bacon and guacamole together, especially on bunless burgers. This is my favorite burger in soup form—complete with "fries" in the form of tender potatoes and a tart, salty punch from the pickle juice.

Prep time 25 minutes
Serves 6

6 to 8 slices thick-cut bacon
1 pound (455 g) ground beef
1 tablespoon steak seasoning
1 cup (160 g) diced onion
1 large stalk celery, diced
2 cloves garlic, minced
1 quart (946 ml) Homemade Beef Stock (page 281)

1 pound (455 g) red potatoes, cut into 1-inch (2.5 cm) pieces (or 1 large sweet potato)
1 14.5-ounce (411 g) can diced tomatoes
1 6-ounce (170-gram) can tomato paste
¼ cup (60 ml) pickle juice
2 tablespoons (22 g) Dijon mustard
1 tablespoon (20 g) honey
2 teaspoons sea salt
1 batch Simple Guacamole (see below)

1 Cut the bacon slices in half and cook them in a large skillet over medium heat until they reach the desired crispness. Remove them from the pan and set them aside. When cool, chop or break up the bacon into small bits.

2 Remove all of the bacon drippings except for 2 to 3 tablespoons (26 to 39 g). Maintain medium-high heat and add the ground beef to the skillet. Add the steak seasoning to the meat. Cook for 10 to 12 minutes until the meat is browned, breaking it into little bits.

3 Add onions, celery, and garlic to the pan. Cook the mixture for another 2 to 3 minutes, then transfer it to a 4-quart (3.8 liter) slow cooker along with the beef stock, potatoes, tomatoes, tomato paste, pickle juice, mustard, honey, and sea salt.

4 Cover and cook on low heat for 7 to 8 hours (or on high heat for 3 to 4 hours).

5 Serve the soup with a scoop of guacamole and a sprinkle of bacon bits.

Simple Guacamole

Prep time 5 minutes
Makes about 1⅓ cups (307 g)

2 avocados
2 tablespoons (30 ml) fresh lime juice
¼ cup fresh cilantro, chopped
¼ teaspoon onion powder
Sea salt

Cut the avocados in half, removing the pit, and scoop the avocado flesh into a medium bowl. Smash the avocado flesh with a fork or a potato masher. Add the lime juice, cilantro, onion powder, and a generous pinch of salt. Mix well.

Chipotle Beef and Avocado Soup

I love this Tex-Mex take on beef vegetable soup! The creamy bites of avocado take the place of the cheese and sour cream usually added to Tex-Mex soups, giving it a guacamole-type flavor. You can adjust the heat level by the amount of chipotle pepper you use. To make a milder version, use only the adobo sauce from a can and omit the chipotle pepper itself.

Prep time 35 minutes
Serves 8 to 10

1½ pounds (680 g) beef-stew meat (like chuck or round cuts)

2 teaspoons (12 g) sea salt, plus optional salt to taste

1½ teaspoons ground cumin

1 teaspoon dried oregano

½ teaspoon black pepper

1 or 2 chipotle peppers plus 1 tablespoon (20 g) sauce, from a can of chipotle peppers in adobo sauce

4 tablespoons (59 ml) avocado oil

5 cups (1.2 liters) Homemade Beef Stock (page 281)

4 large carrots, peeled and cut into 1-inch (2.5 cm) chunks

1 medium onion, diced

1 large potato (12 ounces, or 340 grams), russet or sweet

2 cloves garlic, minced

3 tablespoons (90 g) tomato paste

1 teaspoon chili powder

1 lime, zested and juiced

2 avocados, peeled, pitted, and diced

1 Place the beef in a medium bowl. Add 2 teaspoons salt, the cumin, oregano, black pepper, chipotle pepper, and adobo sauce. Toss the beef and seasonings with your hands, ensuring that the beef is evenly coated.

2 Measure 1 cup (235 ml) of stock and set it next to the stove. Heat 2 tablespoons (29 ml) of avocado oil in a large cast-iron or stainless-steel skillet over medium-high heat. Brown the meat in two batches, until it is golden brown in spots. It does not need to be cooked through. Transfer the meat to a 4- or 6-quart (3.8 or 5.7 liter) slow cooker. While the pan is still very hot, pour ½ cup (120 ml) of stock into it and scrap the browned bits on the bottom until they release. Pour the liquid into the slow cooker with the meat.

3 Add the carrots, onion, potatoes, and garlic to the slow cooker.

4 Whisk the tomato paste into a ½ cup (120 ml) of stock and pour it into the cooker, along with the chili powder, 1 teaspoon lime zest, and juice from the lime.

5 Add the remaining 3½ cups (830 ml) of stock. Cover and cook on low for 3 to 4 hours. Meat should be tender and potatoes should easily pierce with a fork.

6 Taste, adding more salt and lime juice if necessary. Add the diced avocado and cook for another 10 minutes before serving.

Beef Vegetable Soup

This might be the best classic beef vegetable soup I've ever had. And you don't need an onion soup mix either! Searing the beef might seem like an unnecessary step, but it adds so much flavor—especially those browned bits scraped from the bottom of the skillet.

Prep time 25 minutes

Serves 6

1 pound (455 g) stew meat, cut into ½-inch (1 cm) pieces

Sea salt

Black pepper

½ teaspoon onion powder

4 cups (946 ml) beef broth

2 tablespoons (29 g) Homemade Ghee (page 287), avocado oil (29 ml), or coconut oil

3 large carrots, cut into ½-inch (1 cm) pieces

12 ounces (340 g) red potatoes (or sweet potatoes), cut into ½-inch (1 cm) pieces

½ cup (80 g) diced yellow onion

2 large stalks celery, thinly sliced

1 tablespoon (30 g) tomato paste

1 tablespoon Dijon mustard

⅓ cup (80 ml) coconut aminos

3 tablespoons (45 ml) freshly squeezed lemon juice

2 dried bay leaves

2 cloves garlic, minced

1 sprig fresh rosemary

1 teaspoon salt

Black pepper, to taste

1 Sprinkle the meat with generous pinches of sea salt, black pepper, and onion powder. Toss the meat to coat evenly.

2 Pour ½ (120 ml) cup of broth into a measuring cup and set it next to the stove.

3 Heat the ghee in a large stainless-steel or cast-iron skillet to medium-high heat. When the oil begins to "shimmer," add half of the stew meat to the pan in one layer. Let the meat cook undisturbed for 2 to 3 minutes, and then flip them around to sear the other sides. You don't need to sear all sides of the meat or cook them all the way through. The meat should have golden brown crusts scattered throughout. Transfer the meat to a 4-quart (3.8 liter) slow cooker. Repeat with the remaining meat, adding more oil if necessary.

4 Immediately after you transfer the last batch of meat to the slow cooker—and while the pan is still screaming hot—pour the ½ cup (120 ml) broth into the pan and scrape up the browned bits stuck to the bottom that will begin to loosen. Pour the liquid into the slow cooker.

5 Add the carrots, potatoes, onion, and celery to the cooker. Whisk the tomato paste, mustard, coconut aminos, and lemon juice together and pour over the top. Add the bay leaves, garlic cloves, rosemary sprig, and 1 teaspoon of salt (add a second teaspoon of salt if you're using unsalted broth). Pour the remaining 3½ cups of broth over the top.

6 Cover and cook on low for about 5 hours, until the beef is tender and the flavors have combined well. Taste, and add additional salt if necessary.

Italian Beef and Zoodle Soup

Grass-fed beef isn't cheap, so it's nice to have recipes like this one that use less-expensive cuts, like stew meat. Slow cooking turns them into bits of melt-in-your-mouth goodness. But making soups and stews with pricier meat means you can use less and it will stretch further. How often can you feed six people with one pound of meat?

Prep time 30 minutes

Serves 6

1 pound (455 g) stew meat, cut into 1-inch (2.5 cm) pieces

2 cloves garlic, minced

1 teaspoon Italian seasoning

1 teaspoon onion powder

1 teaspoon sea salt

½ teaspoon black pepper

Pinch of crushed red pepper flakes

2 to 4 tablespoons (29 to 59 ml) avocado oil

2 quarts (1.9 liters) beef broth

1 15-ounce (425 g) can diced tomatoes

1 heaping cup (130 g) diced carrots (about 3 medium)

½ cup (60 g) diced celery (about 3 stalks)

1 tablespoon (30 g) tomato paste

1 teaspoon Dijon mustard

2 tablespoons (30 ml) red wine vinegar

2 tablespoons nutritional yeast

2 medium zucchini, thinly spiralized (See Squash Noodles, page 248)

1 Cut any unwanted fat or connective tissue from the stew meat.

2 Combine the garlic, Italian seasoning, onion powder, salt, black pepper, and crushed red pepper flakes in a small bowl. Sprinkle the seasoning over the stew meat.

3 Heat 2 tablespoons (29 ml) avocado oil in a large skillet over medium-high heat. Sear the meat in two batches until much of the meat is covered in a golden brown crust, adding more oil when necessary. It does not need to be cooked all the way through. Transfer the seared meat to a 4-quart (3.8 liter) slow cooker.

4 Return the pan to the stove and heat the pan up again, but not enough for it to start smoking. Pour ½ cup (120 ml) of beef broth into the skillet, and while it sizzles, scrape the browned bits from the bottom of the pan. Pour the liquid into the slow cooker with the stew meat.

5 Add the remaining beef broth, diced tomatoes, carrots, celery, tomato paste, and mustard to the slow cooker. Give it a stir.

6 Cover and cook on low for 6 to 7 hours, until the carrots and beef are tender.

7 Stir in the red wine vinegar, nutritional yeast, and spiralized zucchini. Cover and cook for another 15 minutes, until the zoodles are tender, before serving.

Pizza Soup with Greens

Letting go of cheese on pizza can be a hard transition when you start a paleo lifestyle—perhaps more difficult than finding a good grain-free crust. If you're strictly eliminating dairy, nutritional yeast has an interesting cheesy taste and is a good replacement for a sprinkle of Parmesan. And eating pizza in soup form eliminates the need for a crust. A win-win.

Prep time 25 minutes

Serves 6

1 bell pepper, seeded and diced

3 brown or white button mushrooms, chopped

1½ cups (225 g) cooked pizza topping meat (such as diced pepperoni, ham, or cooked Italian sausage)

2 large carrots, peeled and diced

½ small bunch kale, leaves removed from stems and cut into bite-sized pieces

1 tablespoon dried minced onion

1 teaspoon garlic powder

1 15-ounce (425 g) can tomato sauce

1 teaspoon Italian seasoning

¼ teaspoon oregano

Pinch of crushed red pepper flakes

1 quart (946 ml) Simple Chicken Stock (page 280)

Sliced peperoncini peppers and nutritional yeast, for garnish

1 Place all the ingredients (except the garnishes) in a 4- or 6-quart (3.8 or 5.7 liter) slow cooker. Cover and cook on low for 6 to 8 hours.

2 Serve with peppers, a sprinkle of nutritional yeast, and extra crushed red pepper flakes if you want more heat.

Note: You can find nutritional yeast at health food stores and in some grocery stores that sell bulk foods.

Italian Sausage and Kale Soup with Sweet Potatoes

This is my version of Olive Garden's zuppa toscana—slow cooker, paleo style with sweet potatoes. We like this recipe even better than the restaurant version! It also doubles well, and it's freezer-friendly.

Prep time 15 minutes

Serves 6

2 tablespoons (28 g) Homemade Ghee (page 287) or bacon drippings

1 pound (455 g) bulk uncooked sweet Italian chicken sausage

1 medium onion, diced

4 cloves garlic, minced

1 large sweet potato, peeled and cut into 1-inch (2.5 cm) pieces

½ large bunch kale, leaves removed from stems and cut into bite-sized pieces

1½ quarts (1.4 liters) Simple Chicken Stock (page 280)

2 tablespoons (15 ml) red wine vinegar

pinch of crushed red pepper flakes

1 Heat the ghee in a large skillet over medium-high heat. Add the chicken sausage to the pan and break it up into small bits as it cooks.

2 When most of the sausage is cooked, add the onion to the pan. Cook for 3 to 4 minutes, until the onion begins to soften and become translucent. Add the garlic to the pan and cook for another minute or so.

Transfer the sausage mixture to a 4-quart (3.8 liter) slow cooker.

3 Add the sweet potato cubes, kale, chicken stock, vinegar, and red pepper flakes.

4 Cover and cook on low for 6 to 7 hours (or 3 to 4 hours on high).

5 Taste and add more salt or vinegar if necessary before serving.

Note: If you can't find bulk uncooked Italian sausage, you can use diced precooked Italian sausage.

Spicy Andouille Sausage and Collard Greens Soup

My Southern Grandma Inez grows collard greens in her garden and cooks them in batches to freeze. We never saw them in anything she prepared us, perhaps because hearty greens are a hard sell for kids. I didn't appreciate how flavorful and tender they could be until I was an adult—especially paired with spicy andouille sausage.

Prep time 25 minutes
Serves 6

1 tablespoon avocado oil

12 ounces (340 g) andouille sausage, cut into ½-inch pieces

1½ cup (240 g) chopped sweet onion

1 large stalk celery, diced

1 green bell pepper, diced

1½ teaspoons Cajun Spice Blend (page 284)

1 teaspoon sea salt, divided

1 bay leaf

3 cloves garlic, minced

1 15-ounce (425 g) can diced tomatoes

3 large collard leaves, chopped into bite-sized pieces

2 quarts (1.9 liters) Simple Chicken Stock (page 280)

2 tablespoons (30 ml) coconut aminos

2 tablespoons (30 ml) red wine vinegar

Hot sauce, for serving

1 Heat the oil in a medium skillet. Add the sausage and cook 4 to 5 minutes, until they are golden brown in spots. Transfer the sausage to a 4-quart (3.8 liter) slow cooker.

2 Add the onion, celery, green pepper, Cajun seasoning, and ½ teaspoon salt to the skillet. Cook 2 to 3 minutes, until the onion is translucent, then transfer the vegetables to the slow cooker.

3 Add the other ½ teaspoon salt, bay leaf, garlic, tomatoes, collard greens, chicken stock, coconut aminos, and vinegar.

4 Cover and cook on low for 6 hours.

5 Taste and add more salt and vinegar if necessary.

6 Serve with hot sauce.

Cold Remedy Chicken Soup

Several years ago, our whole family came down with colds during the same week, and because we don't run to the medicine cabinet straight away, I searched online for natural remedies. I saw repeated references to coconut oil, ginger, lemon, and bone stock to promote healing and immune support. Since I was planning to make chicken soup anyway, I tossed all those ingredients into the pot for good measure and ended up with one of the most flavorful chicken soups I've ever eaten! Ginger might be an odd addition, but it simply adds more flavor. If you love ginger (as I do), add more for a stronger ginger flavor.

Prep time 20 minutes
Serves 6

1 to 1½ pounds (455 to 680 g) chicken (boneless, skinless breasts or thighs)

Sea salt and black pepper

2 tablespoons (28 g) coconut oil

4 large carrots, peeled and diced small

1 leek, white part only, quartered and thinly sliced

1 large stalk celery, diced

4 cloves garlic

Juice from 1 small lemon

2-inch (5 cm) knob of ginger, finely grated

6 cups Simple Chicken Stock (page 280)

½ teaspoon dried thyme

1 teaspoon sea salt

Hot sauce, for serving

1 Sprinkle the chicken liberally with sea salt and black pepper.

2 Heat the coconut oil in a skillet over medium-high heat. Sear the chicken on both sides, creating a nice, golden brown crust, and transfer to a 4-quart (3.8 liter) slow cooker. (The chicken does not need to be cooked through at this point.)

3 Add the rest of the ingredients and 1 teaspoon sea salt into the cooker. Cover and cook on low for 6 to 7 hours (or high for 3 to 4 hours).

4 Taste, and add more salt if necessary. If you used homemade unsalted stock, you might want to add up to an additional 1 teaspoon of salt.

5 Serve. We really liked it with hot sauce, which can also help clear out stuffy sinuses.

Mulligatawny

Tell me this soup doesn't remind you of the Soup Nazi on Seinfeld. I understand why Mulligatawny was such a sought-after soup on that crazy episode! It's comforting, with all of those warm Indian spices and creaminess from the coconut milk. It's also a good way to use up leftover cooked chicken and Cauliflower Rice (pages 249 and 250) or jasmine rice.

Prep time 20 minutes
Serves 8 to 10

6 tablespoons (87 g) Homemade Ghee (page 287) or coconut oil

1 large sweet onion, diced

2 large carrots, diced

2 large celery stalks, diced

1 green bell pepper, diced

1 jalapeño, seeded and diced

3 tablespoons (24 g) tapioca flour

2 quarts (1.9 liters) Simple Chicken Stock (page 280)

1 tablespoon good-quality curry powder

2 teaspoons sea salt

½ teaspoon ground nutmeg

⅛ teaspoon ground cloves

¼ teaspoon black pepper

1 15-ounce (425 g) can diced tomatoes

1 14-ounce (400 ml) can coconut milk

2 cups (280 g) cooked chicken, diced or shredded 2 cups leftover Cauliflower Rice (pages 249 and 250) or jasmine rice

1 lime

Thinly sliced green onions, for garnish

1 Heat the ghee in a large skillet over medium-high heat. Add the onion, carrots, celery, bell pepper, and jalapeño to the skillet and cook for 4 to 5 minutes, until onion turns translucent. Transfer vegetables to a 6-quart (5.7 liter) slow cooker.

2 Whisk the tapioca flour into the chicken stock. Pour the mixture into the slow cooker.

3 Add the curry powder, sea salt, nutmeg, cloves, black pepper, and diced tomatoes.

4 Cover and cook on high for 3 hours. (Or low for 5 to 6 hours.) Puree, preferably with an immersion blender.

5 Stir in the coconut milk, cooked chicken, and cauliflower rice or jasmine rice. Squeeze in the juice from half the lime. Taste the soup, and add salt or more lime juice if needed.

6 Serve with a sprinkle of green onions.

Southwest Chicken and Summer Vegetable Soup

This soup came from my website, Perry's Plate, and used to call for rice, corn, beans, and barley. It was a staple, and everyone in my family (including my extended family) loves it. After swapping out the grains and legumes with more nutritious alternatives, it's still super tasty, is more colorful, and is a perfect way to use fresh summer vegetables!

Prep time 20 minutes

Serves 10 to 12

1½ to 2 pounds (680 to 905 g) boneless, skinless chicken (breasts or thighs)

1 large onion, diced

2 bell peppers, seeded and diced

2 cloves garlic, minced

1 medium zucchini, diced

1 medium yellow squash, diced

4 to 5 large stems of Swiss chard

1 7-ounce (198 g) can diced green chillies

1 14.5-ounce (411 g) can crushed tomatoes

1 15-ounce (425 g) can tomato sauce

1 tablespoon chili powder

1 tablespoon ground cumin

½ teaspoon chipotle powder

6 cups (1.4 liters) Simple Chicken Stock (page 280)

1 teaspoon sea salt

Juice from 1 lime

1 cup (16 g) fresh, chopped cilantro

Diced avocados and hot sauce, for serving

1 Add the chicken, onion, bell peppers, garlic, zucchini, and yellow squash to the cooker. Remove the leaves from the Swiss chard stems. Chop the leaves into bite-sized pieces and dice the stems. Place the leaves and the stems into the cooker.

2 Add the green chillies, crushed tomatoes, tomato sauce, chili powder, cumin, chipotle powder, stock, and salt to the slow cooker.

3 Cover and cook on low for 7 to 8 hours (or 3 to 4 hours on high).

4 Remove the chicken, shred it, and stir it back into the soup. Squeeze the juice from the lime into the soup, and stir in the cilantro. Taste, and add more salt if necessary. If the soup tastes acidic, add 2 tablespoons (40 g) of honey.

5 Serve with diced avocados and hot sauce.

Thai Chicken Coconut Soup (Tom Kha Gai)

Thai home cooking used to be a mystery to me since I had a hard time finding a few commonly used ingredients, like lemongrass, galangal, and lime leaves. Lemongrass has been easier to find recently, and I've come to love its floral, lemony aroma. If you can't find any fresh lemongrass, use 2 teaspoons lemongrass paste or substitute ½ teaspoon of lemon zest and an extra ½ teaspoon of grated ginger.

Prep time 15 minutes

Serves 6

1½ pounds (680 g) boneless, skinless chicken breasts or thighs

1½ quarts (1.4 liters) Simple Chicken Stock (page 280)

12 ounces (340 g) sliced cremini or baby portobello mushrooms

3 cloves garlic, minced

2 limes

1 Thai chilli, seeded and minced (a serrano pepper or small jalapeño would be okay)

2-inch (5 cm) knob of ginger, finely grated

3 tablespoons (57 g) fish sauce

1 tablespoon (20 g) honey

1 teaspoon sea salt

½ teaspoon black pepper

2 3-inch (7.5 cm) pieces lemongrass

1 14-ounce (400 ml) can coconut milk

1 cup (65 g) snow peas

⅓ cup chopped fresh cilantro, plus more for garnish

3 green onions, thinly sliced

1 Place the chicken in a 4-quart (3.8 liter) slow cooker with the stock, mushrooms, garlic, zest and juice from 1 of the limes, chilli, ginger, fish sauce, honey, sea salt, and black pepper.

2 Place the lemongrass on a cutting board. Lay a flat side of your knife over the stalks. Hit your fist firmly on the knife, bruising the lemongrass. Do this a few times until the stalk is smashed in several places. Transfer the lemongrass to the slow cooker.

3 Cover and cook on low for 6 to 7 hours (or 3 to 4 on high).

4 Remove the chicken from the cooker, shred into small pieces, and return them to the pot. Stir in the coconut milk, snow peas, and ⅓ cup of cilantro. Cover and cook for another 15 minutes. Cut the remaining lime into wedges.

5 Remove the lemongrass stalks. Taste and add more salt and lime if necessary. Serve with a sprinkle of cilantro, green onions, and lime wedges.

Note: If you can find galangal, use that in place of the fresh ginger. You can also use 2 teaspoons lemongrass paste instead of the fresh lemongrass.

Chipotle Chicken and Sweet Potato Soup with Kale

This soup rocks. It was a huge hit the first night we ate it, and for lunches a few days after, too. I also love the technique of blending some of the soup to create a creamy effect without using cream. It gives it a lot of body and substance.

Prep time 15 minutes
Serves 10

3 pounds (1.4 kg) sweet potatoes, peeled and cut into ½-inch (1 cm) cubes

1 medium onion, diced small

2 teaspoons dried thyme

2 teaspoons dried marjoram

1 teaspoon sea salt

1½ teaspoon BBQ Dry-Rub Seasoning (page 288)

1½ pounds (680 g) chicken breasts or thighs

3 cloves garlic, minced

1 chipotle pepper from a can of chipotles in adobo sauce, seeds removed (if desired), and minced

2 quarts (1.9 liters) chicken broth

3 ounces (85 g) baby kale or regular kale, cut into small pieces

1 cup (235 ml) full-fat coconut milk

Juice from ½ an orange

Juice from ½ a lemon

1 In a 4-quart (3.8 liter) slow cooker, combine the sweet potatoes, onion, thyme, marjoram, and salt.

2 Rub the BBQ rub all over the chicken and place it in the cooker with the vegetables. Add the garlic, chipotle pepper, and chicken broth to the cooker.

3 Cover and cook on low for about 5 hours, until the chicken is tender and shreds easily.

4 Remove the chicken from the cooker and place it on a large plate. Shred it and set it aside.

5 Ladle out about a quart (946 ml) of the soup and blend it in a blender or use an immersion blender in a large bowl. Pour the blended soup back into the slow cooker. Stir in the reserved chicken, kale, coconut milk, orange juice, and lemon juice. Cover and cook for another 10 minutes.

6 Taste the soup and add a little salt, if necessary, before serving.

BLT Chicken Soup

One of my favorite salads is a BLT spinach salad with tender bits of chicken and a warm bacon vinaigrette. I wanted to re-create those flavors in a warm, comforting soup. I love the addition of sun-dried tomatoes, which bring more tomato flavor to the forefront.

Prep time 15 minutes
Serves 6

1½ pounds (680 g) chicken thighs or breasts

½ teaspoon sea salt

1 teaspoon Italian seasoning

1 pound (455 g) red potatoes, cut into ½-inch pieces

½ cup (28 g) dry or oil-packed (55 g) sun-dried tomatoes, chopped

3 cloves garlic

1 teaspoon dried minced onion

1 quart (946 ml) chicken broth

10 slices thick-cut bacon

1 cup (235 ml) full-fat coconut milk

2 handfuls baby spinach, torn

1 tablespoon (15 ml) red wine vinegar

3 Roma tomatoes, seeded and diced

1 Lay the chicken on a plate and sprinkle both sides with the salt and Italian seasoning.

2 Place the chicken in the slow cooker with the potatoes, sun-dried tomatoes, garlic, dried onion, and chicken broth.

3 Cover and cook on low for 5 to 6 hours, until the chicken is tender and the potatoes are cooked through.

4 Meanwhile, cut the bacon into ½-inch (1 cm) pieces and cook them in a large skillet over medium heat until crisp. Remove them with a slotted spoon and place on a folded paper towel to drain.

5 Remove the chicken from the slow cooker, shred the meat with two forks, and return the shredded meat to the pot.

6 Add the coconut milk, spinach, and vinegar to the slow cooker. Cover and cook for another 10 minutes. Taste, and add more salt or vinegar if necessary.

7 Serve the soup with the crispy bacon and diced tomatoes as garnishes.

Easy Chicken Pho with Zoodles

Pho (pronounced "fuh") is a flavorful broth filled with noodles, thin slices of meat, and a little salad of fresh herbs and tender greens sitting on top. In the United States, it's developed a cult following, and my family is just as crazy about it. They loved the tender chicken, flavorful broth, and customizing their bowls with the toppings they wanted. When my husband came home from work the first night we had it, my three-year-old ran up to him and excitedly said, "Dad! We had fffff for dinner!"

Prep time 15 minutes

Serves 6

2½ quarts (2.4 liters) chicken broth

3 star anise pods

1-inch (2.5 cm) knob of ginger, sliced

1 cinnamon stick

1 garlic clove, minced

3 tablespoons (45 ml) coconut aminos

1 tablespoon (20 g) honey

1 teaspoon fish sauce

1 teaspoon sea salt

1½ pounds (680 g) boneless, skinless chicken breasts, partially frozen

2 medium zucchini, spiralized into thin noodles (See Squash Noodles, page 248)

½ cup chopped fresh cilantro

½ cup (20 g) chopped fresh basil

2 to 3 limes, cut into wedges

Additional toppings: shredded carrots, sliced jalapeños, mung bean sprouts, chili garlic paste

1 Pour the chicken broth into a 4-quart (3.8 liter) slow cooker. Add the star anise pods, ginger slices, cinnamon stick, garlic, coconut aminos, honey, fish sauce, and sea salt.

2 Cover and cook on low for 5 to 6 hours, until broth is flavorful and fragrant.

3 Meanwhile, prepare the chicken by slicing it as thinly as you can with a sharp knife. Chill until ready to use. Finish preparing the herbs, lime wedges, and additional toppings.

4 About 20 minutes before serving, remove the ginger, cinnamon stick, and anise pods from the broth with a slotted spoon. Add the thinly sliced chicken and zucchini noodles, and stir the soup around. Cover and cook for another 20 minutes, until chicken is cooked through and the zoodles are tender.

5 Ladle the soup into bowls and top with desired herbs, limes, and toppings.

Salsa Verde Chicken Chili

I'm a big fan of white-chicken chili, but creating a paleo white chili can be difficult, given that all of the "whites" are off limits. I decided to take the backbone of white chili—the chillies and chicken—add a few more green components, and make a green chicken chili instead. The jicama stays crisp and tender, and adds an unexpected crunchy bite!

Prep time 15 minutes
Serves 6

2 boneless, skinless chicken breasts, cut into 1-inch (2.5 cm) cubes

½ teaspoon sea salt

1 teaspoon lime zest

3 tablespoons (45 ml) lime juice

½ teaspoon dried Mexican oregano

1 teaspoon ground cumin

½ teaspoon ground coriander

3 cloves garlic, minced

¼ teaspoon black pepper

¼ teaspoon cayenne pepper

2 bell peppers, any color, diced

2½ cups (325 g) chopped jicama (½-inch [1 cm] pieces)

½ bunch of kale, leaves ripped from the stems and cut into bite-sized pieces

1 16-ounce (454 g) jar of *salsa verde*

½ cup (120 ml) coconut milk

1 cup (16 g) fresh, chopped cilantro

Diced avocado, for serving

1 Place chicken in a medium bowl and sprinkle with ½ teaspoon of salt.

2 Combine the lime zest and juice, oregano, cumin, coriander, garlic, black pepper, and cayenne pepper in a small bowl. Add spice mixture to the chicken and, using your hands, toss to evenly coat. Place the chicken in a 4-quart (3.8 liter) slow cooker.

3 Add the peppers, jicama, kale, salsa verde, coconut milk, and 2 cups (475 ml) of water to the cooker.

4 Cover and cook on low for 6 to 7 hours, until the chicken is very tender.

5 Stir the cilantro into the chili and taste, adding more salt or lime juice if necessary.

6 Serve with diced avocado.

Note: If you'd like this spicier, use poblano peppers instead of bell peppers.

Moroccan Turkey Stew

The mild turkey in this chili takes a supporting role for the exotic spices, and the almond butter not only thickens it, but also gives it a rich, nutty flavor that you can't quite put your finger on. It's excellent over Cauliflower Rice (pages 249 and 250) or simply eaten alone.

Prep time 25 minutes
Serves 8 to 10

2 tablespoons (28 g) avocado or coconut oil

1½ pounds (680 g) ground turkey or chicken

1½ teaspoon ground cumin

1½ teaspoon curry powder

1½ teaspoon ground coriander

1½ teaspoon chili powder

1 teaspoon black pepper

½ teaspoon sea salt

¼ teaspoon cinnamon

1 medium onion, diced

1 cup (100 g) chopped celery

1 green bell pepper, diced

2 cloves garlic, minced

2 tablespoons (12 g or 16 g) fresh minced or grated ginger

1 15-ounce (425 g) can diced tomatoes

3 cups (710 ml) Simple Chicken Stock (page 280)

Juice from 1 lemon (about ¼ cup, or 60 ml)

1 large sweet potato, peeled and diced

1 cup (145 g) unsweetened golden raisins

3 tablespoons (48 g) unsweetened almond butter

¼ cup fresh chopped cilantro

Cauliflower Rice (pages 249 and 250) or Squash Noodles (page 248), for serving

1 Heat the oil in a large skillet over medium-high heat. Add the turkey and cook, breaking up the meat into small chunks, for 6 to 8 minutes or until it is cooked through. Add the seasonings (cumin through cinnamon) and onion. Cook, stirring frequently, for another 3 to 5 minutes, until the onion begins to soften and the mixture is fragrant. Transfer the meat to a 6-quart (5.7 liter) slow cooker.

2 Add the celery, bell pepper, garlic, ginger, tomatoes, stock, lemon juice, and sweet potato to the cooker. Give it a good stir, then cover it and cook on low for 5 to 6 hours.

3 Stir in the raisins and almond butter, and cook for another 30 minutes, covered.

4 Stir in the cilantro and serve with Cauliflower Rice or Squash Noodles.

Peppery Clam Chowder with Bacon

My grandma makes amazing clam chowder. When I saw her recipe, I understood why—the ingredient list included a quart (946 ml) of half and half and more than a stick of butter. Planning a paleo version of this decadent soup had me reaching for some bacon as a flavor booster, but I was surprised when I created a creamy, peppery version that could stand on its own—without a bacon crutch (though a sprinkle of bacon is still nice). I was also surprised how well turnips fare in this soup. Certain little humans in our house thought they were potatoes, which you can also use if you prefer.

Prep time 30 minutes
Serves 8 to 10

6 slices uncooked thick-cut bacon

1½ cups (240 g) minced onion (about 1 large onion)

1½ cups (165 g) minced celery

2 pounds (905 g) turnips, peeled and cut into ½-inch (1 cm) pieces

2 6.5-ounce (184 g) cans chopped or minced clams, undrained

16 ounces (475 ml) clam juice

⅓ cup (43 g) tapioca flour

2 cups (475 ml) Simple Chicken Stock (page 280)

2 teaspoons sea salt

1 teaspoon black pepper

1 sprig of fresh thyme

1 13.5-ounce (398 ml) can coconut milk, chilled

1 Cut the bacon into ½-inch (1 cm) strips and cook in a skillet over medium heat until you reach the desired crispness. Remove it from the pan with a slotted spoon and set it aside for later. Drain all but 2 to 3 tablespoons (26 to 39 g) of the drippings.

2 Return the pan to medium-high heat and sauté the onion and celery, scraping the browned bits from the bottom of the pan. Cook for 4 to 5 minutes, until the onion is translucent. Transfer the vegetables to a 6-quart (5.7 liter) slow cooker.

3 Add the turnips, clams, and clam juice to the slow cooker. Whisk tapioca flour into the chicken stock, removing any lumps, and pour it into the cooker. Stir in the salt and pepper.

4 Cover and cook on low for 4 to 4½ hours, until the turnips are tender.

5 Add the thyme to the cooker. Open the coconut milk from the bottom and pour out the clear liquid (save it and add it to smoothies later) and spoon the coconut cream into the slow cooker. Stir until the coconut is incorporated into the soup.

6 Cover and cook for another 30 minutes.

7 Serve with bacon bits.

Note: You can use ⅛ teaspoon dried thyme in place of the fresh sprig—just add it earlier, in step 3.

Thai-Spiced Seafood Soup with Zoodles

This soup is fun. Using my favorite spice blend is fun. Spiralizing anything is fun—seriously, have you tried it? It never gets old. Dipping your spoon into a creamy, opaque exotic-looking soup—not knowing what it will hold when it comes out—is fun. It might be a bright-colored bell pepper or a flaky piece of cod or one of many looooooong zoodles because you decided not to trim them before adding them to the soup.

Prep time 25 minutes
Serves 6

1 cup (160 g) diced sweet onion

1 bell pepper (red, orange, or yellow), seeded and thinly sliced

3 cloves garlic

1-inch (2.5 cm) knob of fresh ginger, minced or grated

3 limes

5 teaspoons Thai Spice Blend (page 285), divided

3 cups (710 ml) Simple Chicken Stock (page 280)

1 tablespoon (19 g) fish sauce

1 teaspoon sea salt

8 ounces (225 g) uncooked, thawed cod, cut into 1-inch (2.5 cm) chunks

8 ounces (225 g) uncooked, thawed shrimp, shelled and tails removed

1 medium zucchini, spiralized into noodles or thinly julienned (See Squash Noodles, page 248)

1 handful of fresh snow peas

1 13.5-ounce can (398 ml) full-fat coconut milk

Fresh chopped cilantro, for serving

1 Place the onion, bell pepper, garlic, ginger, and juice from 1 lime (about 3 to 4 tablespoons, or 45 to 60 ml) into a 4-quart (3.8 liter) slow cooker. Add 4 teaspoons of Thai spice, stock, fish sauce, and salt.

2 Cover and cook on low for 5 hours.

3 Sprinkle the remaining 1 teaspoon of Thai spice and the juice from half of a lime on the cod and shrimp. Toss to coat evenly. Let it sit for 5 minutes.

4 Add the seafood, zucchini, snow peas, and coconut milk to the slow cooker. Stir well. Cover, turn the cooker to high heat, and cook for another 30 to 45 minutes, until the seafood is cooked through and the noodles are tender.

5 Slice the remaining 1½ limes into wedges. Serve the soup with the chopped cilantro and lime wedges.

Creamy Avocado Soup with Jalapeño-Garlic Shrimp

This soup was an experiment with a happy, delightful ending. "What if I put a bunch of avocados in there and made a pureed soup?" Guacamole in soup form, that's what. Jalapeño-garlic shrimp made this a heartier, tastier meal.

Prep time 15 minutes
Serves 6

For the soup:

½ large sweet onion, sliced

2 quarts (1.9 liters) Simple Chicken Stock (page 280)

5 ripe avocados, pitted, peeled, and cut into large chunks

4 cloves garlic, smashed

¼ cup (60 ml) freshly squeezed lime juice (about 2 limes)

½ teaspoon ground cumin

1 tablespoon (18 g) sea salt

1 tablespoon tapioca flour

1 tablespoon (20 g) honey (if needed)

1 14-ounce (400 ml) can full-fat coconut milk

1 handful fresh cilantro, chopped

For the shrimp:

2 tablespoons (30 g) Homemade Ghee (page 287)

1 jalapeño, seeded and minced

2 cloves garlic, minced

⅛ teaspoon chipotle powder or cayenne pepper

1 pound (455 g) uncooked 31 to 40 count shrimp, shells and tails removed

Sea salt and black pepper

1 cup (180 g) diced cherry or grape tomatoes

1 Place the onion, chicken stock, avocados, garlic, lime juice, cumin, and sea salt in a 4-quart (3.8 liter) slow cooker. Whisk in the tapioca flour.

2 Cover and cook on low for 5 to 6 hours.

3 Blend, preferably using an immersion blender. Taste, and add the honey if it tastes too acidic—it may depend on how ripe the avocados are. Add the coconut milk and cilantro. Blend again, leaving small bits of cilantro. Cover and keep warm while you prepare the shrimp.

4 Heat the ghee in a medium skillet over medium-high heat. Add the jalapeño, garlic, and chipotle powder. Cook for 1 to 2 minutes. Add the shrimp and sprinkle them with sea salt and black pepper. Cook for another 3 to 4 minutes, until the shrimp is completely pink and cooked through.

5 Transfer the shrimp mixture and pan juices to a small serving dish. Stir in the tomatoes.

6 Serve the soup with a couple spoonfuls of the shrimp mixture in each bowl.

Creamy Cod and Macadamia Chowder

A few years ago I found a recipe for cream of macadamia nut soup in a magazine, but somehow lost it. I attempted to create my own tropical version with coconut milk, lemongrass, and warm spices. Macadamia nuts and coconut both have large amounts of healthy saturated fat, but are very rich. The addition of light, flaky cod and fresh lime juice cuts through that richness, creating a lovely balance.

Prep time 20 minutes
Serves 6

3 tablespoons (43.5 g) Homemade Ghee (page 287) or coconut oil

1 cup (165 g) chopped leeks (2 small)

1 large shallot, chopped

2-inch (5 cm) piece lemongrass, smashed

⅛ teaspoon freshly ground nutmeg

⅛ teaspoon allspice

¼ teaspoon ground coriander

2 to 3 medium red potatoes (or 1 medium russet)

1½ cups (198 g) dry roasted macadamia nuts

1 quart (946 ml) Simple Chicken Stock (page 280)

1 tablespoon (19 g) fish sauce

1 tablespoon (15 ml) coconut aminos

1 pound (455 g) wild-caught cod, cut into 1½-inch (3.5 cm) pieces

1 lime

Sea salt

Chopped fresh cilantro and additional limes, for serving

1 Melt the ghee in a medium skillet over medium heat. Add the leeks, shallot, and lemongrass. Cook for 2 to 3 minutes, stirring frequently, until the leeks soften and the shallots turn translucent.

2 Add the nutmeg, allspice, and coriander. Cook for another 30 seconds, and then transfer the mixture to a 4-quart (3.8 liter) slow cooker.

3 Add the potatoes, 1 cup (132 g) of the macadamia nuts, the chicken stock, fish sauce, and coconut aminos.

4 Cover and cook on low for 5 to 6 hours. Potatoes should be fork tender.

5 Puree the soup either using an immersion blender—or, if you want it silky smooth, a high-powered blender. Return the soup to the slow cooker if you used a blender.

6 Toss the cod in the juice from the lime and ½ teaspoon salt. Add the cod to the slow cooker and cook for another 15 minutes. The cod should flake easily when cooked through.

7 Taste, and add more salt and lime juice if necessary. Chop the remaining ½ cup (66 g) of macadamia nuts.

8 Serve with fresh cilantro, chopped macadamia nuts, and lime wedges.

Note: Nuts are often hard to blend smoothly with an immersion blender. To create a super smooth soup, use a high-powered countertop blender instead.

Smoky Shredded Chicken and Chorizo Chili

This chili has a lot going on—tender threads of chicken, spicy chorizo, and lots of paprika, both hot and smoked. Some dishes get better a day or two after you make them, and this is one. It's almost a shame to eat it the same day you make it.

Prep time 35 minutes
Serves 6

2 tablespoons (29 ml) avocado oil

6 ounces (170 g) uncured Spanish-style chorizo, diced (if precooked)

1 large boneless, skinless chicken breast

Sea salt

Black pepper

1½ cups (240 g) chopped sweet onion

1 8-ounce (227 g) jar diced roasted red peppers

1 medium sweet potato (about 8 ounces, or 225 g), cut into ½-inch (1 cm) cubes

2 cups (134 g) chopped kale leaves

1 large tomato, diced

3 cloves garlic, minced

1 tablespoon chili powder

1 teaspoon steak seasoning

1½ teaspoons smoked paprika

½ teaspoon hot paprika or ¼ teaspoon cayenne pepper

1 cup (235 ml) Simple Chicken Stock (page 280)

3 tablespoons (45 ml) coconut aminos

2 tablespoons (60 g) tomato paste

Diced avocado, for serving

1 Heat the avocado oil in a large skillet over medium-high heat. Add chorizo and cook until edges begin to turn golden brown, 5 to 7 minutes. Transfer the chorizo to a 4-quart (3.8 liter) slow cooker.

2 Sprinkle the chicken generously with salt and pepper. In the same skillet, sear the chicken over medium-high heat until both sides have a golden brown crust. (It doesn't have to be cooked through.) Transfer the chicken to the slow cooker.

3 Add the onion, roasted red peppers, sweet potato, kale, tomato, garlic, chili powder, steak seasoning, and both types of paprika to the cooker with the meat.

4 Whisk together the stock, aminos, and tomato paste in a large measuring cup. Pour into the slow cooker.

5 Cover and cook on low for 6 to 7 hours (or on high for 3 to 4).

6 Fish the chicken out of the cooker with tongs. Place it on a plate, shred it with two forks, and stir it back into the chili. Taste the chili, and add more salt if necessary.

7 Serve with diced avocado.

Turkey Enchilada Chili with Zucchini

One of the things I love about ground turkey is that its mild flavor lets other flavors shine while providing a substantial, meaty backbone for a recipe. This chili recipe is more like thick taco soup, and what really makes it great is the Easy Enchilada Sauce (page 292), which comes together in about the time it takes to prep the rest of the chili ingredients. If your enchilada sauce is on the spicy side, then hold back on the ground chipotle.

Prep time 20 minutes
Serves 6

2 tablespoons (29 ml) avocado oil or Homemade Ghee (29 g) (page 287)

2 pounds (905 g) ground turkey

2 teaspoons ground cumin

1 teaspoon sea salt

½ teaspoon black pepper

¼ teaspoon ground chipotle pepper or cayenne pepper

1 medium zucchini, diced

1 cup (160 g) diced red onion

1 jalapeño, seeded and diced

1 15-ounce (425 g) can diced tomatoes

1 4-ounce (113 g) can diced fire-roasted green chillies

4 cloves garlic, minced

2 tablespoons nutritional yeast

1 recipe Easy Enchilada Sauce (about 2½ cups, or 665 g)

⅓ cup chopped fresh cilantro

Diced avocado, lime wedges, and thinly sliced green onions, for serving

1 Heat the oil in a large pan over high heat. Add the ground turkey to the skillet and stir frequently, breaking the meat into small bits, until browned and cooked through. The juices from the turkey should be cooked off and the pan should be dry.

2 Add the cumin, salt, black pepper, and chipotle pepper to the turkey. Stir well, then transfer the seasoned meat to a 4-quart (3.8 liter) slow cooker.

3 Add the zucchini, red onion, jalapeño, diced tomatoes, diced green chillies, garlic, and nutritional yeast to the slow cooker. Pour the enchilada sauce over everything and give it a good stir.

4 Cover and cook on low for 4 to 5 hours.

5 Stir in the cilantro and serve with avocado, lime wedges, and green onions.

Sloppy Joe and Sweet Potato Chili

My Grandma LaRue proclaimed many times over the years that she was a horrible cook. Although I got the impression that she would have rather been sitting at her sewing machine than in the kitchen, I liked her cooking. Her sloppy joes (and chocolate cake) have been a favorite for four generations. When we eat sloppy joes, 99 percent of the time we have sweet potato fries on the table too—often with sloppy joe meat on top of the fries. (A fabulous variation on chili fries!) It was a natural progression to cook them in the same pot. I think Grandma would have liked this chili. (See the recipe Sloppy Joes for a Crowd on page 168.)

Prep time 25 minutes
Serves 6

2 tablespoons (29 ml) avocado oil
1½ pounds (680 g) ground beef
1 15-ounce (425 g) can tomato sauce
¼ cup (44 g) mustard
1 tablespoon dried minced onion
1 tablespoon chili powder
1 tablespoon (20 g) honey
1 teaspoon dried sage

1½ pounds (680 g) sweet potatoes, peeled and cut into 1/2-inch cubes
2 tablespoons (16 g) tapioca flour
2 cups (475 ml) Homemade Beef Stock (page 281)
½ cup (120 ml) pickle or sauerkraut juice
Chopped pickles or sauerkraut, for serving

1 Heat the avocado oil in a large skillet over medium-high heat. Add the ground beef and cook, breaking the meat into small pieces, until it is browned and cooked through. Transfer the meat to a 4-quart (3.8 liter) slow cooker.

2 Add tomato sauce, mustard, onion, chili powder, honey, and sage to the slow cooker. Stir well. Stir in the sweet potatoes.

3 Whisk the tapioca flour into the stock and add it, along with the pickle juice, to the slow cooker.

4 Cover and cook on low for 6 to 8 hours or on high for 3 to 4 hours.

5 Taste, and add salt if needed. Serve with chopped pickles or sauerkraut.

Smoky BBQ Beef Chili

The barbecue sauce in this recipe may make you wonder "Am I eating chili or brisket?" If you're particular about the ingredients in your barbecue sauce, try making your own! You'll find a few recipes in the Pantry Basics chapter (page 279). For this chili I'd recommend the Balsamic BBQ Sauce (page 290) or Blackberry-Chipotle BBQ Sauce (page 291).

Prep time 20 minutes

Serves 6

2 tablespoons (29 ml) avocado oil

1½ pounds (680 g) ground beef

1 large onion, diced

2 tablespoons (15 g) chili powder

1 tablespoon steak seasoning

1 tablespoon ground cumin

1 teaspoon chipotle powder

3 tablespoon (45 ml) coconut aminos

2 bell peppers (red, orange, or yellow), stemmed, seeded, and diced

3 cloves garlic, minced

1½ cups (355 ml) Homemade Beef Stock (page 281)

1 15-ounce (425 g) can tomato sauce

⅔ cup (170 g) smoky barbecue sauce

Thinly sliced green onions and chopped avocado, for serving

1 Heat avocado oil in a large skillet over medium-high heat. Add the ground beef and cook over medium-high heat until brown.

2 Add onion, chili powder, steak seasoning, cumin, chipotle powder, and aminos, and cook for an additional 5 to 7 minutes, until the onions are soft and translucent. Transfer beef and onion mixture to a 4-quart (3.8 liter) slow cooker.

3 Add bell peppers, garlic, ½ cup (120 ml) of stock, tomato sauce, and barbecue sauce to the slow cooker. Stir to combine.

4 Cover and cook on low for 6 to 8 hours or on high for 3 to 4 hours.

5 Taste, and add salt if necessary. Add more stock to reach desired consistency, and serve with green onions and avocado.

Citrus Pork Chili with Mango

This chili gave me grief for a while. At first it was missing something, and I couldn't figure out what it was. A friend of mine and her husband tried it out for me and tinkered with it. After some tweaks, they entered it into a chili cook-off and won second place—in Texas, mind you. It's a slightly exotic take on chili, with lots of citrus, sweet mango, and coconut milk. And clearly, it is a winner.

Prep time *20 minutes*
Serves 6

2 pounds (905 g) pork shoulder roast, cut into large chunks

2 teaspoons sea salt

½ teaspoon black pepper

2 teaspoons (15 g) chili powder

1 teaspoon ground cumin

1 teaspoon coconut sugar

1 teaspoon orange zest

1 teaspoon lemon zest

¼ cup (60 ml) orange juice

¼ cup (60 ml) lemon juice

3 tablespoons (45 ml) melted Home-made Ghee (page 287)

1 15-ounce (425 g) can diced tomatoes

1 8-ounce (227 g) can tomato sauce

1 cup (160 g) diced onion

2 cloves garlic, minced

1 jalapeño, seeded and minced

2 tablespoons (45 ml) coconut aminos

1 4-ounce (113 g) can diced green chillies

1 mango, peeled, pitted, and cut into 1-inch (2.5 cm) cubes

½ cup chopped fresh cilantro

1 sprig fresh mint, leaves removed and minced

1 cup (235 ml) full-fat coconut milk

1 Place the pork in a medium bowl.

2 In a small bowl, combine the salt, pepper, chili powder, cumin, coconut sugar, and citrus zest. Sprinkle over the pork and, using your hands, toss until pork is evenly coated. Place the pork in a 4-quart (3.8 liter) slow cooker.

3 Add the citrus juice, ghee, tomatoes, tomato sauce, onion, garlic, jalapeño, aminos, and green chilies to the cooker and give the mixture a stir.

4 Cover and cook on low for 6 to 7 hours (or 3 to 4 on high), until pork is very tender. Remove the pork from the cooker and shred it into bite-sized pieces. Return the pork to the chili.

5 Stir in the mango chunks, cilantro, mint, and coconut milk. Cover and let the chili cook for another 15 minutes before serving.

3

CHICKEN AND TURKEY

Chicken and turkey make the perfect clean slate for just about any flavor. As an added bonus, they cook beautifully in a slow cooker—especially bone-in cuts. You can use bone-in or boneless for any recipe in this section that doesn't require pre-chopped chicken.

Recipes

Basic Seasoned Shredded Chicken (for freezing)

This recipe started out on a smaller scale as a way to keep small batches of cooked, simply seasoned chicken on hand for my one-year-old. He started eating solids while I was working on recipes for this book and he developed a taste for slow-cooked meat and vegetables. When my other kids kept eating "his" chicken, we realized it would be great to make a bunch of it in bulk and freeze it for future meals and recipes.

Prep time 5 minutes

Makes 3 to 4 quarts (2.8 to 3.8 liters) of shredded chicken

3 to 4 pounds (1.4 to 1.8 kg) chicken breasts or thighs

1 tablespoon (18 g) all-purpose salt-free seasoning

1½ teaspoons sea salt

¼ cup (60 ml) chicken broth

1 Sprinkle the salt-free seasoning and salt over the chicken. Use your hands to spread the seasoning over the meat evenly.

2 Put the meat into a 4- or 6-quart (3.8 or 5.7 liter) slow cooker. Pour the chicken broth down the side of the cooker. Cover and cook on low for 6 to 7 hours, until the chicken is tender.

3 Remove the chicken pieces from the pot, shred them into bite-sized pieces, and return the chicken to the juices. Using a pair of tongs, mix the cooking liquid back into the chicken.

4 Let the chicken cool to room temperature. Divide the chicken and juices into freezer-safe zip-top bags or containers. Freeze until you're ready to use it.

Lemon-Herb Whole Chicken

Whole, roasted chickens are an easy and beloved meal once you get over the trauma of wrangling a raw chicken. Confession: I had an extremely hard time handling raw meat until I was in my mid-twenties. My experience was limited to boneless, skinless chicken breasts and ground beef. Prepping a whole chicken was a big hurdle for me, but once I did it, I felt much more comfortable with raw meat in general. And I was shocked about how easy it was! You'll love this classic lemon-herb chicken. You can always throw one in the slow cooker to shred and use later or even freeze.

Prep time 15 minutes, plus marinating time
Serves 6

1 whole chicken, 3 to 4 pounds (1.4 to 1.8 kg)

1 tablespoon (18 g) sea salt

1 teaspoon black pepper

1 teaspoon dried rosemary

1 teaspoon dried thyme

1 teaspoon dried tarragon

1 whole bulb of garlic plus 2 cloves garlic, minced

1 lemon

2 tablespoons (29 ml) avocado oil

1 Remove the neck and any organs from the cavity of the chicken. (Put them in a freezer zip-top bag and add the rest of the bones later for making stock.) Loosen the skin of the chicken by slipping your fingers under the skin and—without ripping the skin—separate it from the flesh. Start on the breast side and do this with the thigh and leg, too. I like to cut a small hole with a pair of kitchen shears or a knife on the side of the chicken between the thigh and leg, and stick a finger under the skin to loosen it. Place the chicken on a large plate or small pan.

2 In a small bowl, combine the salt, pepper, rosemary, thyme, tarragon, 2 minced garlic cloves, and zest from the lemon. Stir the avocado oil into the salt-herb mixture. Take this mixture and get as much of it as you can underneath the skin—on the breast, thighs, and legs. It helps to maneuver the seasoning from the outside of the skin, massaging it with your fingers. Rub the remaining seasoning over the outside of the chicken.

3 Cover the chicken with plastic wrap and chill for 4 to 12 hours.

4 When you're ready to cook the chicken, make 4 balls out of aluminum foil, about 2 to 3 inches (5 to 7.5 cm) each. Arrange them in the bottom of a 6-quart (5.7 liter) slow cooker, forming a square.

5 Place the chicken, breast-side down, in the prepared slow cooker.

6 Take the garlic bulb and cut about an inch from the top, exposing the cloves. Cut the lemon in half. Put the bulb into the cavity of the chicken. Squeeze the juice from the lemon over the chicken and put the lemon halves into the cavity with the garlic bulb. Pour ¼ cup water (60 ml) into the bottom of the cooker.

7 Cover and cook on low for 4 to 5 hours. Internal temperature should be about 160°F (71°C).

8 Remove the chicken from the slow cooker and serve. (You probably won't be able to get it all out in one piece.)

Spicy Cajun Whole Chicken

After making this spicy, flavorful, rotisserie-like chicken at home, you'll never want to buy one again. This chicken also makes excellent taco meat or you can add it to soups and chili.

Prep time 15 minutes, plus marinating time
Serves 6

1 whole chicken, 4 to 5 pounds (1.8 to 2.3 kg)

3 tablespoons (18.8 g) Cajun Spice Blend (page 284)

2 teaspoons sea salt

½ teaspoon crushed red pepper flakes

3 tablespoons (44 ml) avocado oil

1 Remove the neck and any organs from the cavity of the chicken. (Put them in a freezer zip-top bag and add the rest of the bones later for making stock.) Loosen the skin of the chicken by slipping your fingers under the skin and—without ripping the skin—separate it from the flesh. Start on the breast side and do this with the thigh and leg, too. I like to cut a small hole with a pair of kitchen shears or a knife on the side of the chicken between the thigh and leg, and stick a finger under the skin to loosen it. Place the chicken on a large plate or small pan.

2 Combine the remaining ingredients in a small bowl to make a paste. Take this mixture and get as much of it as you can underneath the skin—on the breast, thighs, and legs. It helps to maneuver the seasoning from the outside of the skin, by massaging it with your fingers. Rub the remaining seasoning over the outside of the chicken.

3 Cover the chicken with plastic wrap and chill for 4 to 12 hours.

4 When you're ready to cook the chicken, make 4 balls out of aluminum foil, about 2 to 3 inches each. Arrange them in the bottom of a 6-quart (5.7 liter) slow cooker, forming a square.

5 Place the chicken, breast-side down, on top of the foil balls.

6 Cover and cook on low for 4 to 5 hours. Using a meat thermometer, check the temperature of the chicken in the thigh or the thickest part of the breast. It should register 160°F (71°C).

7 Remove the chicken from the slow cooker and serve. (You probably won't be able to get it all out in one piece.)

Salt-and-Vinegar–Brined Whole Chicken with Rosemary

Sometimes you just need an easy, basic, flavorful chicken recipe for a meal or to use in other recipes. This simple salt-and-vinegar brine is easy to whip up (no heating required!) and thoroughly seasons the chicken, resulting in tender, juicy meat you can shred and freeze, or dive in and eat right away.

Prep time 15 minutes, plus brining time
Serves 6

2 cups (475 ml) white vinegar
¼ cup (75 g) kosher salt
3 to 4 pounds (1.4 to 1.8 kg) whole chicken

2 sprigs fresh rosemary
Freshly ground black pepper

1 Combine the vinegar, salt, and 4 cups (946 ml) water in a bowl large enough to hold the chicken. Stir until the salt dissolves.

2 Remove the neck and any organs from the cavity of the chicken. Submerge the chicken in the brine, adding up to 4 more cups (946 ml) of water. Cover and chill for 12 to 18 hours.

3 When you're ready to cook the chicken, make 4 balls out of aluminum foil, about 2 to 3 inches each. Arrange them in the bottom of a 6-quart (5.7 liter) slow cooker, forming a square.

4 Loosen the skin from the flesh by gently working your fingers underneath the skin. Insert the rosemary sprigs under the skin—one on each breast. Sprinkle the chicken generously with freshly ground black pepper.

5 Place the chicken, breast-side down, in the prepared slow cooker.

6 Cover and cook on low for 4 to 5 hours. Internal temperature should be about 160°F (71°C).

Green Chilli Shredded Chicken

Christina Lane, a blogger, cookbook author, and friend, paid me the highest compliment when she tried this recipe—"It tastes like Texas!" That's a pretty bold statement coming from a Texan. You'll love how easy this recipe is, too, when you toss the sauce ingredients into the blender, buzz it up, and pour it over the chicken.

Prep time 15 minutes
Serves 10 to 12

4 4-ounce (113 g) cans mild (or hot) diced green chillies

1 large sweet onion, chopped

6 cloves garlic, peeled

1½ teaspoons ground cumin

1½ teaspoons ground coriander

1 tablespoon (18 g) sea salt

½ teaspoon black pepper

1 jalapeño, seeded (seeding optional)

1 lime, zested and juiced (about ¼ cup juice, or 60 ml)

5 to 6 pounds (2.3 to 2.7 kg) uncooked chicken (boneless, skinless or skin-on, breasts or thighs)

1 cup (16 g) chopped fresh cilantro

2 green onions, thinly sliced

1 Combine chillies, onion, garlic, cumin, coriander, salt, pepper, jalapeño, lime zest, and lime juice in a blender or large food processor. Blend until smooth.

2 Place chicken in a 4- or 6-quart (3.8 or 5.7 liter) slow cooker. Pour the chilli mixture over the top. Push and lift the chicken around a bit so the chilli mixture can get between the chicken pieces.

3 Close and cook for 6 to 7 hours on low or 4 hours on high.

4 Remove the chicken, shred it, and place it back into the slow cooker. Stir in the cilantro, green onions, and additional salt if necessary.

Note: If you'd rather have chunks of chilli and onion, you don't have to blend anything. Just mix the sauce ingredients together in a bowl and pour it over the chicken.

Easy Shredded Chicken for Tacos

This chicken is really versatile. It's great in tacos, but you can also use it in egg dishes, salads, or even a quick chicken taco soup. Save about two cups of chicken and make a soup by cooking it with a quart (946 ml) of chicken stock, a couple handfuls of diced vegetables, a teaspoon or so of taco seasoning, and a sliced avocado. My kids love soups like this in their lunches, which I can throw together while I'm getting breakfast ready in the morning.

Prep time 5 minutes

Makes about 5 cups (700 g) of shredded chicken

4 large boneless, skinless chicken breasts

Juice from half a lime

1 cup (250 mg) salsa or fresh *pico de gallo*

4 teaspoons Homemade Taco Seasoning (page 284)

Paleo Tortillas (page 256), Simple Guacamole (page 59), additional salsa, and hot sauce, for serving

1 Place the chicken breasts in a 4-quart (3.8 liter) slow cooker. Pour the lemon juice over the chicken.

2 Add the salsa to the cooker and sprinkle the taco seasoning over the top. Lift the chicken breasts to ensure the salsa and seasoning gets in between them.

3 Cover and cook on low for 6 to 7 hours (or on high for 3 to 4 hours).

4 Remove the chicken, shred it, and place it back in the cooker for 10 more minutes to soak up some of the pot juices.

5 Serve with your favorite taco fixings.

Island Balsamic BBQ Shredded Chicken

Every slow-cooking repertoire needs a good shredded BBQ chicken recipe—and this is mine. I love the addition of fresh, sweet pineapple and how it mingles perfectly with the tart, smoky Balsamic BBQ Sauce (page 290). Making barbecue sauce from scratch is incredibly easy, and a necessity when living a paleo lifestyle, given that almost all commercial BBQ sauces contain refined sugar in some form. I like to make a double batch of sauce and use it in a couple of meals during the month. The sauce keeps for several weeks refrigerated and also freezes well.

Prep time 20 minutes

Serves 8

3 pounds (1.4 kg) boneless, skinless chicken breasts or thighs

1 teaspoon sea salt

3 cups (495 g) chopped fresh pineapple or unsweetened pineapple tidbits

1 cup (160 g) diced sweet onion

1 large jalapeño, seeded (if desired) and diced

2 cloves garlic, minced

2 cups (500 g) Balsamic BBQ Sauce (page 290)

1 Sprinkle the salt over the chicken, then place it in a 4-quart (3.8 liter) slow cooker. Add the pineapple, onion, jalapeño, garlic, and 1 cup (250 g) of the BBQ sauce.

2 Cover and cook on low for 6 to 7 hours, until the chicken is tender and pulls apart easily with a fork.

3 Remove the chicken from the slow cooker, shred the meat into bite-sized pieces, and return them to the slow cooker. Add another ½ cup (125 g) of BBQ sauce to the chicken. Toss, and add more if desired.

4 Serve the chicken with your preferred side dish, such as Southwest Cabbage Slaw (page 252), Squash Noodles (page 248), Zucchini Flatbread (page 254), or "Baked" Sweet Potatoes (page 253).

Chicken Tikka Masala with Cauliflower

Marinating chicken overnight in coconut milk and spices really gives a boost of flavor! Garam masala is a common Indian spice blend and is now widely available in the spice section of many grocery stores. If you have a well-stocked spice cabinet, you may have the ingredients to make your own—just do a quick Internet search to find a simple recipe. I prefer the ones that are heavy on cinnamon and cloves.

Prep time 30 minutes, plus overnight marinating

Serves 8 to 10

1½ pounds (680 g) boneless, skinless chicken breasts or thighs, cut into 1-inch (2.5 cm) pieces

1 13.5-ounce (398 ml) can coconut milk

2 tablespoons (14 g) ground cumin

1 tablespoon ground coriander

1 teaspoon turmeric

6 cloves garlic, minced

1-inch (2.5 cm) knob of ginger, minced (about 1 tablespoon)

1 teaspoon sea salt

1 jalapeño, minced

½ cauliflower head

1 medium yellow onion, cut into large chunks

1 red bell pepper, cut into large chunks

2 large tomatoes, cut into large chunks

3 tablespoons (90 g) tomato paste

1 teaspoon garam masala

Juice from ½ lime

½ cup fresh chopped cilantro

Cauliflower Rice (pages 249 and 250) or Squash Noodles (page 248), for serving

1 The day before you make this, place the chicken pieces in a zip-top bag. Mix the coconut milk, cumin, coriander, turmeric, garlic, ginger, salt, and jalapeño in a large measuring cup or small mixing bowl. Pour the mixture into the bag with the chicken and mash the bag around to ensure that all of the chicken is coated. Chill for 4 to 12 hours.

2 On cooking day, place the chicken, marinade, and cauliflower into a 6-quart (5.7 liter) slow cooker.

3 Place the onion, bell pepper, tomatoes, and tomato paste into a food processor. Pulse until everything is chopped fine. Pour it over the chicken and cauliflower in the slow cooker. Give it a stir to coat everything in the marinade and vegetable mixture.

4 Cover and cook on low for 6 to 7 hours (or 3 to 3½ hours on high).

5 Stir in the garam masala, lime juice, and cilantro.

6 Serve with Cauliflower Rice, zucchini noodles, or roasted potatoes.

Thai Chicken Curry

Store-bought curry paste is a great time saver. Its wide range of spices and seasonings makes it a solid foundation for a good curry. You can find it in the Asian section of most grocery stores or in an Asian market. Be sure to read the label to make sure there aren't any undesirable ingredients in there!

Prep time 20 minutes
Serves 6

2 medium zucchini, cut into 1-inch (2.5 cm) pieces

3 large carrots, peeled and cut into 1-inch (2.5 cm) pieces

1 large sweet potato or 2 medium Yukon gold potatoes, cut into 1-inch (2.5 cm) pieces

3 tablespoons (42 g) coconut oil, divided

3 large boneless, skinless chicken breasts

Sea salt

1 large onion, diced

1½-inch (3.5 cm) knob of fresh ginger, minced

1 to 2 tablespoons red or green curry paste

1 14-ounce (400 ml) can full-fat coconut milk

1 lime, zested and juiced

2 tablespoons (38 g) fish sauce

1 teaspoon sea salt

1 bunch fresh basil, thinly sliced

Cauliflower Rice (pages 249 and 250) or Squash Noodles (page 248), for serving

1 Place chopped zucchini, carrots, and potatoes into a 4-quart (3.8 liter) slow cooker.

2 Heat coconut oil in a large skillet over medium-high heat. Sprinkle chicken generously with salt and add it to the skillet. Sear both sides until they are golden brown. The chicken does not need to be cooked through. Transfer the chicken to the slow cooker.

3 Add another tablespoon of coconut oil to the skillet. Add the onion and ginger. Cook, stirring occasionally, until the onion is translucent and slightly brown, about 7 to 9 minutes. Add the curry paste to the skillet and cook for another minute. Add coco-nut milk, zest and juice from the lime, fish sauce, and sea salt. Heat until bubbly, then remove from heat.

4 Pour the curry sauce over the chicken and vegetables. Cook on low for 5 to 6 hours or on high for 3 to 4 hours, until the chicken is tender and shreds easily with a fork.

5 Remove the chicken from the cooker. Shred the chicken into large chunks, then return it to the cooker. Stir in half of the basil a few minutes before serving. Reserve the rest for garnish.

6 Serve curry over Cauliflower Rice or Squash Noodles.

Southeast Asian Coconut Chicken Curry

My seven-year-old was researching Micronesia for a school project, and, much to my delight, was required to bring a dish to share. After pulling her away from the cakes and desserts she found after a quick Internet search, I convinced my little sweet-toothed daughter that some curry and jasmine rice would be fun to bring instead. (She's obsessed with rice.) After doing a little research of my own, I came up with this gem of a curry. It's a little Indian, with aromatic spices, and a little Thai, with a touch of lemongrass and fish sauce.

Prep time 20 minutes
Serves 6

2 large boneless, skinless chicken breasts, cut into 1-inch (2.5 cm) pieces

1 teaspoon sea salt

1½ tablespoons good-quality curry powder

4 cloves garlic, minced

1 tablespoon lemongrass, finely grated (or 1 tablespoon [17 g] lemongrass paste)

¼ teaspoon ground nutmeg

⅛ teaspoon ground cloves

1 red bell pepper, seeded and thinly sliced

1 medium zucchini, halved and cut into ¼-inch (5 mm) half-moons

2 cups (140 g) thinly sliced baby portobello mushrooms

2 medium carrots, peeled and sliced into ¼-inch (5 mm) pieces

1 Thai chilli or jalapeño, seeded and minced

1 cup (160 g) chopped sweet onion

½ cup (120 ml) Simple Chicken Stock (page 280)

3 tablespoons (57 g) fish sauce

1 13.5-ounce (398 ml) can full-fat coconut milk

Cauliflower Rice (pages 249 and 250), limes, and chopped fresh cilantro, for serving

1 Place the chicken pieces in a medium bowl. In a small bowl, combine the salt, curry powder, garlic, lemongrass, nutmeg, and cloves. Mix well, and rub the seasoning blend into the chicken.

2 Place the bell pepper, zucchini, mushrooms, carrots, chilli, onion, stock, and fish sauce in a 4-quart (3.8 liter) slow cooker. Add the chicken on top of the vegetables. Cover and cook on low for 6 to 7 hours (or on high for 3 to 4 hours). Stir halfway through to break up the chicken if it has clumped together.

3 Stir coconut milk into the curry, and cook for another 15 minutes.

4 Taste, and add more salt or lime juice if necessary.

5 Serve with Cauliflower Rice, cilantro, and limes.

Sweet and Sour Pineapple Chicken

Attempting to re-create a classic Chinese dish full of umami flavors is quite a task when soy sauce isn't an option. You'll see a couple of not-so-traditional ingredients in this: coconut aminos and fish sauce. They give this a deep, salty underlying flavor that is similar to soy sauce. You can find coconut aminos in health food stores and fish sauce in the Asian section of most grocery stores. Just be sure to check the ingredients, as some brands of fish sauce contain sugar.

Prep time 30 minutes
Serves 6

2 large boneless, skinless chicken breasts, cut into 1-inch (2.5 cm) pieces

½ of a red bell pepper, diced small

1 cup (165 g) pineapple chunks (fresh or canned)

2 cloves garlic, minced

¼ cup (60 ml) pineapple juice

Juice from ½ a lemon (about 3 tablespoons, or 45 ml)

2 tablespoons (30 ml) rice vinegar

2 tablespoons (16 g) finely grated fresh ginger

2 tablespoons (30 ml) tomato sauce

4 tablespoons (85 g) honey

1 tablespoon (15 ml) apple cider vinegar

⅓ cup (80 ml) coconut aminos

1 tablespoon tapioca flour

1 tablespoon (19 g) fish sauce

Cauliflower Rice (pages 249 and 250), for serving

1 In a 4-quart (3.8 liter) slow cooker, add the chicken, bell pepper, pineapple chunks, garlic, pineapple juice, lemon juice, rice vinegar, and ginger. Give it a stir.

2 Cook on low for 5 to 6 hours (or on high for 2 to 3).

3 When the chicken is cooked through and very tender, remove the chicken and other chunks from the pot. Set aside.

4 Transfer the cooking juices to a medium skillet. Return the chicken and vegetables to the cooker to keep warm.

5 Add the tomato sauce, honey, cider vinegar, aminos, tapioca flour, and fish sauce to the skillet. Whisk well. Bring to a boil and let it cook for about 10 minutes or until slightly thickened.

6 Pour sauce over the chicken. Cook on high for about 10 to 15 minutes, until everything is heated through and bubbly.

7 Serve with Cauliflower Rice or another side dish.

Orange-Sesame Chicken

In the early years of my marriage—when my husband and I ate fast food more often—I had a "usual" at a nearby Chinese food place: orange chicken, stir-fried vegetables, and chow mein. I really, really loved their orange chicken. But since learning about food-processing practices and the biological effects certain foods have on the body, I can't look at a piece of that chicken without thinking about the sourcing of the animals, the starchy, gluten-filled breading,

and the oxidized oils and sugary sauce in which it was fried and tossed. Not to mention the preservatives and flavorings.

Learning about food sourcing and nutrition can be enlightening and life-changing, but sometimes it's just a plain old buzzkill. All joking aside, this is now my go-to orange chicken recipe, and it doesn't make me think of anything but how delicious it is.

Prep time 15 minutes

Serves 6

2½ pounds (1.1 kg) skinless, boneless chicken breasts or thighs, cut into 1-inch (2.5 cm) pieces

1 teaspoon sea salt

½ medium onion, thinly sliced

3 cloves garlic, minced

1-inch (2.5 cm) knob of fresh ginger, minced or grated

2 oranges, zest and juice

Juice from 1 large lemon

2 tablespoons (30 ml) sesame oil, divided

⅛ teaspoon black pepper

Pinch of crushed red pepper flakes

⅓ cup (115 g) honey

⅓ (80 ml) cup coconut aminos

2 tablespoons (16 g) tapioca flour

1 tablespoon toasted sesame seeds

Cauliflower Rice (pages 249 and 250), for serving

1 Place the chicken in a 4-quart (3.8 liter) slow cooker. Sprinkle with salt, and toss to coat evenly.

2 Add the onion, garlic, ginger, 2 teaspoons orange zest, half of the lemon juice, 1 tablespoon (15 ml) sesame oil, black pepper, and red pepper flakes. Give it a quick stir.

3 Cover and cook on low for 5 to 6 hours, until chicken is very tender.

4 You'll need to transfer the cooking liquid in the pot to a medium skillet on the stove. You can do this by pouring the contents of the cooker into a large mesh strainer with a container to catch the liquid. Or you can remove the chicken mixture from the cooker with a slotted spoon and transfer the remaining liquid to the skillet.

5 Return the chicken mixture to the cooker to keep warm.

6 To the skillet, add the honey, coconut aminos, the remaining orange zest, the juice from both oranges, the remaining lemon juice, and 1 tablespoon (15 ml) sesame oil. Whisk in the tapioca flour to remove any lumps. Bring the mixture to a boil, reduce the heat to medium, and let it cook at a medium boil for about 15 minutes, until the mixture is reduced and has thickened enough to coat the back of a spoon. Taste, and add more salt or honey if desired.

7 Pour the orange-sesame sauce over the chicken mixture in the slow cooker. If the chicken needs to be warmed again, cover and cook it for about 10 to 15 minutes on high.

8 Transfer the chicken and sauce to a serving platter and sprinkle with toasted sesame seeds.

9 Serve with Cauliflower Rice.

Note: Feel free to add more crushed red pepper if you'd like this spicier.

Kung Pao Chicken and Vegetables

I love pretty food, and I'm a very visual person. Sometimes I add certain vegetables to a recipe solely to add color. In this case I chose orange and yellow bell peppers and green snow peas so I could add them to the red from the chillies and create a rainbow. Nerdy? Perhaps. But I think there's some truth to the saying, "We eat with our eyes first." My eyes fell in love with this dish instantly, and luckily, my mouth followed suit.

Prep time 25 minutes

Serves 6

2 large skinless, boneless chicken breasts (about 1½ pounds, or 680 g), cut into 1-inch (2.5 cm) pieces

1 teaspoon sea salt

⅔ cup (160 ml) coconut aminos

2 tablespoons (30 ml) mirin or rice vinegar

2 tablespoons (20 g) fresh minced garlic (6 to 8 cloves)

2 tablespoons (16 g) freshly grated ginger

1 tablespoon (19 g) fish sauce

2 bell peppers (any color), seeded and cut into 1-inch (2.5 cm) pieces

½ of a medium onion, thinly sliced

2 teaspoons (20 g) tomato paste

5 to 10 dried red chillies

3 tablespoons (60 g) honey

1 tablespoon (15 ml) balsamic vinegar

1 tablespoon (15 ml) sesame oil

¼ teaspoon Szechuan peppercorns, crushed

A large handful of snow peas

2 green onions, cut into 1-inch (2.5 cm) pieces

¼ cup (69 g) cashew halves

¼ cup chopped fresh cilantro

1 tablespoon toasted sesame seeds

Cauliflower Rice (pages 249 and 250), for serving

1 Sprinkle 1 teaspoon of salt on the chicken, toss it around to coat evenly. Place the chicken in a 4-quart (3.8 liter) slow cooker.

2 In a medium bowl combine the aminos, vinegar, garlic, ginger, and fish sauce. Pour half of the mixture over the chicken and set the rest aside for later. Add the bell peppers and onions to the slow cooker, too.

3 Cover and cook on low for 5 to 6 hours. Chicken should be tender, but not dry.

4 Pour the cooking juices into a medium skillet. I just tilt the cooker until most of the juices run out of it, but you can remove the chicken and vegetables with a slotted spoon if that is easier. Return the chicken and vegetables to the cooker if you choose to strain the juices that way.

5 To the juices in the skillet, add the reserved aminos mixture, tomato paste, chillies, honey, balsamic, sesame oil, and peppercorns. Cook over medium-high heat for about 15 minutes, until mixture has reduced and thickened slightly. Pour the sauce back into the cooker with the chicken and vegetables.

6 Stir in the snow peas, green onions, cashews, and cilantro. Cook on high for about 15 minutes.

7 Serve with Cauliflower Rice and a sprinkle of sesame seeds.

Notes:

Use 3 to 4 chillies for a kid-friendly dish with a slight kick (just don't let them eat the chillies) and add more chillies for more heat.

To toast your own sesame seeds, put them in a small skillet and cook over medium heat, shaking the pan occasionally, for 3 to 4 minutes until they are fragrant and slightly golden brown.

Szechuan peppercorns are a signature ingredient in Kung Pao chicken, but sometimes they can be hard to find. If you can't find them, just use regular black peppercorns.

Greek Chicken Thighs with Zucchini, Fennel, and Garlic Aioli

There's this little Greek restaurant in Sacramento (Opa! Opa!—and you must say it in an excited voice) that has incredibly garlicky hummus. It's fantastic. I wanted the same punch of garlic in this dish, so I added it in the form of an aioli—which is basically a flavored mayonnaise. It also adds a creamy complement to the chicken, vegetables, and salty olives.

Prep time 20 minutes
Serves 8

For chicken thighs:
½ teaspoon sea salt
1 teaspoon dried oregano
½ teaspoon dried thyme
2 cloves garlic, minced
½ teaspoon black pepper
10 boneless, skinless chicken thighs
3 medium zucchini, cut into ¼-inch (5 mm) half-moons
2 cups (174 g) sliced fennel (1 whole fennel bulb), reserving a few fronds
¼ cup (25 g) sliced kalamata olives

1 or 2 large lemons
2 tablespoons (30 ml) extra-virgin olive oil

For garlic aioli:
1 cup (225 g) Paleo-Friendly Mayonnaise (page 286)
3 cloves garlic, minced
3 tablespoons (45 ml) lemon juice
Sea salt
1 teaspoon honey (optional)

1 Combine the salt, oregano, thyme, garlic, and pepper in a small bowl. Rub the herb mixture on the chicken, coating both sides. Place the chicken in a 6-quart (5.7 liter) slow cooker.

2 Place the zucchini, fennel, and olives over the chicken.

3 Slice the lemons into ¼-inch (5 mm) rings and lay them over the vegetables. Place the reserved fennel fronds on top of the lemons. Drizzle the olive oil over the top.

4 Cover and cook on high for 3 to 4 hours (or on low for 6 to 7 hours).

5 To make the aioli, combine the mayonnaise, garlic, and lemon juice in a small bowl. Stir it together and add a couple generous pinches of salt. Taste, and add more salt or lemon juice as needed. Cover and chill until ready to use. Aioli is best if it chills for at least 30 minutes.

6 Transfer the chicken and vegetables to a serving platter (lemons included).

7 Serve with garlic aioli.

Easy Italian Chicken Sausage and Peppers with Marinara

I always keep some precooked, uncured Italian sausages around because they make such fast, easy meals. Our family loved these saucy sausages and peppers over "Baked" Sweet Potatoes (page 253), but Cauliflower Rice (pages 249 and 250) or Squash Noodles (page 248) would also be good options.

Prep time 10 minutes

Serves 6

12 ounces (340 g) precooked Italian chicken sausages, cut into 1-inch (2.5 cm) pieces

½ medium onion, thinly sliced

2 bell peppers (any color), thinly sliced

2 cups (500 g) Basic Marinara (page 283)

2 tablespoons (30 ml) balsamic vinegar

Cauliflower Rice (pages 249 and 250), Squash Noodles (page 248), or "Baked" Sweet Potatoes (page 253), for serving

1 Place all ingredients into a 2- or 4-quart (1.9 or 3.8 liter) slow cooker. Stir to cover everything with marinara.

2 Cover and cook on low for 5 hours.

3 Serve with Cauliflower Rice, Squash Noodles, or "Baked" Sweet Potatoes.

Maple-Mustard Chicken with Carrots and Brussels Sprouts

I love the combination of maple and mustard: sweet playing off of tangy. But the carrots and Brussels sprouts nearly stole the show, because the sauce created in the cooker was the perfect complement to the vegetables.

Prep time 15 minutes
Serves 6

1 pound (455 g) carrots, peeled and cut into 1-inch (2.5 cm) chunks

2 pounds (905 g) boneless chicken breasts or thighs

Sea salt

Black pepper

½ cup (88 g) Dijon mustard

¼ cup (80 g) pure maple syrup

1 clove garlic, minced

1 tablespoon (15 ml) apple cider vinegar

8 ounces (225 g) trimmed Brussels sprouts (cut the larger ones in half)

1 Place the carrots in a 4-quart (3.8 liter) slow cooker.

2 Sprinkle the chicken generously on both sides with salt and pepper, and place it on top of the vegetables.

3 Whisk together the mustard, syrup, garlic, and vinegar. Pour over the chicken, lifting the chicken to coat both sides.

4 Cook for 5 hours on low. Add the Brussels sprouts to the top of the pot; cover and cook for another hour, until all of the vegetables are tender and the chicken pulls apart easily with a fork.

5 Transfer the chicken to a plate and separate into large pieces. Serve with the vegetables and maple-mustard sauce from the pot.

Note: This goes well with Cauliflower Rice (pages 249 and 250) or a salad.

Chicken and Sausage Peperoncini Stew

This recipe is based on a shrimp recipe I found in Bon Appétit *magazine several years ago. I had recently fallen in love with* peperoncini *peppers, so I did some ingredient swaps and adapted it for my slow cooker. The peperoncini add a little kick, so I use sweet Italian sausage when I make it for my kids. If you'd like to turn it up a notch, try using spicy Italian sausage.*

Prep time 25 minutes
Serves 6

1 tablespoon avocado oil

1 pound (455 g) bulk Italian sausage (sweet or spicy), casings removed, if necessary

1 to 1½ pounds (455 to 680 g) boneless, skinless chicken breasts or thighs, cut into 1-inch (2.5 cm) cubes

½ cup (68 g) sliced peperoncini peppers, plus ½ cup (120 ml) liquid from jar

½ cup (57 g) chopped shallots

2 cloves garlic, chopped

1 teaspoon smoked paprika

1 teaspoon dried thyme

1 teaspoon dried oregano

1 teaspoon dried basil

A pinch of cayenne pepper (more if you'd like it spicier)

2 cups (500 ml) Basic Marinara (page 283) or paleo-friendly marinara

½ cup (120 ml) full-fat coconut milk

Cauliflower Rice (pages 249 and 250) or Squash Noodles (page 248), for serving

1 Heat oil in a large skillet over medium-high heat. Add sausage to the pan and brown the meat, stirring frequently, breaking it up into small chunks. It doesn't need to be cooked all the way through.

2 Transfer the sausage to a 4-quart (3.8 liter) slow cooker.

3 Turn the heat up to high and add chicken pieces. Brown the chicken quickly (again, it doesn't have to be cooked through). Transfer chicken and any juices to the slow cooker.

4 Add the peperoncini slices and liquid, shallots, garlic, smoked paprika, thyme, oregano, basil, cayenne pepper, and marinara to the slow cooker and give everything a quick stir.

5 Cover and cook on low for 4 to 5 hours or on high for 2 to 3 hours. Stir in the coconut milk, cover, and cook for another 10 minutes.

6 Serve over desired side dish.

Strawberry-Balsamic Chicken

It saddens me that I'm late to the strawberry-balsamic game. I'm a convert now, and I've made up for it with this recipe. Adding a strawberry-balsamic reduction at the end really amps up the tangy-sweet flavors. This is the same sauce that goes on the vanilla cake on page 272. Talk about versatile!

Prep time 15 minutes
Serves 8

3 pounds (1.4 kg) chicken breasts or thighs
¼ teaspoon sea salt
¼ teaspoon black pepper
1 tablespoon Dijon mustard
½ teaspoon Italian seasoning

4 cloves garlic
½ cup (245 g) tomato sauce
1 cup (235 ml) balsamic vinegar
1½ pounds (680 g) strawberries, diced
2 tablespoons (40 g) honey

1 Place the chicken in a 4-quart (3.8 liter) slow cooker. Sprinkle the salt and pepper over the chicken. Add the mustard, Italian seasoning, garlic, and tomato sauce. Give the chicken a stir to coat evenly.

2 Cover and cook on low for 5 to 6 hours, until the chicken is tender.

3 While the chicken is cooking, combine the balsamic vinegar, two-thirds of the strawberries, and the honey in a medium skillet. Cook over medium heat for 20 to 25 minutes, until it has reduced by half and tastes sweeter and less like vinegar. Blend and set aside until the chicken is finished cooking.

4 Break the chicken into large chunks. Pour the strawberry vinegar sauce over the chicken and give it a stir.

5 Serve the chicken with the cooking juices and remaining diced fresh strawberries.

Blackberry-Chipotle BBQ Chicken with Carrots and Sweet Potatoes

Let's face it—the star of this recipe is the Blackberry-Chipotle BBQ Sauce. It's smoky, tangy, and the fruity sweetness from the blackberries plays well with the chicken and vegetables. Raspberries and chipotle have become a popular combination lately, but after a side-by-side sauce test, the members of my family unanimously preferred blackberries.

Prep time 20 minutes

Serves 6

8 to 10 chicken drumsticks or 6 to 8 boneless or bone-in chicken thighs

1 tablespoon BBQ Dry Rub Seasoning (page 288)

½ teaspoon sea salt

4 large carrots, peeled and cut into 1-inch (2.5 cm) chunks

1 large or two small sweet potatoes, peeled and cut into 1-inch (2.5 cm) chunks

1½ cups (275 g) Blackberry-Chipotle BBQ Sauce (page 291)

1 cup (145 g) fresh blackberries

1 Place the chicken in a large bowl. Sprinkle with dry rub and salt. Work the seasoning into the chicken with your hands.

2 Place the carrots and sweet potatoes in a 4-quart (3.8 liter) slow cooker. Add the chicken on top of the vegetables. Pour 1 cup (250 g) of the BBQ sauce over the chicken, and add the blackberries on top.

3 Cover and cook on low for 4 to 5 hours, until the chicken is cooked through and very tender.

4 Transfer the chicken and vegetables to a serving platter. Spoon some of the cooking juices over the top and serve with the remaining ½ cup (125 g) BBQ sauce (warmed, if necessary).

Prosciutto-Wrapped Drumsticks and Butternut Squash

Wrapping a drumstick in prosciutto is a great technique—it's as if the drumstick is getting a big, salty hug. The butternut squash below gets basted by prosciutto-spiked chicken juices. There's some serious flavor sharing going on in this slow cooker. I don't usually purchase chopped vegetables, but butternut squash is one exception. If you're pinched for time, it makes things a lot faster and easier.

Prep time 15 minutes

Serves 6

3 to 4 cups (420 to 560 g) cubed butternut squash

3 cloves garlic

Sea salt

Black pepper

1 tablespoon avocado oil

8 skin-on chicken drumsticks

3 tablespoons (45 ml) freshly squeezed lemon juice

¼ teaspoon dried thyme

½ teaspoon dried rosemary

8 slices prosciutto

1 Place the squash and garlic in a 2.5- or 4-quart (2.4 or 3.8 liter) slow cooker. Sprinkle generously with sea salt and black pepper, and drizzle with 1 tablespoon avocado oil.

2 Place the drumsticks in a large bowl and add lemon juice, thyme, rosemary, and a few generous pinches of sea salt and black pepper. Using your hands, toss the drumsticks to ensure that they're all coated in lemon juice and seasonings.

3 Wrap each drumstick in one slice of prosciutto and place on top of the squash in the slow cooker. Try to arrange them in one layer, if possible.

4 Cover and cook on low for 7 to 8 hours (or 3 to 4 hours on high). Chicken should be pulling from the bone and be juicy and tender.

5 Transfer the drumsticks to a large serving dish and scoop out the squash. Spoon some of the drippings over the meat and vegetables, and serve.

Note: This recipe can easily be doubled in a 6-quart (5.7 liter) cooker. Cooking times should be on the long end of the range listed.

Orange-Cumin Drumsticks with Sweet Potatoes and Cranberries

Everything about this recipe reminds me of November—the sweet potatoes, cranberries, and sweet oranges mixed with warming cumin spice. It's autumn with winter approaching on its heels. This recipe would also be good using a whole chicken.

Prep time 15 minutes
Serves 4 to 5

8 to 10 chicken drumsticks
2 teaspoons sea salt
1 tablespoon ground cumin
½ teaspoon turmeric
2 cloves garlic, minced
Zest and juice from 1 orange

2 tablespoons (29 ml) avocado oil or other high-heat cooking oil
2 pounds (907 g) sweet potatoes, peeled and sliced into 1-inch (2.5 cm) cubes
⅓ cup (40 g) dried cranberries (naturally sweetened, if you can find them)
3 green onions, thinly sliced

1 Place the drumsticks in a large bowl and sprinkle the salt, cumin, turmeric, garlic, and orange zest over the top. Rub the mixture into the chicken to evenly coat, then add the orange juice and avocado oil. Mix well.

2 Place sweet potatoes in a 4-quart (3.8 liter) slow cooker. Pour the chicken and marinade mixture over the top. Cover and cook on low for 6 to 7 hours.

3 During the last 30 minutes of cooking, add the cranberries and green onions to the slow cooker. You don't need to mix it.

4 When the chicken is cooked through and the cranberries have plumped a bit, remove the chicken and sweet potatoes, using a slotted spoon if necessary, into a serving dish and cover to keep warm.

5 Transfer the pot drippings to a small saucepan and cook over high heat for 5 to 10 minutes to thicken the sauce slightly.

6 Pour the sauce over the chicken and sweet potatoes before serving.

Chinese Five-Spice Drumsticks with Beets and Carrots

Chinese five spice seasoning is a unique, peppery blend with a hint of licorice and baking spices. It is fairly easy to find in well-stocked grocery stores, but if you have trouble tracking down a jar, you can make your own by combining equal parts of these ground spices: anise, cinnamon, clove, fennel, and Szechuan or black pepper.

Prep time 20 minutes, plus marinating time
Serves 6

10 to 12 chicken drumsticks
4 teaspoons Chinese five spice seasoning
2 teaspoons sea salt
3 cloves garlic, minced, divided
4 teaspoons grated or minced fresh ginger, divided

1 tablespoon coconut or avocado oil
1 pound (455 g) beets, trimmed, peeled, and cut into 1-inch (2.5 cm) pieces
4 to 5 medium carrots, peeled and cut into 1-inch (2.5 cm) pieces
Sea salt and black pepper

1 Place the drumsticks in a large bowl. In a small bowl, combine the Chinese five-spice, salt, 2 minced garlic cloves, 3 teaspoons grated ginger, and the oil. Mix to form a paste, and pour over the drumsticks. Using your hands, toss the drumsticks to coat them evenly with the spice mixture. Chill for 4 to 12 hours.

2 When you're ready to cook, place the beets and carrots into a 4-quart (3.8 liter) slow cooker. Add 1 clove of minced garlic, 1 teaspoon of grated ginger, and a generous pinch of sea salt and pepper. Give it a stir to combine.

3 Arrange the drumsticks over the vegetables, layering if necessary.

4 Cover and cook on low for 5 to 6 hours, until the chicken is tender and pulls off the bone easily. The vegetables should also be tender.

5 Transfer the drumsticks and vegetables to a large serving dish. Spoon some of the cooking juices over the top and serve.

Spicy Chicken Sausage and Pineapple Stuffed Peppers

I've always loved stuffed peppers. I made them several times when my husband and I were first married, but it wasn't until around year five that Steve admitted he doesn't like cooked peppers. I wasn't sure whether to be annoyed that he didn't tell me sooner or touched that he didn't want to hurt my feelings. When I made these, Steve happily ate—the filling. And gave it a thumbs-up.

Prep time 15 minutes
Serves 4, generously

4 bell peppers, any color

2 cups (215 g) leftover Roasted Cauliflower Rice (pages 249 and 250)

1 cup (175 g) chopped precooked spicy-sweet chicken sausage

½ cup (80 g) chopped fresh or canned pineapple

¼ teaspoon chili powder

¼ teaspoon garlic powder

¼ teaspoon ground cumin

¼ teaspoon sea salt

¼ cup chopped fresh cilantro

Chopped avocados, for serving

1 Cut the tops from the peppers and remove seeds and large, white membranes. Line a 6-quart (5.7 liter) slow cooker with aluminum foil or parchment paper.

2 In a medium bowl, combine cauliflower rice, sausage, pineapple, spices, salt, and 2 tablespoons of the cilantro.

3 Spoon mixture into the peppers and place them in the slow cooker.

4 Cover and cook on low for 4 to 5 hours (or on high for 2 to 2½ hours). Peppers should be tender, but not mushy, and the filling should be heated through.

5 Sprinkle with the remaining 2 tablespoons of chopped cilantro and serve with chopped avocados.

Note: Using leftover Roasted Cauliflower Rice is important here. Cooked cauliflower has a lot less moisture than raw cauliflower does, and it keeps the pepper filling from turning into soup.

Chicken and Andouille Sausage Lettuce Wraps with Creamy Celery Slaw

When I nailed this dish, I couldn't keep my fingers out of it. I probably ate two or three lettuce wraps worth of chicken and sausage before we even sat down to eat. It was a tad spicy (which I love), but luckily, the celery slaw helped cool it off for my little eaters. We have them enrolled in spicy food training.

Prep time 30 minutes
Serves 8

For the lettuce wraps:

3 cloves garlic, minced

1 tablespoon Cajun Spice Blend (page 284)

1 tablespoon avocado oil

1 teaspoon sea salt

4 chicken breasts (or 8 thighs)

12 ounces (340 g) precooked andouille sausage, diced

½ large red onion, thinly sliced

For the slaw:

4 celery stalks, thinly sliced

2 large carrots, peeled and grated

⅔ cup fresh chopped cilantro

2 green onions, thinly sliced

4 tablespoons (56 g) Paleo-Friendly Mayonnaise (page 286)

2 tablespoons (30 ml) red wine vinegar

¼ teaspoon sea salt

3–4 heads butter or baby romaine lettuce, ends cut off and leaves separated

Hot sauce, for serving

1 Combine the garlic, Cajun seasoning, oil, and salt in a small bowl to form a paste. Rub the paste on both sides of the chicken.

2 Place the chicken in a 4-quart (3.8 liter) slow cooker. Place the sausage and onion on top of the chicken.

3 Cover and cook on low for 6 to 7 hours, flipping chicken halfway through to submerge the onions in the cooking liquid. The chicken should be very tender and easy to pull apart with a fork.

4 Remove the chicken from the cooker, shred, and return to the pot. Give it a good stir to combine it with the sausage and onions. Cover and turn off the cooker.

5 Combine all of the slaw ingredients in a medium bowl. Chill until ready to use.

6 To serve, place a couple spoonfuls of the chicken-andouille mixture into a lettuce leaf and top with a bit of slaw and a few shakes of hot sauce.

Ranch Chicken with Broccoli and Bacon

Have you ever made ranch seasoning? It's awfully hard to compete with the green "MSG packets" (as my husband affectionately calls them), but I think I did rather well. The ranch seasoning in this recipe adds great flavor and texture when you stir some mayo into the cooking juices at the end, creating a creamy coating for the chicken, broccoli, and bacon. Be sure to use boneless, skinless chicken for this one; bones and skin would make the "dressing" too greasy.

Prep time 20 minutes

Serves 6

3 large boneless, skinless chicken breasts

1 tablespoon homemade Dry Ranch Seasoning Mix (page 285)

1½ teaspoon steak seasoning

3 shallots, peeled and sliced

6 cups (426 g) broccoli florets

12 strips bacon

⅔ cup (160 g) Paleo-Friendly Mayonnaise (page 286)

3 tablespoons (45 ml) red wine vinegar

¼ teaspoon sea salt

1 Place the chicken breasts in a 3- or 4-quart (2.8 or 3.8 liter) slow cooker. Sprinkle the ranch mix and steak seasoning over the top. Add the shallots.

2 Cover and cook on low for 3 to 4 hours, until the chicken is cooked thoroughly and pulls apart easily with a fork.

3 Add the broccoli to the pot. Cover and cook for another 30 to 45 minutes, until the broccoli is crisp and still tender.

4 Meanwhile, cook the bacon strips until they're as crisp as you like. Set aside to cool.

5 When the broccoli is finished cooking, remove the chicken from the cooker, shred with two forks, and return it to the cooker. Do not drain the juices in the pot. Stir in the mayonnaise and red wine vinegar. Crumble the bacon into the mixture. Taste, and adjust salt if needed before serving.

Cider-Brined Turkey Breast

This recipe was truly a labor of love. For the second testing, I couldn't find a turkey breast so I bought a smallish turkey to try instead. I brought it home, made the brine, and let it soak up all of the sweetness and flavor from the cider and seasonings. I pulled the turkey from the brine, rinsed it off, and lowered it into my biggest slow cooker.

IT. WAS. TOO. BIG.

Why didn't I check to see if it would fit before I brined it?! Determined, I dropped the turkey on a large cutting board, sharpened my knife, and for the first time in my life, dismantled an entire raw turkey. Luckily, the breast fit in my slow cooker. And as it turns out, it was one of the juiciest, best-tasting turkey breasts I've ever eaten.

Prep time 25 minutes, plus cooling and brining time

Serves 6

2 quarts (1.9 liters) unsweetened apple cider

2 oranges

1 lemon

2 cinnamon sticks

½ teaspoon whole cloves

2 teaspoons whole peppercorns

3 bay leaves

3 sprigs fresh thyme

1 sprig fresh rosemary

½ cup (150 g) kosher salt

1 whole turkey breast or 2 bone-in turkey breast halves

1 In a large pot, combine all of the ingredients except for the turkey. Bring to a low simmer and stir until the salt is dissolved. Remove from heat and let it cool to room temperature. Feel free to add several cups of ice cubes to speed up the cooling.

2 When the brine has cooled, place the turkey breast in a large bowl or stockpot. Add brine to the container and enough water to completely cover the turkey.

3 Cover the bowl or pot containing the turkey and chill. Let it brine for 12 to 24 hours.

4 When you're ready to cook the turkey breast, place four aluminum foil balls in the bottom of a 6-quart (5.7 liter) slow cooker.

5 Remove the turkey breast from the brine and run it under cool water for a minute or two to remove any excess brine.

6 Place the turkey, breast-side down, on top of the aluminum foil balls.

7 Cover and cook for 2½ to 3 hours or until a meat thermometer reaches 160°F (71°C) when inserted into the thickest part of the breast.

8 Remove from the cooker and cover, letting it rest for 15 minutes before slicing and serving.

Turkey Tamale Pie

Instead of spending hours wrapping shredded meat and masa dough in a corn husk, you can layer the filling and masa dough in a pan and bake it. Genius, right? I made my own paleo version by creating a flavorful chili-like filling with ground turkey, Tex-Mex sausage, and spices, and topped it with a grain-free dough. I added the pumpkin puree to the dough because it needed something to keep it moist, and I happened to have an open can of pumpkin in the fridge. But I think it was destiny—I love how the pumpkin blends with Tex-Mex flavors!

Prep time 30 minutes
Serves 6

For the filling:
2 tablespoons (29 ml) avocado oil
1½ pounds (680 g) ground turkey
½ teaspoon sea salt
1 teaspoon ground cumin
1 teaspoon chili powder
1 cup (160 g) diced onion
2 links of precooked Tex-Mex style sausage or chorizo, diced
1 15-ounce (425 g) can tomato sauce
1 cup (260 g) salsa

For the topping:
1 cup (96 g) almond flour
½ cup (64 g) tapioca flour
1 teaspoon baking soda
½ teaspoon sea salt
¼ teaspoon ground cumin
¼ teaspoon (15 g) chili powder
⅛ teaspoon cayenne powder
3 tablespoons (42 g) solid coconut oil
1 egg
½ cup (123 g) pumpkin puree

1 Heat the avocado oil in a large skillet and add the ground turkey. Cook, stirring to break the meat into small chunks, for 6 to 8 minutes, until no longer pink. Transfer the meat to a 4-quart (3.8 liter) slow cooker.

2 Add the salt, cumin, chili powder, onion, sausage, tomato sauce, and salsa to the cooker. Stir well.

3 For the topping, combine the almond flour, tapioca flour, baking soda, salt, cumin, chili powder, and cayenne powder in a food processor. Pulse a few times to blend. Add the coconut oil and pulse several times until the oil breaks into pieces and the mixture resembles wet sand.

4 Add the egg and pumpkin puree, and pulse until a loose dough forms.

5 Spoon the dough over the turkey mixture.

6 Cover and cook on low for 4 to 5 hours, until topping is cooked through. A toothpick inserted into the center should come out clean.

7 Serve hot.

Sun-Dried Tomato Turkey Meatballs in Marinara

Meatballs and red sauce is a favorite easy meal— particularly these meatballs. I love using ground organic turkey because it has such a mild flavor and is truly a blank canvas for any flavor you add. These meatballs—like all of the meatballs in this book—can be frozen raw on a large baking sheet and once firm, placed into freezer bags and stored until you're ready to use them. Just add them to a slow cooker, still frozen, and add an hour or two of cooking time.

Prep time 25 minutes

Makes about 28 meatballs

⅔ cup (73.3 g) olive oil–packed sun-dried tomatoes

6 cloves garlic

2 pounds (905 g) ground turkey

1 tablespoon nutritional yeast

1 teaspoon sea salt

1 teaspoon dried basil

½ teaspoon black pepper

¼ teaspoon crushed red pepper flakes

2 tablespoons (28 g) avocado or coconut oil

3 cups (750 ml) Basic Marinara (page 283)

1 Combine the sun-dried tomatoes and garlic in a food processor. Pulse until a smooth paste forms. (If you don't have a food processor, chop them as fine as you can.)

2 Place the turkey in a large bowl. Add the sun-dried tomato paste, nutritional yeast, salt, basil, black pepper, and pepper flakes. Toss the mixture with your hands gently to combine everything thoroughly.

3 Form the turkey into tight 1½-inch (3.5 cm) balls and place them on a large plate.

4 Heat the oil in a large skillet over medium-high heat. Sear the meatballs in batches (don't overcrowd the pan) on two sides until a golden brown crust forms. Transfer the meatballs to a 4-quart (3.8 liter) slow cooker.

5 Pour the marinara over the meatballs. Cover and cook on low for 3 to 4 hours, until the meatballs are cooked through.

6 Serve the meatballs with the sauce or with some Squash Noodles (page 248).

Turkey, Apple, and Brussels Sprouts Potpie with Sauerkraut Biscuit Topping

Back in my early twenties, I spent a year and a half in Austria as a representative for my church, and there, I fell head over heels for sparkling water, Nutella, and sauerkraut. I also grew to love new flavor combinations, and although this recipe is far from Austrian, the way the mustard, sauerkraut, apples, and turkey combine makes me a little homesick for that breathtaking place.

Prep time 25 minutes
Serves 6

For the filling:

1½ pounds (680 g) uncooked turkey cutlets or breast meat, cut into 1-inch (2.5 cm) pieces

1 teaspoon sea salt

8 ounces (225 g) Brussels sprouts, trimmed and cut in half

1 tart apple, diced

1 tablespoon tapioca flour

⅛ teaspoon black pepper

1 tablespoon whole-grain mustard

1 tablespoon (15 ml) apple cider vinegar

¼ teaspoon dried thyme

3 tablespoons (42 g) Paleo-Friendly Mayonnaise (page 286)

For the topping:

1 cup (96 g) blanched almond flour

½ cup (64 g) tapioca flour

1 teaspoon baking soda

½ teaspoon sea salt

½ teaspoon black pepper

2 tablespoons (28 g) solid coconut oil

2 teaspoons whole-grain mustard

2 egg whites

1 cup (150 g) sauerkraut, drained

1 Place the turkey in a 4-quart (3.8 liter) slow cooker. Sprinkle with salt and toss the turkey to coat evenly.

2 Add the Brussels sprouts, apple, tapioca flour, black pepper, 1 tablespoon mustard, apple cider vinegar, thyme, and mayonnaise. Stir well.

3 To make the topping, combine the almond flour, tapioca flour, baking soda, ½ teaspoon sea salt, and ½ teaspoon black pepper in a food processor. Pulse a few times to combine. Add the coconut oil and pulse until the mixture resembles wet sand. Add the mustard, egg whites, and drained sauerkraut. Pulse until the mixture turns into a loose dough.

4 Spoon the topping over the chicken mixture.

5 Cover and cook on low for 4 to 5 hours, until biscuit mixture is cooked through. When you insert a toothpick into the center, it should come out clean.

6 Serve hot.

Note: You can substitute chicken breast or thigh meat if you like.

Mediterranean Turkey Meatloaf with Sun-Dried Tomato Aioli

This meatloaf takes a bit of prep work, but the result is something special. The roasted vegetables and bits of olives and peppers keep this dish incredibly moist. You'll love it with the creamy sun-dried tomato aioli!

Prep time 25 minutes

Serves 6

For the meatloaf:

1 eggplant, peeled and cut into ½-inch (1 cm) cubes

1 cup (160 g) chopped onion

4 cloves garlic, chopped

2 tablespoons (29 ml) avocado oil

1½ pounds (680 g) ground turkey

Sea salt

¼ teaspoon black pepper

2 tablespoons (16 g) minced kalamata olives

⅓ cup (45 g) chopped *peperoncini* peppers

¼ teaspoon oregano

2 tablespoons (30 ml) balsamic vinegar

For the aioli:

⅔ cup (73 g) olive oil–packed sun-dried tomatoes

1 cup (225 g) Paleo-Friendly Mayonnaise (page 286)

1 tablespoon (15 ml) freshly squeezed lemon juice

1 Preheat the oven to 425°F (218°C).

2 Combine the eggplant, onion, and garlic on a rimmed baking sheet. Drizzle oil over the top, add a couple generous pinches of salt, and toss everything together to coat well. Spread the vegetables evenly over the pan and roast for 15 to 18 minutes, flipping them once or twice during cooking, until the eggplant is cooked through and golden brown.

3 Prep a 6-quart (5.7 liter) slow cooker by adding "handles" made of aluminum foil. This is easy: Tear off two sheets of aluminum foil about 2 feet (60 cm) long each. Fold each piece in half lengthwise, and then in half again to make long, narrow strips. Lay one strip across the bottom and up the sides of your slow cooker. Lay the other strip perpendicular to the first one. You should have foil pieces hanging off all sides of the slow cooker and a foil "rack" lining the bottom.

4 Place the turkey in a medium bowl. Add the roasted vegetable mixture, ½ teaspoon sea salt, pepper, kalamata olives, peperoncini peppers, and oregano. Using your hands, carefully blend the mixture.

5 Place the mixture in the slow cooker, forming it into a loaflike mound. Pour the balsamic vinegar over the top.

6 Cover and cook on low for 3 to 3½ hours.

7 Puree the sun-dried tomatoes in a food processor, then add the mayonnaise, lemon juice, and a pinch of salt. Pulse until smooth and blended. Chill until ready to use. If you don't own a food processor, mince the sun-dried tomatoes as fine as you can and combine with the other ingredients in a small bowl.

8 Remove the slow cooker lid. Gather all of the aluminum foil ends to the center and lift out the meatloaf, transferring it to a large plate or platter. Discard cooking juices. Cover the meatloaf with the aluminum strips and let it rest for 10 minutes before slicing.

9 Serve with aioli.

Thanksgiving Turkey Meatloaf

This meatloaf has almost all of my favorite paleo Thanksgiving components in one dish—turkey, herbs, cranberries, and aromatics. Pair this with some mashed potatoes and you've got a simplified Thanksgiving dinner anytime you want.

Prep time 20 minutes
Serves 6

2 tablespoons (29 g) Homemade Ghee (page 287) or avocado oil (29 ml)

1 medium onion, diced small

2 pounds (905 g) ground turkey

1½ teaspoons sea salt

¼ teaspoon black pepper

2 celery stalks, diced small

1 teaspoon dried, rubbed sage or ½ teaspoon ground

1 tablespoon minced fresh rosemary or 1 teaspoon dried

1 teaspoon fresh thyme or ¼ teaspoon dried

¼ cup (30 g) dried cranberries

1 Prep a 6-quart (5.7 liter) slow cooker by adding "handles" made of aluminum foil. This is easy: Tear off two sheets of aluminum foil about 2 feet (60 cm) long each. Fold each piece in half lengthwise, and then in half again to make long, narrow strips. Lay one strip across the bottom and up the sides of your slow cooker. Lay the other strip perpendicular to the first one. You should have foil pieces hanging off all sides of the slow cooker and a foil "rack" lining the bottom.

2 Heat the ghee in a medium skillet over medium heat. Add the diced onion and cook, stirring frequently, for 8 to 10 minutes, until the onion has deep golden brown spots. Set aside to cool for 5 to 10 minutes.

3 Meanwhile, place the turkey in a large mixing bowl. Add the salt, pepper, celery, sage, herbs, and cranberries. Add the cooked onion to the bowl. Use your hands and mix everything together gently, being careful not to squeeze the meat in your fists.

4 Gather the meat mixture into one large mass and transfer it to the prepared slow cooker. Form the mixture into an oblong shape.

5 Cover and cook on low for 3 to 3½ hours, until the meat is cooked through.

6 Remove the slow cooker lid. Gather all of the aluminum foil ends to the center and lift out the meatloaf, transferring it to a large plate or platter. Discard cooking juices. Cover the meatloaf with the aluminum strips and let it rest for 10 minutes before slicing and serving.

Creamy Sage-Rubbed Turkey and Mushrooms

I'm a fairly recent convert to mushrooms, and I have to say, this is my favorite mushroom-heavy dish of all the ones I've tried. Using two kinds of mushrooms really brings more flavor to the chicken—and that creamy sauce made from paleo mayo and the pot juices? Divine. I would eat this every day. I did, in fact, until it was gone.

Prep time 15 minutes
Serves 6

8 ounces (225 g) baby portobello mushrooms, sliced

1½ ounces (43 g) dried porcini mushrooms

1 sprig fresh rosemary or ¼ teaspoon dried

1 shallot, sliced

4 cloves garlic, minced

1½ pounds (680 g) uncooked turkey cutlets or breast meat

1 teaspoon dried, rubbed sage or ¼ teaspoon ground sage

1 teaspoon sea salt

½ teaspoon coarsely ground black pepper

1 tablespoon avocado oil

½ cup (115 g) Paleo-Friendly Mayonnaise (page 286)

1 tablespoon (15 ml) red wine vinegar

Cauliflower Rice (pages 249 and 250) or Squash Noodles (page 248), for serving

1 Place the mushrooms, rosemary, shallot, and garlic in a 4-quart (3.8 liter) slow cooker. Sprinkle with a pinch or two of sea salt and black pepper.

2 Place the turkey on top of the mushrooms.

3 In a small bowl, combine the sage, salt, pepper, and avocado oil. Stir to form a paste. Rub the paste on the chicken breasts.

4 Cover and cook for 5 to 6 hours, until the chicken is very tender and shreds easily with a fork.

5 Transfer the turkey to a plate and shred with two forks. Return the meat to the cooker. Add the mayonnaise and red wine vinegar. Toss to coat evenly and to mix the turkey with the mushrooms.

6 Serve with Cauliflower Rice or Squash Noodles.

Note: If you'd like, you can substitute chicken for the turkey.

4

BEEF

One of the best things about buying a beef share is all of the big roasts you get. Cooking large, inexpensive cuts of beef is an economical way to feed a crowd or build a stash of meal starters in the freezer. And who doesn't love tender shreds of saucy beef? Beef is perfect for slow cooking.

Recipes

Asian Beef Short-Rib Lettuce Wraps

The first time I had beef short ribs, they were prepared in a manner similar to this. These deep Asian flavors mixed with the spicy, cool bite from the slaw is still my favorite way to eat them. If your short ribs aren't so meaty, throw in a couple of extra ribs so you'll have enough meat to go around. (And save those bones to make beef stock later!)

Prep time 20 minutes

Serves 6

For the wraps:

4 to 5 pounds (1.8 to 2.3 kg) meaty beef short ribs

Sea salt and black pepper

2-inch (5 cm) knob of fresh ginger, minced

4 cloves garlic

½ cup (120 ml) coconut aminos

½ cup (120 ml) rice vinegar

3 tablespoons (45 ml) sesame oil

1 teaspoon crushed red pepper flakes

⅓ cup (115 g) honey

½ lime

2 heads butter lettuce or baby Romaine, trimmed and leaves separated

For the slaw:

1 English cucumber, julienned

1 large carrot, julienned or grated

1 green onion, thinly sliced

⅓ cup chopped fresh cilantro

¼ cup (60 ml) rice vinegar

¼ teaspoon crushed red pepper flakes

¼ teaspoon sea salt

1 teaspoon honey

1 Sprinkle the short ribs generously with sea salt and black pepper. Place in a 4- or 6-quart (3.8 or 5.7 liter) slow cooker.

2 Combine ginger, garlic, aminos, vinegar, sesame oil, pepper flakes, and honey in a small bowl. Mix well and pour over the short ribs. Cover and cook on low heat for 9 to 10 hours (or on high for 4 to 5 hours).

3 Meanwhile, combine the cucumber, carrot, green onion, and cilantro in a medium bowl. Whisk together the vinegar, pepper flakes, salt, and honey in a small bowl and pour over the slaw vegetables. Toss to combine. If you aren't using this right away, cover the bowl and chill until you are ready to use it. For best results, let it sit for at least 30 minutes to allow the flavors to combine.

4 When the meat pulls off of the ribs easily, remove them from the slow cooker. Use a slotted spoon to remove bits and pieces of undesirables from the pot. Remove meat from the ribs; discard the bones and return the meat to the pot with the strained juices. Taste the meat, and add more salt if necessary. Squeeze the juice from the lime over the meat.

5 Serve the shredded meat inside of lettuce leaves and top with the slaw.

Orange Balsamic Short Ribs

If you have leftover cooking juices, save them and use a few spoonfuls when you reheat the leftover rib meat. It will moisten and give more flavor to the meat, which may have dried out a bit while it was chilled. Also, slow-cooked meat tends to be more tender when reheated. I'm not sure why, but it's magical.

Prep time 15 minutes
Serves 4

4 to 5 pounds (1.8 to 2.3 kg) meaty short ribs

1 teaspoon sea salt

½ teaspoon black pepper

Zest from 1 orange (about 1 teaspoon)

Juice from 2 oranges (about ⅔ cup, or 160 ml)

1 cup (235 ml) balsamic vinegar

1 cup (235 ml) Homemade Beef Stock (page 281)

2 cloves garlic, minced

1 medium onion, sliced

2 sprigs fresh rosemary

Cauliflower Rice (pages 249 and 250) or Squash Noodles (page 248), for serving

1 Sprinkle the ribs with salt and pepper. Place them in a 4- or 6-quart (3.8 or 5.7 liter) slow cooker.

2 In a large measuring cup, combine the orange juice and zest, vinegar, beef stock, and garlic.

3 Place the onion and rosemary over the beef and pour the liquid mixture over the top.

4 Cover and cook for 8 to 10 hours on low (or 4 to 5 hours on high) until the rib meat pulls away from the bone easily with a fork.

5 Transfer the ribs to a serving dish and spoon some of the cooking juices over the top.

Smoky Short Ribs with Mushrooms

Anyone who knows me well knows my fondness for bacon. I have a quote on my kitchen wall that says "Bacon is like a little hug from God." Well, these short ribs have been hugged by bacon, so I guess that makes them secondhand-edly hugged by the divine. And pretty tasty.

Prep time 15 minutes
Serves 6

1½ pounds (680 g) sliced baby portobello mushrooms

3 tablespoons (45 ml) coconut aminos

1½ tablespoons (45 g) tomato paste

3 cloves garlic, minced

1½ teaspoon dried minced onion

¾ teaspoon smoked paprika

¾ teaspoon black pepper

¾ teaspoon sea salt

½ teaspoon dried thyme

3 pounds (1.4 kg) short ribs (about 8 meaty ribs)

4 slices thick-cut bacon

1 Place the sliced mushrooms in a 4- or 6-quart (3.8 or 5.7 liter) slow cooker.

2 In a small bowl, combine the coconut aminos, tomato paste, garlic, onion, smoked paprika, black pepper, sea salt, and thyme to form a paste. Rub the paste all over the short ribs. Place the short ribs on top of the mushrooms and lay the bacon slices on top of the ribs.

3 Cover and cook on low for 6 to 8 hours, until the short ribs are tender.

4 Discard the bacon slices and serve the short ribs with the mushrooms and some cooking juices.

Taqueria-Style Shredded Beef

I've always lived in places with large Mexican populations, and with that, wonderful things like Latin markets, taqueria restaurants, and food trucks. If your experience has been limited to Americanized "Mexican" fast food, you're missing out. My favorite tacos are filled with red-orange, slightly spicy shreds of tender beef that drip juices out of the tortilla and onto your hands.

This recipe brings a whole pot of that wonderfully seasoned and tender meat into your kitchen. I've made large batches of this and froze it for meals later on. It reheats beautifully and you can use it for lettuce tacos, soups, omelets and baked dishes.

P.S. The strained cooking juices make the most spectacular enchilada sauce I've ever eaten.

Prep time 30 minutes
Serves 10 to 12

5 to 7 dried chilli peppers (*pasilla* or *guajillo* or both)

1 medium onion, roughly chopped

3 cloves garlic, halved

1 lime, juiced (3 to 4 tablespoons, or 45 to 60 ml)

2 chipotle peppers, from a can of chipotles in adobo sauce (seeded, to reduce spiciness, if desired)

2 tablespoons (60 g) tomato paste

1 tablespoon ground coriander

1 tablespoon ground cumin

1 tablespoon (18 g) sea salt

1 tablespoon (20 g) honey

1 teaspoon dried oregano

3 to 5 pounds (1.4 to 2.3 kg) beef roast (any cut)

3 tablespoons (42 g) avocado or coconut oil

Paleo Tortillas (page 256) or lettuce wraps, for serving

1 Break the chillies in half and discard most of the seeds. Place the chillies in a bowl and pour boiling water over them. Keep them submerged for 20 minutes.

2 Drain the chillies (reserving the liquid). Remove the stems and place them in a blender or large food processor with the remaining ingredients except for the oil and beef. Add some of the chilli liquid if the mixture is too thick; it should be the consistency of applesauce.

3 Heat the oil in a large skillet over high heat. The oil should appear to shimmer. Place the beef in the skillet. You should hear some crazy sizzling or the pan isn't hot enough. Let the beef sit, untouched, in the pan for a couple of minutes. Turn the meat to sear on all sides. It should have a deep brown crust in spots.

4 Transfer beef to a 6-quart (5.7 liter) slow cooker. Pour the blended chilli sauce over the top. Cover and cook on low for 8 to 10 hours, until the beef pulls apart easily.

5 Remove the roast from the cooker and shred it with a couple of forks. Set the meat aside and keep warm.

6 Strain the sauce in the cooker, discarding the fatty solids.

7 If you are using the meat right away, return it and the sauce to the slow cooker and toss to combine.

8 If you aren't using the meat right away, let it and the sauce cool. Cover each and chill. The sauce will turn into a gelatinous mixture with a layer of fat on top. Remove that fat and discard. Reheat some meat and a few spoonfuls of sauce in a skillet.

9 Serve in Paleo Tortillas, lettuce wraps, or add meat to soups.

Notes: You can find dried chillies in the Latin section of many grocery stores or at a Latin market.

You can make the chilli sauce 2 to 3 days ahead if you like. Chill until ready to use.

Shredded Barbacoa Beef

Here's another take on tender shredded beef. I guess you could say it's a knockoff of the barbacoa beef served at the Chipotle Mexican Grill, a popular restaurant in North America and some parts of Europe. It's spicy, but not too spicy, and the herbs and spices give it great depth. It might be my new favorite!

Prep time 15 minutes
Serves 8 to 10

3- to 4-pound (1.4 to 1.8 kg) beef roast

2 teaspoons sea salt

1 or 2 chipotle peppers, plus 1 tablespoon (20 g) of sauce from a can of chipotles in adobo sauce

6 cloves garlic, minced

2 limes

1 tablespoon ground cumin

2 teaspoons chili powder

1 teaspoon dried oregano

1 teaspoon black pepper

¼ teaspoon ground cloves

2 bay leaves

1 small onion, cut in half and thinly sliced

1 15-ounce (425 g) can diced tomatoes, undrained

½ cup chopped fresh cilantro

Paleo Tortillas (page 256), Southwest Cabbage Slaw (page 252), and Simple Guacamole (page 59), for serving

1 Rub the sea salt all over the roast.

2 Slice the chipotle pepper(s) in half, scrape out the seeds, and discard them. Mince the peppers and put them in a small bowl with the adobo sauce, garlic, juice from 1 lime, cumin, chili powder, oregano, black pepper, and cloves. Stir well and rub the paste all over the beef.

3 Place the bay leaves, onions, and tomatoes in a 4- or 6-quart (3.8 or 5.7 liter) slow cooker, depending on the size of the beef. Place the beef on top of the vegetables in the slow cooker. Cover and cook on low for 7 to 8 hours, until the meat pulls apart easily with a fork.

4 Remove the roast from the cooker, shred it, and return it to the cooker. Toss the meat with the onions and tomatoes to combine. Stir in the fresh cilantro and the juice from half of the other lime. Cut the other half into wedges for serving.

5 Serve the beef with the tortillas, slaw, and Simple Guacamole (page 59).

Greek Peperoncini Beef Lettuce Wraps with Cucumber Salad

I've always been fascinated with Greece—the whitewashed buildings, the deep blue water, the history, and the bright, briny Mediterranean flavors.

My college degree had a travel and tourism emphasis, and for one of my class projects, I planned a week-long, painfully detailed (yet, budget-less) dream trip to Greece. In truth, if I were to go to Greece, I think I would spend most of the time eating or sitting on the beach. That wouldn't have flown with my professor, so I added some cultural and outdoor destinations to my itinerary. While I'm saving up for my dream trip, I can make Greek-inspired food at home, starting with these lettuce wraps.

Prep time 40 minutes, plus overnight marinating

Serves 6

For the lettuce wraps:

3- to 4-pound (1.4 to 1.8 kg) beef roast (bone-in or boneless)

1½ teaspoons sea salt

½ teaspoon black pepper

4 cloves garlic, minced

1 tablespoon dried oregano

2 teaspoons dried minced onion

½ teaspoon dried mint

½ teaspoon dried thyme

½ teaspoon dried basil

½ teaspoon dried marjoram

2 tablespoons (29 ml) avocado oil

½ cup (68 g) sliced Greek *peperoncini* peppers

2 to 3 heads baby Romaine or butter lettuce, leaves separated

Chopped kalamata olives, for serving (optional)

For the salad:

1 English cucumber, quartered lengthwise and chopped

2 medium Roma tomatoes, seeded and chopped

8 to 10 narrow strips of thinly sliced red onion

¼ cup (60 ml) lemon juice (about 1 large lemon)

2 cloves garlic

2 tablespoons (30 ml) extra-virgin olive oil

¾ teaspoon sea salt

¼ teaspoon black pepper

¼ teaspoon dried oregano

1 Trim the roast of any unwanted fat and place on a large plate. Rub the salt and pepper into the meat on all sides.

2 In a small bowl, combine the rest of the roast ingredients (except the peperoncini peppers, lettuce, and olives) to make a paste. Rub the paste over the entire roast, then cover it with plastic wrap and let it marinate, chilled, for 8 to 24 hours.

3 Place the roast in a 4- or 6-quart (3.8 or 5.7 liter) slow cooker. Cover and cook on low for 8 to 9 hours or on high for 4 to 5 hours. The beef should be tender and pull apart easily with a fork.

Notes: If you eat dairy, I highly recommend adding a small amount of high-quality feta cheese to the wraps. If you can't find dried mint, use fresh mint. About 1½ teaspoons minced will do.

4 When the roast is nearly finished, prep the salad by combining the cucumber, tomatoes, and onion in a medium bowl. Whisk the remaining salad ingredients together in a measuring cup and pour over the salad. Toss everything together to coat well. Taste, and add more salt if needed. Cover and chill until ready to serve.

5 When the beef is finished cooking, it should pull apart easily with a fork. Transfer the roast to a large plate or platter and shred it into bite-sized pieces. Return the meat to the slow cooker with the peperoncini peppers and toss it around with a pair of tongs so that the beef and peperoncini are combined and everything is coated with the cooking juices.

6 Assemble the wraps by placing a small amount of beef inside a lettuce leaf, top it with a spoonful or two of the salad, and sprinkle with kalamata olives.

Indian-Style Shredded Beef

Beef isn't commonly served in India because of the religious beliefs of most people, but it pairs well with the strong, complex spices in Indian cuisine. This tender, shredded beef is one of my favorite Indian-style dishes to date.

Prep time 15 minutes
Serves 8

1 tablespoon (18 g) sea salt

2 teaspoons ground cumin

2 teaspoons ground coriander

1 teaspoon black pepper

1 teaspoon ground turmeric

½ teaspoon cinnamon

½ teaspoon cardamom

½ teaspoon fennel seed

¼ teaspoon ground cloves

3- to 4-pound (1.4 to 1.8 kg) beef roast

2 shallots, thinly sliced

2-inch (5 cm) knob of ginger, grated

1 jalapeño, seeded and diced

2 dried bay leaves

½ cup (120 ml) beef broth

½ cup (120 g) coconut cream or 1 cup (235 ml) full-fat coconut milk

½ cup fresh, chopped cilantro, plus more for serving

3 limes

Cauliflower Rice (pages 249 and 250), for serving

1 In a small bowl, combine the salt, cumin, coriander, black pepper, turmeric, cinnamon, cardamom, fennel seed, and cloves.

2 Rub the spice blend over the entire roast and place it in a 4-quart (3.8 liter) slow cooker. Add the shallots, ginger, jalapeño, and bay leaves to the slow cooker. Pour the beef broth down the side of the cooker.

3 Cover and cook on low for 7 to 8 hours, until the meat is tender and pulls apart easily.

4 Remove the roast from the slow cooker, shred it into bite-sized pieces, and put it back into the cooking juices. Add the coconut cream, cilantro, and the juice from half of a lime. Stir it well. Taste, and add more lime juice or salt if necessary. Cut the remaining limes into wedges.

5 Serve beef over Cauliflower Rice with a sprinkle of cilantro and a couple of lime wedges.

Blackberry-Chipotle Shredded BBQ Beef

Every slow-cooker recipe collection must include a classic BBQ shredded beef recipe. This one is easy—and you can substitute any dry rub or BBQ sauce you like. The Blackberry-Chipotle BBQ Sauce (page 291) with this beef had me weak in the knees. And it's really great with Zucchini "Flatbread" (page 254).

Prep time 15 minutes
Serves 8 to 10

3- to 4-pound (1.4 to 1.8 kg) beef roast
2 tablespoons BBQ Dry-Rub Seasoning (page 288)
6 cloves garlic, minced

1 tablespoon dried minced onion
½ cup (120 ml) beef broth or water
2 cups (500 g) Blackberry-Chipotle BBQ Sauce (page 291)

1 Trim any excess fat from the roast. Rub the dry-rub seasoning all over the roast, and place it in a 4-quart (3.8 liter) slow cooker.

2 Add the garlic and dried minced onion on top of the roast. Pour the broth down the side of the slow cooker, then cover it and cook on low for 8 to 9 hours, until the beef pulls apart easily with a fork.

3 Transfer the roast to a large sheet pan or plate, leaving the juices in the pot. Shred the meat with a couple of forks into bite-sized pieces. Discard all but 1 cup (235 ml) of the juices from the slow cooker. Return the shredded meat to the slow cooker and add the BBQ sauce. Toss the meat with a pair of tongs to combine it with the pot juices and BBQ sauce. Cover and cook for another 15 minutes, until the meat has absorbed some of the sauce and everything is heated through.

4 Serve alone with a green salad, as a filling for "Baked" Sweet Potatoes (page 253), or however you like.

Spiced Pomegranate Beef Roast

One of the reasons I love beef is that its earthy taste can stand up to loud, bold flavors. Braising a pot roast with sweet-tart pomegranate juice and an exotic spice blend for hours will make your kitchen—and entire house—smell like a Moroccan spice market.

Prep time 20 minutes
Serves 8

2- to 3-pound (900 g to 1.4 kg) beef roast
1 tablespoon (18 g) sea salt
1 teaspoon black pepper
3 tablespoons (90 g) tomato paste
2 cloves garlic, minced
2 teaspoons ground coriander
½ teaspoon fresh or dried orange zest
½ teaspoon crushed red pepper flakes
½ teaspoon cinnamon
½ teaspoon ground cloves
¼ teaspoon ground allspice
1 cup (235 ml) unsweetened pomegranate juice
¼ cup (60 ml) red wine vinegar
½ of a large red onion, thinly sliced
Arils from 1 small pomegranate (about 1 cup, or 174 g)
Cauliflower Rice (pages 249 and 250) or mashed potatoes, for serving

1 Place the beef roast on a large plate. Rub the salt and pepper all over the roast.

2 Combine the tomato paste, garlic, coriander, orange zest, pepper flakes, cinnamon, cloves, and allspice in a small bowl. Mix thoroughly to form a paste and rub the paste all over the roast.

3 Place the roast in a 4-quart (3.8 liter) slow cooker. Pour the pomegranate juice and vinegar into the cooker and place the onions on top of the roast.

4 Cover and cook on low for 7 to 8 hours until the roast is tender and pulls apart easily.

5 Transfer the roast to a large plate and shred. Return the shredded meat to the slow cooker. Stir in the pomegranate arils. Cover and keep warm until ready to serve.

6 Serve with Cauliflower Rice or mashed potatoes.

Note: If you don't plan to serve the beef right away, wait and add the pomegranate arils immediately before serving. They lose their color and vibrancy after spending several hours in the meat juices.

Balsamic Pot Roast

My parents make some pretty mean steaks. My mom always preps the marinade and my dad presides over the grill. I loved the flavor of the meat as a kid, but if there was any resistance at all when I chewed, out it came. Chewy meat wasn't my thing.

My sweet dad, though, wanted me to like steak, so he would give me the most tender fillet pieces out of his T-bone. Now that I have children of my own—one of whom is a daughter who is similar to me (including textural issues)—I find myself giving her the best bites of steak too.

I love my parents' steak marinade so much that I made it into a pot roast recipe— replacing the soy sauce with coconut aminos and balsamic vinegar to make it soy-free. Now I have an entire pot of incredibly tender meat!

Prep time 15 minutes
Serves 6

2- to 3-pound (900 g to 1.4 kg) beef roast
1 tablespoon (18 g) sea salt
1 teaspoon black pepper
½ cup (120 ml) Homemade Beef Stock (page 281)
¼ cup (60 ml) coconut aminos
¼ cup (60 ml) balsamic vinegar
6 cloves garlic, chopped
½ to 1 teaspoon crushed red pepper flakes
½ lemon, juiced
Mashed sweet potatoes or Rosemary-Garlic Mashed Potatoes (page 244), for serving

1 Rub the beef roast with the salt and pepper.

2 Place it in a 4-quart (3.8 liter) slow cooker. Add the remaining ingredients except the lemon juice over the beef.

3 Cover and cook on low for 7 to 9 hours, until the beef is tender and pulls apart easily with a fork.

4 Remove the beef from the cooker, shred it with a couple of forks, and return the meat to the cooker to soak up some of the cooking juices.

5 Sprinkle the lemon juice over the top of the beef, and serve the beef and juices over mashed potatoes.

Sunday Pot Roast

Is it just me or is a Sunday pot roast the most classic slow-cooker recipe of all time? This one comes together so quickly you could make it any day of the week.

Prep time 15 minutes
Serves 6

3- to 4-pound (1.4 to 1.8 kg) beef roast
Sea salt
Black pepper
2 tablespoons (30 g) Homemade Ghee (page 287)
1 cup (235 ml) beef broth, divided
1½ pounds (680 g) large carrots, cut into 1- or 2-inch (2.5 or 5 cm) pieces

2 stalks celery, cut into large pieces
1 medium onion, peeled and cut into wedges
3 or 4 sprigs fresh rosemary
3 or 4 sprigs fresh thyme
1 tablespoon (30 g) tomato paste

1 Sprinkle the roast generously on both sides with salt and pepper.

2 Heat the ghee in a cast-iron or stainless-steel skillet to high heat. Place the roast in the pan and let it cook, undisturbed, for 3 to 4 minutes. Flip the roast, and sear the other side. Put the roast in a 6-quart (5.7 liter) slow cooker. While the pan is still hot, pour in ½ cup (120 ml) of beef broth. As it sizzles, scrape the browned bits off the bottom. Pour the contents of the skillet into the cooker.

3 Place the carrots, celery, and onion around the roast and the fresh herbs on top. Sprinkle the whole thing with 1 teaspoon sea salt and ½ teaspoon black pepper.

4 Whisk the tomato paste into the other ½ cup (120 ml) of broth and pour it around the sides of the slow cooker.

5 Cover and cook on low for 7 to 8 hours. The carrots should be very tender and the meat should pull apart easily with a fork.

6 Remove the roast and carrots from the slow cooker and place them on a large platter. Keep warm.

7 Blend the contents of the slow cooker, preferably with an immersion blender. Taste, and add salt if necessary.

8 Serve the roast and carrots with the gravy.

Leftover Pot Roast with Butternut Squash and Roasted Poblanos

Fortunately, if you cook the same meat in a slow cooker twice, it won't melt away and disappear into the cooking liquid. It's true. Take some leftover basic pot roast and give it a new life by adding some squash, peppers, and Tex-Mex spices.

Prep time 20 minutes
Serves 6

3 poblano peppers

4 to 5 cups (2 to 2½ pounds [905 g to 1.1 kg]) leftover beef pot roast and juice, cut into large pieces

3 cups (420 g) cubed butternut squash (about ½ of a medium squash)

2 teaspoons chili powder

1 teaspoon ground coriander

½ teaspoon ground cumin

¼ teaspoon cayenne pepper (or to taste)

1 Char the poblano peppers. You can do this by putting them on a foil-lined baking sheet under the broiler for several minutes. Or if you have a gas range, turn it on medium heat and place the peppers right on the grates above the flames. With either method, turn the peppers with heat-safe tongs until most of the skin is black and charred. When they're finished, wrap the peppers in foil, creating a packet, and allow them to steam for about 5 minutes. The steaming step makes it easy to remove the black, charred skin. Remove the skin and dice the peppers, also discarding the stem and seeds. Add the peppers to a 4-quart (3.8 liter) slow cooker.

2 Add the rest of the ingredients into the slow cooker. Give it a quick stir.

3 Cover and cook on low for 3 to 4 hours or on high for 2 to 3 hours. The butternut squash should be tender.

4 Serve with Cauliflower Rice (pages 249 and 250) or Squash Noodles (page 248).

Note: Use leftover meat from a roast that has mild or complementary flavors.

Garlicky Mushroom-Rubbed Pot Roast and Gravy

I like to pulverize dried mushrooms in a blender or food processor and add them to spice blends, like the rub for this pot roast. I even added some to the gravy, which made it much richer and more flavorful! Don't be nervous about the amount of garlic in this recipe; stewing in a slow cooker for many hours tames garlic and makes it quite mild.

Prep time 15 minutes
Serves 6

3- to 4-pound (1.4 to 1.8 kg) pot roast
2 tablespoons pulverized dried mushrooms (porcini are recommended)
1 tablespoon granulated garlic
2 teaspoons sea salt
2 teaspoons onion powder
½ teaspoon black pepper
½ cup (120 ml) beef broth
2 bulbs garlic, cloves removed and peeled

1 Place the pot roast on a large plate. In a small bowl, combine 1 tablespoon dried mushrooms, garlic, salt, onion powder, and black pepper. Rub the mixture all over the pot roast.

2 Place the roast in a 4- or 6-quart (3.8 or 5.7 liter) slow cooker. Pour the beef broth down the sides of the cooker and sprinkle the garlic cloves all over.

3 Cover and cook on low for 7 to 8 hours, until the meat is tender and pulls apart easily with a fork.

4 Transfer the roast to a large plate or platter, leaving the garlic cloves in the cooker.

5 Use a slotted spoon to remove any undesirables from the cooking liquid, leaving the garlic cloves. Add the other tablespoon of dried mushroom powder and a generous pinch of salt to the cooking liquid. Blend everything using an immersion blender or transfer the mixture to a blender. Blend until smooth.

6 Break the roast into large chunks or bite-sized pieces, according to your preference. Return the meat to the pot and toss it with the gravy using a pair of tongs. Close the lid and cook for another 10 minutes or so if the meat and gravy need to be warmed up further.

7 Serve the roast and gravy with your choice of sides. Many of the recipes in the Sides chapter (page 236) would work well here: Try Rosemary-Garlic Mashed Potatoes (page 244), Cauliflower Rice (pages 249 and 250), Squash Noodles (page 248), or Zucchini Flatbread (page 254).

Holiday Brisket with Caramelized Onions

Our family used to have Baja-style breaded and fried fish tacos for Christmas dinner—an odd choice, but we had sentimental reasons. This tradition lasted until our kids decided they didn't like fish tacos very much. I'm grateful for this, because although my husband and I adore a good fish taco, the breaded and fried ones are a lot of work and create a huge mess. The last thing I want to do on Christmas is slave all day in the kitchen.

One Christmas, I threw a grass-fed brisket in a slow cooker with a pile of caramelized onions and vegetables. I spent the rest of the day with my husband and kids, enjoying our time together and the gifts we had just opened. And no one complained during dinner. I declared that we had found a new tradition.

Prep time 15 minutes
Serves 8

8 large carrots, cut into 1-inch (2.5 cm) pieces

5 red potatoes, cut into 1-inch (2.5 cm) pieces

6 cloves garlic, smashed

2 teaspoons sea salt

1 teaspoon black pepper

6 tablespoons (87 g) Homemade Ghee (page 287) or avocado oil (88 ml)

1 3- to 4-pound (1.4 to 1.8 kg) beef brisket

3 large sweet onions, thinly sliced

3 sprigs fresh thyme

3 sprigs fresh rosemary

¼ cup (60 ml) balsamic vinegar

¼ cup (60 ml) coconut aminos

1 Place the carrots, potatoes, and garlic into a 6-quart (5.7 liter) slow cooker.

2 Sprinkle the salt and pepper over both sides of the brisket.

3 Bring 3 tablespoons (45 g) of ghee to medium-high heat in a skillet large enough for the brisket.

4 Sear the brisket on both sides until a dark golden brown crust forms. Transfer to the slow cooker and place it on top of the vegetables.

5 Add another 3 tablespoons (45 g) of ghee to the skillet and add the sliced onion. Cook on medium high for a few minutes, until the onions soften and begin to turn brown in spots. Reduce heat to medium and cook, stirring occasionally, for about 15 minutes or until the onions are a medium brown color and very, very soft and caramelized.

6 Pour onions and pan juices over the brisket. Place the fresh herbs on the onions. Pour the balsamic vinegar and coconut aminos over the onions and beef as well.

7 Cover and cook on low for 7 to 9 hours or until the brisket pulls apart easily with a fork and the carrots are tender. Turn the slow cooker off.

8 Transfer the brisket to a large plate or a cutting board. Leave the vegetables in the slow cooker to keep warm.

9 Cut or shred the brisket and transfer the meat and onions to a large serving platter. If there's room, add the vegetables from the slow cooker. Spoon some of the cooking juices over everything and serve.

Cocoa-Chili Crusted Tri-Tip and Potatoes

I love using cocoa and chili together—especially on beef, which can handle bold flavors. If you find certain cuts of beef (like tri-tip) too expensive, consider buying your beef from a grass-fed ranch as part of a beef share. It's more expensive all at once, but by the pound, your tri-tip and filet steaks cost as much as the ground beef. It's an investment my husband and I have never regretted. Plus, seeing where your food comes from and shaking the hand of the rancher is always a good thing.

Prep time 15 minutes
Serves 6

1½ pounds (680 g) red or sweet potatoes, cut into large 2- to 3-inch (5 to 8 cm) pieces

1- to 1½-pound (455 to 680 g) tri-tip roast

2 teaspoons chili powder

1 teaspoon unsweetened cocoa powder

1 teaspoon sea salt

½ teaspoon black pepper

⅛ teaspoon ground cloves

2 tablespoons (28 g) avocado or coconut oil

⅓ cup (80 ml) coconut aminos

4 cloves garlic, minced

2 to 3 tablespoons (30 to 45 ml) freshly squeezed lemon juice

1 Place the potatoes in a 4-quart (3.8 liter) slow cooker.

2 Trim the excess fat from the roast, but not all of it. Combine the chili powder, cocoa powder, salt, pepper, and cloves in a small bowl. Rub the spice mixture all over the roast.

3 Heat the oil in a large nonstick or cast-iron pan over high heat. Sear both sides of the roast until a golden crust forms. Transfer the roast to the slow cooker on top of the potatoes.

4 Pour the coconut aminos into the bottom of the cooker and sprinkle the garlic over the roast.

5 Cover and cook on low for 6 to 7 hours, until the roast pulls apart easily with a fork.

6 Remove the roast from the cooker and let it rest for 10 minutes. (Do not discard cooking juices.)

7 Remove the potatoes from the cooker with a slotted spoon and cover to keep warm. Slice the roast thin and place the meat back into the slow cooker to soak up some of the juices for a few minutes. Sprinkle the lemon juice over the meat. Taste, and sprinkle with a little sea salt if necessary.

8 Serve the roast and potatoes with a few spoonfuls of cooking juices over the top.

Creamy Beef Stroganoff

Good news: You don't need flour, butter, or a container of sour cream to make a delicious beef stroganoff. The gravy that coats the tender beef and mushrooms gets its umami flavor and velvety texture from a handful of clean ingredients, including coconut cream—an unlikely addition, but one that simply adds a nice richness. You won't even detect a coconut flavor.

Prep time 25 minutes
Serves 6

1 to 1½ pounds (455 to 680 g) beef stew meat or steak cut into 1-inch (2.5 cm) pieces

1 teaspoon sea salt, divided

1 teaspoon black pepper, divided

4 tablespoons (59 ml) avocado oil

1 medium onion, diced

1½ cup (355 ml) Homemade Beef Stock (page 281), divided

2 tablespoons (16 g) tapioca flour

1 tablespoon Dijon mustard

1 tablespoon (30 g) tomato paste

⅓ cup (80 ml) coconut aminos

3 cloves garlic, minced

12 ounces (336 g) baby portobello mushrooms, sliced

1 ounce (28.4 g) dried porcini mushrooms

2 sprigs fresh rosemary

1 13.5-ounce (398 ml) can coconut milk

Cauliflower Rice (pages 249 and 250) and Squash Noodles (page 248), for serving

1 Sprinkle the beef with ½ teaspoon sea salt and ½ teaspoon black pepper.

2 Heat 2 tablespoons (29 ml) of the avocado oil in a large stainless-steel or cast-iron pan over medium-high heat. Brown the beef in two batches, until the pieces are covered in deep, golden brown spots. They don't have to be cooked all the way through. Transfer the browned beef to a 4-quart (3.8 liter) slow cooker.

3 Add the onion to the same skillet. Cook for 2 to 3 minutes and then pour ½ cup (120 ml) of beef stock into the pan. Stir, scraping up the browned bits from the bottom of the pan. Pour the onion and pan juices into the slow cooker with the beef.

4 Stir the tapioca flour, mustard, tomato paste, and coconut aminos into the remaining 1 cup (235 ml) beef stock until smooth. Pour the mixture into the slow cooker, and add the garlic, mushrooms, rosemary, and remaining ½ teaspoon of salt and pepper. Give everything a good stir.

5 Cover and cook on low for 6 hours. Put the can of coconut milk in the fridge.

6 When the beef is finished, open the can of coconut milk from the bottom. Pour the clear liquid out into a small container (and save it for a smoothie later). Scrape out the hardened coconut cream and stir it into the stroganoff. Taste, and add more salt if necessary.

7 Serve with a sprinkle of freshly ground black pepper and desired side dish.

Austrian Granny's Goulash

As I described earlier, I spent a year and a half in Austria as a representative for my church. We frequently ate in church members' homes, and that was always a treat. One elderly woman invited us over often. She used to be "Austria's queen yodeler" back in the 1940s and did voice-over work in movies. She told the best stories and served the best goulash every time we came over—with apple strudel for dessert. I love this fiery-looking yet mildly flavored sauce mixed with tender bits of slow cooked beef. We usually ate it with egg noodles, but it would be just as delicious over squash noodles or steamed potatoes.

Prep time 25 minutes
Serves 8

2 to 2½ pounds (900 g to 1.1 kg) beef stew meat, cut into ½-inch (1 cm) pieces

2 teaspoons sea salt, divided

½ teaspoon black pepper

2 to 4 tablespoons (28 to 56 g) Homemade Ghee (page 287) or bacon drippings

2 red bell peppers, seeded and minced

1 large onion, minced

3 cloves garlic, minced

3 tablespoons (21 g) paprika

1 teaspoon hot Hungarian paprika

1 teaspoon caraway seed

3 tablespoons (45 ml) red wine vinegar

2 tablespoons (16 g) tapioca flour

2 tablespoons (60 g) tomato paste

2 to 4 cups (475 to 946 ml) beef broth

Squash Noodles (page 248), cooked potatoes, or Cauliflower Rice (pages 249 and 250), for serving

1 Trim any excess fat from the stew meat. Sprinkle 1 teaspoon sea salt and the black pepper over the meat. Toss to coat evenly.

2 Heat 2 tablespoons (30 g) of the ghee in a large skillet (preferably stainless-steel or cast-iron) over high heat. Working in two or three batches, add some of the beef chunks to the skillet, not overcrowding the pan. Let them cook, undisturbed, for 3 to 4 minutes. Flip them around and let them cook another 3 to 4 minutes, until golden brown crusts form on a few sides. They do not need to be cooked through. Transfer the seared beef to a 4-quart (3.8 liter) slow cooker, and sear the rest of the meat.

3 Add the minced bell pepper and onion, garlic, both paprikas, caraway seed, and 1 teaspoon sea salt to the slow cooker.

4 In a large liquid measuring cup, whisk together the red wine vinegar, tapioca flour, tomato paste, and 2 cups (475 ml) of beef broth. Pour the liquid mixture into the slow cooker, and give the entire contents a good stir.

5 Cover and cook on low for 5 to 6 hours, until the stew meat is tender. If you'd like to thin the stew and make it more souplike, add another cup or two of beef broth.

6 Taste, and add more salt or a splash of red wine vinegar if necessary.

7 Serve with desired side dish.

Note: To save time, use a food processor to mince the bell pepper and onion.

Mongolian Beef and Broccoli

One of my favorite Chinese dishes is Mongolian Beef. I love the addition of broccoli, which gives this a freshness that cuts through the sweet sauce. The slices of beef are thin in this dish, so it cooks up quickly. You could throw this in your cooker after lunch and it'll be ready by dinnertime.

Prep time 15 minutes
Serves 6

1 flank steak
½ teaspoon sea salt
¼ teaspoon black pepper
⅔ cup (160 ml) coconut aminos
¼ cup (85 g) honey
2 cloves garlic, minced
2-inch (5 cm) knob of fresh ginger, finely grated

Pinch of crushed red pepper flakes
1½ pounds (680 g) broccoli crowns
3 green onions, thinly sliced
½ lemon
Cauliflower Rice (pages 249 and 250) or Squash Noodles (page 248), for serving

1 Sprinkle the flank steak on both sides with the salt and pepper. Cut it in half lengthwise, then slice it into thin strips, cutting against the grain of the meat. Place the meat in a 4-quart (3.8 liter) slow cooker.

2 Add the coconut aminos, honey, garlic, ginger, and red pepper flakes. Stir well.

3 Cover and cook on low for 3 to 4 hours, until the beef is tender.

4 Add the broccoli, green onions, and the juice from the half lemon to the slow cooker. Cover and cook for another 15 to 20 minutes, until the broccoli is crisp and tender.

5 Serve with desired side dish.

Creamy Beef and Sauerkraut

If you can find lacto-fermented sauerkraut in the chilled section of the grocery store, it is far superior to the canned varieties on the shelves. You'll love how the tartness balances the rich, tender beef!

Prep time 15 minutes
Serves 8

2 pounds (905 g) stew meat, cut into ½-inch (1 cm) pieces

1 teaspoon sea salt

½ teaspoon black pepper

½ teaspoon caraway seed

½ teaspoon dried dill weed

2 tablespoons (29 ml) avocado oil or Homemade Ghee (29 g) (page 287)

1 medium sweet yellow onion, thinly sliced

2 tablespoons (22 g) whole-grain mustard

2 cups (284 g) sauerkraut (lacto-fermented, if possible)

⅓ cup (75 g) Paleo-Friendly Mayonnaise

Cauliflower Rice (pages 249 and 250), "Baked" Sweet Potatoes (page 253), roasted potatoes, or Squash Noodles (page 248), for serving

1 Remove the excess fat from the meat, if desired.

2 Combine the salt, black pepper, caraway seed, and dill weed in a small bowl. Sprinkle the mixture over the meat and toss to coat evenly.

3 Heat the oil in a large stainless-steel or cast-iron skillet over medium-high heat. Add half of the beef to the skillet, not overcrowding the pan, and let it cook undisturbed for 2 to 3 minutes. Flip the meat around and let it cook for another 2 to 3 minutes, until bits of deep golden crust has formed throughout the meat. You do not need to cook it all the way through. Transfer the meat to a 4-quart (3.8 liter) slow cooker.

4 Add the onion, mustard, and sauerkraut to the slow cooker and stir it a bit.

5 Cover and cook on low for about 5 hours, until the beef is tender.

6 Stir the mayonnaise into the beef mixture to form a creamy sauce. Cover and let it cook for another 10 minutes.

7 Serve with desired side dish.

Note: If your sauerkraut contains caraway seed, either reduce the amount of caraway seed in the recipe or omit it altogether.

Beef and Potato Stew with Cilantro Cream and Kale Chips

There's a steak and potato salad recipe that is possibly my favorite potato salad. It is dressed in a cilantro chimichurri dressing and mixed with crispy grilled kale. I took these flavors and made a warm version, keeping that bright chimichurri flavor in the cilantro cream.

Prep time 40 minutes

Serves 8

2 pounds (905 g) stew meat,
cut into 1-inch (2.5 cm) pieces

1½ teaspoons sea salt

1 teaspoon salt-free all-purpose seasoning

1 teaspoon ground cumin

½ teaspoon black pepper

A generous pinch of crushed
red pepper flakes

6 tablespoons (88 ml) avocado oil

½ cup (120 ml) beef broth

2 pounds (905 g) red or russet potatoes,
cut into 1-inch (2.5 cm) pieces

1 red bell pepper, diced

3 cloves garlic, minced

For the kale chips:

1 bunch kale, stems removed

1 tablespoon avocado oil

For the cilantro cream:

1 bunch cilantro, chopped

2 tablespoons (30 ml) red wine vinegar

⅓ cup (75 g) Paleo-Friendly Mayonnaise
(page 286)

Pinch of salt

Pinch of crushed red pepper flakes

1 Spread the stew meat out on a large plate.

2 Combine the salt, salt-free seasoning, cumin, black pepper, and pepper flakes in a small bowl. Sprinkle the seasoning on the beef and toss to coat.

3 Heat 2 tablespoons (29 ml) avocado oil in a large skillet over medium-high heat. Add one-third of the beef to the skillet. Let it cook, undisturbed, for 3 to 4 minutes. Flip the pieces and let them cook for another 2 to 3 minutes, until they are golden brown in spots. If the meat seems to stick, let it cook longer and it will release easily. Repeat with the remaining bits of beef, adding more oil to the pan between batches, and transferring the seared beef to a 4-quart (3.8 liter) slow cooker. While the pan is still hot, pour in the beef broth and scrape the browned bits from the bottom of the pan. Pour the liquid from the pan into the cooker.

4 Add the potatoes, bell pepper, and garlic to the slow cooker. Give it a stir.

5 Cover the cooker and cook on low for 5 to 6 hours, until the potatoes are cooked through and the beef is tender. Turn off the cooker (or set it to "warm" if you have the option) and cover to keep warm.

6 To make the kale chips, preheat the oven to 400°F (204°C). Place the kale on a rimmed baking sheet. Drizzle a tablespoon of oil over the leaves and sprinkle with a few pinches of sea salt. Rub the oil into the leaves with your hands, then spread the leaves out evenly on the pan. Bake for 8 to 10 minutes, until the leaves are crisp and slightly browned on the edges. Transfer the kale chips to a plate and set aside until ready to serve.

7 To make the cilantro sauce, combine the cilantro and red wine vinegar in a small food processor. Pulse until the cilantro is finely chopped. Scrape the sides of the work bowl with a rubber spatula, then add the mayonnaise and pinches of salt and crushed red pepper flakes. Pulse again, until blended, and process for 10 to 15 seconds until smooth. Transfer to a small serving bowl and chill until ready to use.

8 Serve the stew with a drizzle of cilantro cream and kale chips.

Note: You can make the kale chips and cilantro cream up to three days in advance.

Simple Sausage and Peppers with Sauerkraut

This recipe couldn't be simpler, but sometimes the simplest things yield the best results. Choose brats or similar sausages you really like, because they flavor the whole pot. Also, adding a few forkfuls of sauerkraut on each serving is a must!

Prep time 10 minutes

Serves 6

1½ pounds (680 g) brat-style sausages

1 green bell pepper

2 red, orange, or yellow bell peppers

1 large onion

4 tablespoons (60 ml) melted Homemade Ghee (page 287)

½ teaspoon sea salt

Sauerkraut, for serving

1 Slice the sausage into ½-inch (1 cm) rounds. Slice the peppers and onions into ¼-inch (6 mm) strips.

2 Place the sausage, peppers, and melted ghee into a 3-quart (2.8 liter) slow cooker. Sprinkle with salt.

3 Cover and cook on low for 3 to 4 hours (or on high for 1½ to 2 hours).

4 Serve with sauerkraut.

Note: This is also good with Cauliflower Rice (pages 249 and 250), Baked Sweet Potatoes (page 253), or lettuce cups.

Sweet Potato Foil Packet "Tacos"

This recipe won the North Carolina Sweet Potato Commission's Blogger Recipe Contest (Kid-Friendly Category) several years ago! I created it with my two daughters, who were about two and four years old at the time. They loved assembling their own packets. These would also do well as a camping meal. These "tacos" or foil packets are full of flavor and require a dollop of Simple Guacamole (page 59) on top, whether you're roughing it or not.

Prep time 30 minutes
Serves 6

1 pound (455 g) ground beef

Sea salt and black pepper

1 4-ounce (113 g) can diced green chillies

½ cup (123 g) tomato sauce

2 tablespoons Homemade Taco Seasoning (page 289)

1½ cups (168 g) frozen chopped spinach

2 large sweet potatoes, peeled and cut into 1-inch (2.5 cm) cubes

Simple Guacamole (page 59), salsa, and fresh cilantro, for serving

1 In a large skillet over medium-high heat, add the beef and a few generous pinches of salt and pepper. Cook, breaking the beef up into small chunks, until the meat has crispy brown bits throughout, about 10 to 15 minutes.

2 Add green chillies, tomato sauce, taco seasoning, and spinach to the skillet. Stir and cook for another 6 to 8 minutes, until flavors have blended and the spinach is heated through. Remove from heat and set aside.

3 Tear six sheets of aluminum foil, each about as large as a placemat. In the center of each square, place

1 cup (133 g) of sweet potato cubes and ⅔ cup (133 g) of seasoned ground beef over the top. Fold opposite sides to the center. Then bring the other sides together in the middle and fold them together downward, creating a sealed packet.

4 Place the packets in a 6-quart (5.7 liter) slow cooker. Cook on low for 5 to 6 hours (or 2 to 3 hours on high). Check sweet potatoes for doneness by unwrapping a packet and poking them with a fork.

5 Remove the packets from slow cooker and serve with guacamole, salsa, and fresh cilantro.

Note: These are great reheated at breakfast! Just dump the contents of a packet into a skillet and cook over medium heat. Crack a couple of eggs into the skillet and scramble it all up into a hash.

Sloppy Joes for a Crowd

The benefit of using a slow cooker for sloppy joes is its portability (potlucks!) and the ease of keeping food warm. Eating sloppy joes paleo-style with a couple of lettuce leaves gives "sloppy" a whole new meaning. We've branched out into making sloppy joe salads (salad joes!) and used the meat as a topping for baked sweet potatoes, a bed of sweet potato fries, and over a platter of squash noodles. There's no need to limit yourself to a bun!

Prep time 40 minutes

Serves 12

6 pounds (2.7 kg) ground beef

4 15-ounce (425 g) cans tomato sauce

2 teaspoons dried rubbed sage

½ cup (88 g) yellow mustard

2 tablespoons dried minced onion

4 teaspoons chili powder

4 teaspoons (24 g) sea salt

4 tablespoons (32 g) tapioca flour

4 tablespoons (85 g) honey

1 teaspoon black pepper

Diced pickles and Paleo Ranch (page 285) as garnish (optional)

Salad greens, Squash Noodles (page 248), or "Baked" Sweet Potatoes (page 253), for serving

1 Brown the ground beef in two batches in a large skillet, draining any excess grease. Transfer the beef to a 6-quart (5.7 liter) slow cooker.

2 Add the tomato sauce, sage, mustard, minced onion, chili powder, salt, tapioca flour, honey, black pepper, and 1 cup (235 ml) of water to the cooker. Stir well.

3 Cover and cook on low for 4 hours.

4 Serve along desired side dish with diced pickles and paleo ranch dressing over the top.

Creamy Meatballs and Gravy

My Grandma Inez shows her love through her cooking, and she's always excited for our family to try new things she makes. One slow cooker dish she makes quite often—and that we all love—are her meatballs and gravy. Because the recipe calls for so much mayonnaise and packets of gravy mix, I decided to use the paleo-friendly kind (use good oil!) and a blend of seasonings and tapioca flour to thicken the gravy. It worked like a charm. The meatballs have a lot of flavor from the Italian sausage, and they're coated in a smooth, richly flavored gravy. You'll love these. And I think my grandma would, too.

Prep time 30 minutes
Serves 6

1½ pounds (680 g) ground beef

½ pound (225 g) bulk hot Italian sausage

1 cup (160 g) finely chopped onion

1 egg

¾ cup (188 g) blanched almond flour

2 teaspoons sea salt, divided

¾ teaspoon black pepper

Coconut oil or avocado oil, for cooking

3 cups (710 ml) beef broth

¾ cup (175 g) Paleo-Friendly Mayonnaise (page 287)

1½ teaspoon onion powder

3 tablespoons (45 ml) coconut aminos

3 tablespoons (24 g) tapioca flour

2 teaspoons (22 g) Dijon mustard

1 tablespoon (30 g) tomato paste

Cauliflower Rice (pages 249 and 250), Squash Noodles (page 248), or "Baked" Sweet Potatoes (page 253), for serving

1 Combine the ground beef, sausage, onion, egg, almond flour, 1 teaspoon salt, and ½ teaspoon black pepper in a large mixing bowl. Gently mix everything with your hands (without squeezing it in your fists), form it into tight, 1½-inch (3.5 cm) balls, and transfer them to a large plate.

2 Heat 2 tablespoons (30 ml) of oil in a large skillet over medium-high heat. Place ½ cup (120 ml) of beef broth next to the stove. Sear the meatballs on a couple of sides, working in two batches. Add more oil between batches, if necessary. Transfer the meatballs to a 4-quart (3.8 liter) slow cooker. While the pan is still hot, pour the ½ cup (120 ml) of broth into the pan and scrape the browned bits from the bottom. Pour the contents of the pan into the slow cooker with the meatballs.

3 Combine the remaining 2½ cups (570 ml) beef broth, mayonnaise, onion powder, coconut aminos, 1 teaspoon salt, ¼ teaspoon pepper, tapioca flour, mustard, and tomato paste into a blender or food processor. Blend until smooth. Pour the sauce over the meatballs.

4 Cover and cook on low for 6 to 7 hours.

5 Serve with desired side dish.

Note: This can easily be doubled and cooked in a 6-quart (5.7 liter) slow cooker. You can also freeze large batches of meatballs after you sear them—just let them cool off, arrange them on a baking sheet, and freeze until solid. Transfer them to a freezer bag. When you're ready to use them, put them in a slow cooker with the blended sauce, and cook for the same amount of time.

Sun-Dried Tomato and Pesto Meatballs and Spaghetti Squash

Meatballs, sauce, and "noodles" all in one pot! You could even make a large batch of meatballs and freeze them on a cookie sheet, then divide them into portions in zip-top bags. Throwing a bag of frozen meatballs into a pot with some sauce and a spaghetti squash can be a lifesaving meal on a busy day.

Prep time 30 minutes
Serves 6

1 pound (455 g) ground beef
3 tablespoons (45 g) Paleo Pesto (page 293)
¼ cup chopped sun-dried tomatoes
½ teaspoon sea salt
¼ teaspoon black pepper

1 tablespoon (15 ml) coconut aminos
1 tablespoon nutritional yeast (optional)
1 tablespoon avocado oil
½ large spaghetti squash
3 cups (750 g) Basic Marinara (page 285)

1 Arrange the spaghetti squash halves in the slow cooker. If your squash is too large, you can bake the other half in the oven (see note).

2 In a large mixing bowl combine the ground beef, pesto, sun-dried tomatoes, salt, pepper, coconut aminos, and nutritional yeast. Blend it gently with your hands, being careful not to squish the meat too forcefully. (It makes the meatballs mushy and mealy.)

3 Form the meat into 1½- to 2-inch (2.6 to 5 cm) balls.

4 Drizzle the oil on the inside of the squash halves and sprinkle with salt and pepper.

5 Place the spaghetti squash half in a 4- or 6-quart (3.8 or 5.7 liter) slow cooker. Arrange meatballs in the cooker, behind the squash and in the center cavity. Pour the marinara sauce over the squash and the meatballs.

6 Cover and cook over low heat for 5 to 6 hours (or 2 to 3 hours on high).

7 Carefully transfer meatballs to a serving plate. Remove squash with tongs and scrape out the noodles with a fork. Place the squash noodles on the plate with the meatballs and spoon the marinara sauce over the top before serving.

Note: If you need more spaghetti squash for serving, drizzle the other half of the squash and lay it, cut-side up, on a sheet pan and bake at 400°F (204°C) for 30 to 40 minutes, until the "noodles" pull apart with a fork.

Cilantro Chimichurri Meatballs and Enchilada Spaghetti Squash

This is a Latin spin on spaghetti squash and meatballs, with cilantro-infused meatballs cooked in enchilada sauce. If you have trouble finding paleo-compliant enchilada sauce, make your own: Check out my Easy Enchilada Sauce (page 292).

Prep time 25 minutes
Serves 6

For the meatballs:

½ bunch cilantro, leaves and stems chopped, and extra cilantro for garnish

1 garlic clove, halved

1 tablespoon (15 ml) red wine vinegar

1 teaspoon sea salt, divided

⅛ teaspoon crushed red pepper flakes

3 tablespoons (44 ml) avocado oil, divided

2 pounds (907 g) ground beef

For the squash:

1 medium or large spaghetti squash, halved with seeds removed

Pinch of black pepper

1 recipe Easy Enchilada Sauce (page 292)

Juice from ½ a lime

1 Arrange the spaghetti squash halves in the slow cooker. If your squash is too large, you can bake the other half in the oven (see note on page 171).

2 In a food processor combine the cilantro, garlic, vinegar, ¼ teaspoon salt, pepper flakes, and 2 tablespoons (28 g) oil. Pulse until smooth.

3 Place the ground beef in a medium bowl. Add cilantro mixture and ¾ teaspoon sea salt. Blend it gently with your hands, being careful not to squish the meat too forcefully— or you might end up with mushy meatballs.

4 Form meat into 1½- to 2-inch (2.6 to 5 cm) balls.

5 Drizzle 1 tablespoon oil on the inside of the squash, and sprinkle with sea salt and black pepper.

6 Place the squash in a 6-quart (5.7 liter) slow cooker. Arrange meatballs around and inside the squash. Pour the enchilada sauce over the squash and meatballs.

7 Cover and cook on low for 5 to 6 hours (or 2 to 3 hours on high).

8 Transfer the meatballs to a serving dish. Remove the squash and scrape out the "noodles" with a fork. Place them with the meatballs and spoon the sauce on top. Squirt the lime juice over everything and sprinkle with more fresh cilantro before serving.

BBQ Bacon
Bison Meatballs

Bison has grown more popular in recent years, and is incredibly good for you. It is very lean and can dry out easily, so it's good to pair it with something a little fatty and moist—like bacon. Cover it with some BBQ sauce, too, and you'll have some pretty spectacular meatballs.

Prep time 25 minutes

Serves 6

12 slices thick-cut uncured bacon

2½ pounds (1.4 kg) ground bison

½ cup (80 g) minced yellow onion

4 cloves garlic, minced

2 tablespoons BBQ rub

1½ teaspoons sea salt

1½ (375 g) cups BBQ sauce (pages 289–291)

Cauliflower Rice (pages 249 and 250) or Squash Noodles (page 248), for serving

1 Slice the bacon into small pieces and cook them in a large nonstick or cast-iron skillet over medium heat, stirring frequently, until crispy.

2 Remove the bacon with a slotted spoon and drain off all of the bacon grease except 2 tablespoons. Set the pan aside.

3 In a large mixing bowl, add the ground bison, reserved bacon, onion, garlic, BBQ rub, and sea salt. Mix everything gently with your hands and form the meat into 1½-inch (3.5 cm) balls.

4 Heat the pan with the reserved bacon grease over medium-high heat.

5 Sear the meatballs in two batches, letting them cook undisturbed for 2 to 3 minutes on each side, until a golden brown crust forms. Transfer the meatballs into a 4-quart (3.8 liter) slow cooker and pour ½ cup (125 g) BBQ sauce over the top.

6 Cover and cook on low for 3½ to 4 hours, until the meatballs are cooked through. Pour the rest of the BBQ over the top, cover the cooker, and cook for another 10 minutes (or longer if the sauce is cold).

7 Serve meatballs with desired side dish.

Avocado-Stuffed Taco Meatloaf

One night, I was brainstorming recipes and I had an idea for a taco-flavored meatloaf stuffed with avocados. My husband thought I was a bit nuts to put avocados in a meatloaf, but I learned through this process that you never know how something will turn out unless you give it a shot. Some things end up as complete disasters or they come out beautifully and exceed expectations—like this meatloaf. You could serve it sliced alongside a small salad or stuff it into some Paleo Tortillas (page 256). The leftovers are fantastic for breakfast with a fried egg and some hot sauce on top. (But most leftovers are.)

Prep time 20 minutes
Serves 8

1 pound (455 g) ground beef
1 pound (455 g) ground pork
1 red bell pepper, diced small
1 jalapeño pepper, seeded and diced small
4 cloves garlic, minced
¼ cup (25 g) Homemade Taco Seasoning (page 284)

¼ teaspoon sea salt
¼ teaspoon black pepper
1 avocado, peeled, pitted, and thinly sliced
Salsa or pico de gallo and hot sauce, for serving

1 Prep a 6-quart (5.7 liter) slow cooker by adding "handles" made of aluminum foil. This is easy: Tear off two sheets of aluminum foil about 2 feet (60 cm) long each. Fold each piece in half lengthwise, and then in half again to make long, narrow strips. Lay one strip across the bottom and up the sides of your slow cooker. Lay the other strip perpendicular to the first one. You should have foil pieces hanging off all sides of the slow cooker and a foil "rack" lining the bottom.

2 In a large bowl, combine the beef, pork, peppers, garlic, taco seasoning, salt, and pepper. Toss the mixture around gently with your hands and combine well.

3 Grab the meat mixture in one large mass and place it on the foil "rack" in the slow cooker. Press it together to form an oblong meatloaf shape. Using your fingers, make a 2-inch (5 cm) well across the meatloaf, lengthwise, an inch or two (3 or 5 cm) from each end. Add the avocado slices to the well, then squish it back together and close the well, sealing the avocado inside.

4 Cover and cook on low for 2½ to 3 hours, until the meatloaf is cooked through.

5 Remove the slow cooker lid. Gather all of the aluminum foil ends to the center and lift out the meatloaf, transferring it to a large plate or platter. Discard the cooking juices. Cover the meatloaf with the aluminum strips and let it rest for 10 minutes before slicing.

6 Slice the meatloaf and serve with salsa and hot sauce.

Note: If you use a taco seasoning other than the one in this book, check its salt content. If it contains a lot, you may want to omit the salt in this recipe.

Italian Balsamic BBQ Meatloaf

Here's another spin on meatloaf using bulk Italian sausage to boost the flavor and minced vegetables to keep it moist. I added my Balsamic BBQ Sauce (page 290) over the top to give it a tangy twist.

Prep time 20 minutes
Serves 6

1 pound (455 g) ground beef
1 pound (455 g) uncooked bulk Italian sausage (pork or chicken)
1 cup (124 g) zucchini, diced small
3 cloves garlic, minced
2 tablespoons (30 ml) balsamic vinegar

1 tablespoon dried minced onion
2 teaspoons Italian seasoning
1 teaspoon sea salt
¼ teaspoon black pepper
2 cups (500 g) Balsamic BBQ Sauce (page 290)

1 Prep a 6-quart (5.7 liter) slow cooker by adding "handles" made of aluminum foil. This is easy: Tear off two sheets of aluminum foil about 2 feet (60 cm) long each. Fold each piece in half lengthwise, and then in half again to make long, narrow strips. Lay one strip across the bottom and up the sides of your slow cooker. Lay the other strip perpendicular to the first one. You should have foil pieces hanging off all sides of the slow cooker and a foil "rack" lining the bottom.

2 In a large bowl, combine all of the ingredients except the BBQ sauce. Fold the mixture gently together with your fingers to thoroughly combine. Press it into one large mass and transfer it to the prepared slow cooker. Form it into an oblong shape.

3 Cover and cook on low for 2½ to 3 hours, until cooked through. Pour ½ cup (125 g) BBQ sauce over the meatloaf, cover, and cook for another 10 minutes.

4 Remove the slow cooker lid. Gather all of the aluminum foil ends to the center and lift out the meatloaf, transferring it to a large plate or platter. Discard the cooking juices. Cover the meatloaf with the aluminum strips and let it rest for 10 minutes before slicing.

5 Slice and serve with remaining BBQ sauce.

PORK AND LAMB

I'm not particularly fond of lamb or pork—unless it's bacon. What started out as a tough chapter turned out to be a section containing some of my most favorite recipes in this book! I hope you fall in love with this collection of roasts, chops, and stews—just like I did.

Recipes

Bacon-Wrapped Pork Loin with Fruity Date Sauce

Wrapping bacon around a loin roast gives it a great smoky flavor and pairs beautifully with the sweet orange, date, and ginger flavors in the sauce. As the dates cook, they soften considerably and almost "melt" into the sauce.

Prep time 15 minutes
Serves 6

3-pound (1.4 kg) pork loin roast
1½ teaspoons sea salt
½ teaspoon black pepper
¼ teaspoon crushed red pepper flakes
1 teaspoon dried rosemary
5 slices thick-cut bacon

2-inch (5 cm) knob fresh ginger, grated
4 *Medjool* dates, pitted and chopped
½ cup (120 ml) freshly squeezed orange juice
2 tablespoons (30 ml) rice vinegar

1 Place the pork loin on a large plate. Combine the sea salt, pepper, red pepper flakes, and rosemary in a small bowl. Rub the mixture over the entire roast.

2 Wrap the bacon around the loin in a single layer and tuck the ends underneath. Place the roast in a 6-quart (5.7 liter) slow cooker.

3 Mix together the ginger, dates, orange juice, and vinegar, and pour it over the loin, putting the chopped dates into the bottom of the pot. Cover and cook on low for about 4 hours, until the pork is just barely cooked through.

4 Remove the loin from the slow cooker and let it rest for 10 minutes. Remove the bacon. If you like, throw the bacon into a skillet and cook over medium heat to crisp it up a bit. Slice the roast into thin pieces and place them in a serving dish.

5 Whisk the cooking juices to break the cooked dates into smaller bits. Serve the roast with the sauce.

Balsamic Apple Pork Loin Roast

This pork loin roast is tender and flavorful, but honestly, the sweet-tart gravy is the star of the show. Luckily, you'll have quite a bit, so don't skimp on it.

Prep time 20 minutes
Serves 8

2 tart baking apples
1 large onion
1 3- to 4-pound (1.4 to 1.8 kg) pork loin
2½ teaspoons (15 g) sea salt
¾ teaspoon dried thyme
½ teaspoon crushed red pepper flakes
¾ teaspoon dried rosemary
½ teaspoon freshly ground black pepper
⅔ cup (160 ml) balsamic vinegar
⅓ cup (80 ml) Simple Chicken Stock (page 280)
4 cloves garlic

1 Chop apples into ¼ inch (5 mm) slices, discarding the core. Set them aside. Trim ends off the onion, slice it in half, and cut it into ¼ inch (5 mm) half-moons. Separate the onion layers and place them into a 6-quart (5.7 liter) slow cooker.

2 Place the pork loin on a cutting board or sturdy surface, fat-side up. Trim the excess fat according to your preferences. Using a sharp knife, cut slits into the top of the loin, an inch or two (3 or 5 cm) apart the entire length of the meat, widthwise, and about 2 inches (5 cm) deep. Insert an apple slice into each slit. Place the remaining apple slices into the slow cooker with the onions.

3 Combine the salt, thyme, pepper flakes, rosemary, and black pepper in a small bowl with your fingers. Rub mixture onto both sides of the loin.

4 Place the loin on top of the apples and onions in the slow cooker, fat-side up. Combine the vinegar and stock, and pour into the cooker around the sides. Pour a small amount over the loin, but not too much or you'll rinse off the seasonings you just rubbed on. Drop the garlic cloves into the cooker.

5 Cover and cook on low for 6 to 7 hours (or high for 2 to 3 hours) until the meat is cooked through and tender.

6 Transfer the roast from the cooker to a serving platter and cover to keep warm.

7 For the gravy, pour the juices and cooked apples and onions into a blender or a food processor, and process until smooth.

8 Slice or shred the loin roast, and serve with a heavy drizzle of gravy.

Prosciutto-Wrapped Pork Chops with Peach Sauce

Prosciutto is one of my favorite ingredients. It gives these pork chops a deep, salty flavor and goes beautifully with the peach sauce! Be sure you don't skip the step of broiling the chops for a few minutes when they come out of the cooker. It'll crisp up that prosciutto nicely!

Prep time 15 minutes
Serves 6

1½ teaspoons sea salt

½ teaspoon black pepper

1 tablespoon chopped fresh rosemary

4 cloves garlic, minced

Pinch of red pepper flakes

1 tablespoon avocado oil

6 thick-cut pork chops

12 slices prosciutto

1 pound (455 g) fresh or frozen peach slices

¼ cup (60 ml) chicken or vegetable broth

1 In a small bowl, combine the salt, pepper, rosemary, garlic, pepper flakes, and oil to form a paste. Rub the paste on both sides of each pork chop.

2 Cover each pork chop with two slices of prosciutto. Drape each piece over the top and sides—it's not necessary to cover the bottoms.

3 Put half of the peach slices and the broth in the bottom of a 6-quart (5.7 liter) slow cooker. Arrange the pork chops in a single layer over the peaches, packing them tightly if necessary. If you are using frozen peaches, leave the remaining peaches on the counter in a bowl to thaw.

4 Cover and cook for 6 hours on low.

5 Preheat the broiler. Transfer the chops to a rimmed baking sheet and cover them to keep warm. If the frozen peaches are still cold, place them on the baking sheet as well. Broil for 5 to 10 minutes, until the prosciutto crisps up a bit. Transfer the chops to a serving platter and dice the warm peaches.

6 Blend the peaches and juices together in the pot, preferably using an immersion blender. Stir in the diced peaches.

7 Serve the pork chops with the peach sauce.

Honey Dijon Pork Chops

You can eat these pork chops whole or shred them and put them back into the slow cooker to soak up all the juices. They're great shredded— especially the next day with a side of sauerkraut.

Prep time 15 minutes
Serves 6

6 thick-cut pork chops
1 teaspoon sea salt
1 teaspoon black pepper
4 tablespoons (56 g) Homemade Ghee (page 287) or bacon drippings

½ cup (170 g) honey
½ cup (88 g) Dijon mustard
4 cloves garlic, minced
1 teaspoon mustard seeds
Sauerkraut, for serving

1 Sprinkle both sides of the pork chops with salt and pepper. Heat the ghee in a medium skillet over medium-high heat. Sear the pork chops on both sides, then place them in a 6-quart (5.7 liter) slow cooker.

2 Whisk together the honey, mustard, garlic, and mustard seeds in a small bowl. Pour the mixture over the pork chops.

3 Cook on low for 5 to 6 hours (or on high for 2 to 3 hours), until the pork chops are tender and pull apart easily with a fork.

4 Remove pork chops from the slow cooker. You can either shred them and return them to the pot with the juices or serve them whole with the juices spooned over the top. Serve with sauerkraut.

Caribbean Jerk Pork Chops with Mango Salsa

Caribbean jerk seasoning is typically very spicy—featuring habanero peppers. Feel free to use half of a habanero pepper in place of the jalapeño, but be warned—long, slow braising tends to intensify the heat of chilli peppers and other spicy ingredients. The mango salsa adds a nice cooling element, though. Make sure to keep a glass of cold almond milk on hand. Just in case.

Prep time 20 minutes
Serves 6

For the pork chops:

6 thick-cut pork chops

Sea salt

3 tablespoons (19 g) Dry Caribbean Jerk Rub (page 288)

1 orange, zest and juice

2 limes (zest from 1 and juice from 2)

1 jalapeño, diced (seeded, if desired) or ½ a habanero chilli, seeded

1 13.5-ounce (398 ml) can coconut milk

1 cup (235 ml) chicken or vegetable stock

2 bay leaves

1½ tablespoons (30 g) honey

1½ tablespoons tapioca flour

For the mango salsa:

2 large tomatoes, seeded and diced

1 mango, peeled and diced

Juice from 1 lime

1 jalapeño, minced (seeded, if desired)

¼ cup chopped fresh cilantro

½ cup (80 g) diced yellow onion

2 tablespoons (16 g) of finely grated ginger

Pinch of sea salt

1 Sprinkle both sides of the pork chops with sea salt.

2 In a small bowl, combine the jerk seasoning, orange zest, and lime zest. Rub the mixture together between your fingers and then rub it on both sides of each pork chop. Set aside.

3 In a 6-quart (5.7 liter) slow cooker, combine the orange juice, lime juice, jalapeño, coconut milk, stock, bay leaves, honey, and tapioca flour. Place the pork chops in the coconut mixture.

4 Cover and cook on low for 5 to 6 hours until the chops are tender, but not dry.

5 Combine all salsa ingredients and chill until ready to use.

6 When the pork chops are finished cooking, they should break apart easily with a fork. Remove the bay leaves and squirt the juice from one lime over the entire pot. Taste, and add more salt if needed.

7 Remove pork chops from the slow cooker and serve with a few spoonfuls of cooking liquid and some mango salsa. If you like, you can also shred the chops and place the meat back into the slow cooker to soak up more of the juices.

Pork Satay Stew

This dish is a spin-off of chicken satay—a common Thai-style appetizer made with strips of marinated, grilled chicken on skewers with a spicy peanut sauce for dipping. I had some cubed pork loin in the fridge, and I thought a stew version would be good to incorporate those satay flavors—and to use up the rest of the pork. A fabulous idea! The almond butter made the sauce rich and nutty—perfect over a bed of Squash Noodles.

Prep time 25 minutes
Serves 6

1½ to 2 pounds (680 to 905 g) cubed pork loin or shoulder

1 teaspoon sea salt

⅓ cup (80 ml) freshly squeezed lime juice (2 to 3 juicy limes)

1 tablespoon (19 g) fish sauce

1 tablespoon (15 g) *sambal oelek* or other Asian chili garlic sauce

1 tablespoon (20 g) honey

1 teaspoon ground turmeric

2-inch (5 cm) knob of fresh ginger, grated or finely minced

2 cloves garlic, minced

3 medium carrots, cut into ¼-inch (5 mm) slices

½ cup (80 g) yellow onion, diced small

1 cup (235 ml) unsweetened coconut milk

⅓ cup (76 g) unsweetened almond butter

½ cup (120 ml) chicken broth

1 tablespoon tapioca flour

Additional lime wedges and Asian chili garlic paste, for garnish

Squash Noodles (page 248) or Cauliflower Rice (pages 249 and 250), for serving

1 Sprinkle the pork pieces with salt. Toss to combine and transfer the pork to a 4-quart (3.8 liter) slow cooker.

2 Add the lime juice, fish sauce, chili paste, honey, turmeric, ginger, and garlic to the cooker, and give the whole thing a good stir.

3 Add the carrots and onions to the cooker.

4 Whisk together the coconut milk, almond butter, broth, and tapioca flour, and pour over the vegetables.

5 Cover and cook on low for about 5 hours or until the pork is tender. Taste, and add salt and lime juice if necessary.

6 Serve over desired side dish with lime wedges and chili paste.

Deconstructed Egg Rolls with Toasted Sesame Cashews

Egg rolls are a popular Chinese food, but nothing fried in vegetable oil is a very healthy choice. I took the filling—a mixture of flavorful ground pork, vegetables, and seasoning—and cooked them together. To give them some crispy texture, I added water chestnuts and a sprinkling of toasted sesame cashews. This dish is perfect over a bowl of Cauliflower Rice (pages 249 and 250) or you can simply eat it alone.

Prep time 25 minutes

Serves 6

1 to 1½ pounds (455 to 680 g) ground pork

1 teaspoon sea salt, divided

⅛ teaspoon Chinese five-spice seasoning

1 medium head green cabbage, cored, and chopped into bite-sized pieces

1½ cup (165 g) chopped carrots (½- inch [1 cm] pieces)

1 8-ounce (227 g) can sliced water chestnuts, drained and chopped

½ cup (80 g) chopped yellow onion

⅓ cup (80 ml) coconut aminos

2 cloves garlic, minced

1-inch (2.5 cm) knob of fresh ginger, grated

1 tablespoon (15 ml) lemon juice

4 teaspoons (20 ml) sesame oil, divided

1 tablespoon (15 ml) mirin (optional)

2 tablespoons (40 g) honey, divided

Pinch of crushed red pepper flakes

1 cup (143 g) raw cashews

¼ teaspoon roasted sesame seeds

Asian chili paste and Cauliflower Rice (pages 249 and 250), for serving (optional)

1 Cook the pork in a large skillet over medium-high heat. Stir it frequently and break the pork into small bits until the pork is cooked through and browned. Sprinkle with ½ teaspoon of sea salt and the Chinese spice mixture. Drain off any excess grease. Set the pork aside.

2 Place the cabbage in a 4-quart (3.8 liter) slow cooker. Add the carrots, water chestnuts, onion, and cooked pork on top of the cabbage.

3 In a large measuring cup, combine the coconut aminos, garlic, ginger, lemon juice, 3 teaspoons (15 ml) of sesame oil, mirin, 1 tablespoon (20 g) honey, crushed red pepper, and ½ teaspoon sea salt. Pour the mixture over the pork and vegetables.

4 Cover and cook on low for 4 hours, until the vegetables are cooked through. Toss the mixture in the cooking juices to coat.

5 Put the cashews in a skillet with the remaining 1 tablespoon (20 g) honey, 1 teaspoon (5 ml) sesame oil, and a pinch of salt. Heat over medium heat until the cashews are golden brown and fragrant. Sprinkle with the sesame seeds.

6 Serve the pork and vegetable mixture with a sprinkle of toasted sesame cashews and Cauliflower Rice, if desired.

Note: Chinese five-spice seasoning is a unique, peppery blend of spices that has a hint of licorice. You'll likely find it in well-stocked grocery stores, but if you have trouble tracking down a jar, you can make your own by combining equal parts of these ground spices: anise, cinnamon, clove, fennel, and Szechuan or black pepper.

Easy Pork Chili Verde

Pork chili verde *is a staple in Latin American cuisine, and it's naturally paleo! The blend of peppers, chillies, and tomatillos makes a tart and spicy filling for Paleo Tortillas (page 256) or a topping for Cauliflower Rice (pages 249 and 250) or "Baked" Sweet Potatoes (page 253). It's especially good for breakfast with a fried egg.*

Prep time 15 minutes
Serves 8

3½ pounds (1.6 kg) boneless pork loin, cut into 1-inch (2.5 cm) chunks
1½ teaspoons sea salt
2 teaspoons ground cumin
2 teaspoons ground coriander
½ teaspoon chipotle powder
½ teaspoon black pepper
2 to 4 tablespoons (29 to 59 ml) avocado oil

1 16-ounce (454 g) jar of salsa verde
6 cloves garlic, minced
Juice from 1 lime
Juice from ½ of a large orange
1 cup (16 g) chopped fresh cilantro
Cauliflower Rice (pages 249 and 250), sliced radishes, and toasted pepitas, for serving

1 Place the pork chunks in a medium bowl.

2 Combine the salt, cumin, coriander, chipotle, and black pepper in a small bowl. Sprinkle the spice blend over the pork, and using your hands, mix thoroughly until the pork is coated in spices.

3 Heat 2 tablespoons (28 g) of oil in a large cast-iron or stainless-steel skillet over medium-high heat. Sear the pork in two batches, adding more oil if necessary. The meat should have a golden brown crust on most sides. It does not have to be cooked through. Transfer the pork to a 4- or 6-quart (3.8 or 5.7 liter) slow cooker.

4 Add the salsa verde, garlic, lime juice, and orange juice to the slow cooker. Give it a stir, then cover and cook on low for about 5 hours (or on high for 3 to 4 hours).

5 Stir in the fresh cilantro and taste, adding more salt or lime juice, as needed.

6 Serve with Cauliflower Rice, sliced radishes, and toasted pepitas.

Easy BBQ Spareribs with Potatoes and Carrots

I've only recently started liking pork ribs. Crazy, right? My dislike stemmed from chewy, gummy meat covered with overly sweet barbecue sauce on the ribs I had eaten in the past. Well, these ribs fall right off the bone and are covered with just-sweet-enough sauce. Plus, there are potatoes cooked underneath for your loved ones to fight over. One problem solved, another one created.

Prep time 20 minutes
Serves 6

1 full rack of pork spareribs

3 tablespoons (18.8 g) BBQ Dry-Rub Seasoning (page 288)

4 large carrots, peeled and cut into 1-inch (2.5 cm) pieces

6 red potatoes, cut into 1-inch (2.5 cm) pieces

½ cup (120 ml) Simple Chicken Stock (page 280)

Sea salt and black pepper

2 cups (500 g) of your favorite barbecue sauce, plus more for serving

1 The night before you plan to cook the ribs, rub the BBQ rub over both sides. Cover and chill until morning.

2 Add the carrots and potatoes to a 6-quart (5.7 liter) slow cooker. Pour chicken stock over the vegetables. Sprinkle with a couple generous pinches of sea salt and black pepper.

3 Cut the rack of ribs into 2 or 3 large pieces so that they fit in the cooker. It's okay if they overlap or need to be stacked. Place them on top of the vegetables.

4 Cover and cook for 8 to 9 hours on low (or high for 5 to 6 hours). When you can pull the meat from them easily with a fork, they're finished cooking.

5 About 30 minutes before the ribs are finished, pour the barbecue sauce over the top. If they are stacked, lift them up and pour sauce in between the layers to ensure that they're all covered. Cover and cook for another 30 minutes.

6 Transfer the ribs to a large serving dish. Using a slotted spoon, remove the potatoes and carrots from the cooker. Spoon some of the remaining juices over the ribs and the vegetables, and serve with additional barbecue sauce, if desired.

Sweet Chili Spareribs

Overnight marinating makes a big difference with large cuts of meat. This sweet chili paste gets into every nook and cranny on these ribs. They don't even need a sauce after they're cooked!

Prep time 15 minutes
Serves 6

1 6-ounce (170 gram) can tomato paste
⅓ cup (115 g) honey
⅓ cup (50 g) coconut sugar
2 tablespoons chili powder
2 tablespoons (30 ml) apple cider vinegar
1 tablespoon dried cumin

1 teaspoon crushed red pepper flakes
3 cloves garlic, minced
1 full rack spare ribs
1 teaspoon sea salt
1 teaspoon black pepper

1 In a small bowl, stir together the tomato paste, honey, coconut sugar, chili powder, apple cider vinegar, cumin, red pepper flakes, and garlic.

2 Place the ribs on a rimmed baking sheet. Rub the salt and pepper into the ribs on both sides. Then rub the tomato-spice mixture over both sides of the ribs.

3 Cover the ribs with plastic wrap and let them marinate for at least 4 hours or even overnight.

4 Cut the rack in half (or in small enough pieces to fit into your 6-quart [5.7 liter] slow cooker). Place the ribs in the slow cooker. Cover and cook on low for 7 to 8 hours (or 4 to 5 hours on high).

5 Remove the ribs from the slow cooker and serve.

Tangy Mustard Ribs with Balsamic Glaze

Here's a different take on ribs, with flavors of Dijon and a tangy balsamic glaze. My rib-loving 7-year-old could barely contain herself when she saw these come out of the oven. You can serve them with a side of Rosemary-Garlic Mashed Potatoes (page 244) or a big green salad, but those may be ignored when the ribs arrive on the table.

Prep time 15 minutes, plus marinating time
Serves 6

1 full rack of spare or back ribs
3 tablespoons (45 ml) freshly squeezed lemon juice
1 tablespoon (18 g) sea salt
1 tablespoon Dijon mustard
6 cloves garlic, minced

2 teaspoons onion powder
1 teaspoon dried thyme
½ teaspoon black pepper
¼ cup (60 ml) balsamic vinegar
3 tablespoons (60 g) honey

1 Place the ribs on a rimmed baking sheet or large platter.

2 Combine the lemon juice, salt, mustard, garlic, onion powder, thyme, and black pepper in a small bowl. Pour the mixture over the ribs, and using your hands, spread it over both sides. Let the ribs sit for 30 minutes.

3 Transfer the rack to a 6-quart (5.7 liter) slow cooker, cutting the rack in half and layering if necessary. Add ¼ cup (60 ml) water to the bottom of the cooker and cook on low for 5 to 6 hours or until the meat is tender and shreds easily with a fork.

4 Remove the ribs from the cooker and place them on a rimmed baking sheet. Preheat the oven broiler.

5 Pour 1 cup (235 ml) of the cooking juices from the slow cooker into a small skillet. Add the balsamic vinegar and honey to the skillet. Heat to boiling and let it bubble for 6 to 8 minutes, until the glaze has thickened slightly and begins to look syrupy and coat a spoon.

6 Brush some glaze over the ribs and broil them for 2 to 3 minutes, until bubbly. Brush another layer of glaze over them and return to the broiler until bubbly.

7 Serve the ribs with extra glaze.

Asian-Style Ribs with Ginger-Orange Glaze

This glaze. I can't even begin to tell you how deliciously sticky, tangy, and addictive it is. It's the perfect complement to these Asian-style ribs!

Prep time 15 minutes, plus marinating time
Serves 6

1 full rack of spare or back ribs

1 tablespoon (18 g) sea salt

⅓ cup (80 ml) coconut aminos

4 tablespoons (80 g) honey, divided

1½ teaspoons (7.5 ml) sesame oil

1½ teaspoons *sambal oelek* or other Asian chili garlic sauce

1½ teaspoons fish sauce

2-inch (5 cm) knob of fresh ginger, grated or finely minced, divided

1 orange

1 tablespoon (15 ml) rice vinegar

Pinch of red pepper flakes

1 Place the ribs on a rimmed baking sheet or large platter.

2 Combine the salt, coconut aminos, 1 tablespoon (20 g) honey, sesame oil, chili paste, fish sauce, and half of the ginger in a small bowl. Whisk together, then pour it over the rack of ribs. Use your hands to spread the marinade over both sides of the rack. Let it sit for 30 minutes.

3 Transfer the ribs and marinade to a 6-quart (5.7 liter) slow cooker, cutting the rack in half and layering them if necessary. Add ¼ cup (60 ml) of water to the bottom of the cooker, and cook on low for 5 to 6 hours, until the meat is fork tender and shreds easily.

4 Remove the ribs from the cooker and place them on a rimmed baking sheet. Preheat the oven broiler.

5 Pour 1 cup (235 ml) of the cooking juices from the slow cooker into a small skillet. Add ½ teaspoon of orange zest and the juice from the orange to the skillet. Add the other half of the ginger, 3 tablespoons (60 g) of honey, the rice vinegar, and the pepper flakes to the skillet as well. Heat to boiling and let it bubble for 6 to 8 minutes, until the glaze has thickened slightly and begins to look syrupy and coat a spoon.

6 Brush some glaze over the ribs and broil them for 2 to 3 minutes, until bubbly. Brush another layer of glaze over them and return to the broiler until bubbly.

7 Serve the ribs with extra glaze.

BBQ Apple Pulled Pork

I've met only a couple people who eat meat and don't like pulled pork—it seems to be a universally loved potluck or picnic dish. I created a version using apples and my Cider BBQ Sauce (page 289) to create the familiar sweet and tangy flavors.

Prep time 15 minutes
Serves 10 to 12

4- to 5-pound (1.8 to 2.2 kg) pork roast (loin or shoulder)

2 tablespoons BBQ Dry-Rub Seasoning (page 288)

3 tablespoons (45 ml) apple cider vinegar, divided

2 tablespoons (29 ml) avocado oil

2 teaspoons sea salt

¼ teaspoon cinnamon

1 medium onion, halved and thinly sliced

2 medium apples, cored and thinly sliced

2 cloves garlic, smashed

3 cups (750 g) Cider BBQ Sauce (page 289)

1 Remove some—but not all—of the fat from the roast, and place it on a large plate.

2 Stir together the dry rub, 2 tablespoons (30 ml) of vinegar, oil, salt, and cinnamon in a small bowl. Spread the mixture all over the roast. Cover it with plastic wrap and chill for 4 to 12 hours.

3 Place the onion, apple slices, and garlic in a 6-quart (5.7 liter) slow cooker. Set the roast on top, fat-side up.

4 Cover and cook on low for 6 to 7 hours for a loin roast or 7 to 8 hours for a shoulder roast. When finished, the meat should be tender and pull apart easily with a fork.

5 Transfer the meat to a platter and shred it. Return the meat to the cooker and stir in the BBQ sauce.

6 Serve warm.

Note: Serve with Southwest Cabbage Slaw (page 252), Paleo Tortillas (page 256), or Squash Noodles (page 248).

Thai Pulled-Pork Tacos with Creamy Chili Slaw

Prep time 20 minutes, plus marinating time
Serves 10

This is one of my most favorite recipes in this entire book. The combination of Thai-spiced shreds of pork with a slightly spicy, creamy slaw is incredible. I pull out this recipe for a houseful of company, take it to a new mother, bring it to a potluck, or make a giant pot just for our family to eat for several days.

For the tacos:

4- to 5-pound (1.8 to 2.2 kg) pork roast (loin or shoulder)

1 tablespoon Thai Spice Blend (page 285)

1 tablespoon (18 g) sea salt

1 tablespoon avocado oil

2 cloves garlic, minced

2-inch (5 cm) knob of ginger, grated finely

4 limes, cut in half and zested

½ cup (120 ml) chicken broth

2 stalks lemongrass or 1 tablespoon (17 g) lemongrass paste

½ cup fresh chopped cilantro

Paleo Tortillas (page 256) and *sambal oelek* or other Asian chili garlic sauce, for serving

For the slaw:

1 small head cabbage, shredded

½ cup (115 g) Paleo-Friendly Mayonnaise (page 286)

2 tablespoons (30 g) sambal oelek or other chili garlic sauce

¼ teaspoon sea salt

½ cup fresh chopped cilantro

1 Trim some of the excess fat from the pork roast, but not all of it. Place the roast on a rimmed baking sheet or large platter or plate.

2 In a small bowl, combine the Thai spices, salt, oil, garlic, ginger, 2 teaspoons of lime zest, and juice from half of one of the limes to form a paste. (Wrap and chill the other half of the lime.) Rub the paste all over the pork roast. Cover the roast in plastic wrap and chill for 4 to 18 hours.

3 When you're ready to cook the roast, place it in a 6-quart (5.7 liter) slow cooker, fat-side up. Squeeze the reserved half of the lime over the pork. Pour the broth around the sides of the slow cooker. Cut the bottom 4 to 5 inches (10 to 13 cm) off of each lemongrass stalk, and discard the tops. Lay the flat side of your knife on each stalk and smash it with the palm of your hand. Bend and twist the stalks to rough them up, and then add them to the cooker alongside the pork.

4 Cover and cook on low for 5 to 6 hours (or high for 2 to 3 hours) if you're using a loin roast, and 7 to 8 hours on low (or for 3 to 4 hours on high) if you're using a shoulder roast. When finished, the meat should be easy to pull apart with a fork.

5 Remove the roast from the slow cooker, shred it, discard the fatty pieces, and return the shredded meat to the cooker. Add the juice from half of the other lime and chopped cilantro to the pork and stir it all together. Reserve the other half of the lime for the slaw. Cover and keep it warm while you prepare the slaw.

6 Place the shredded cabbage in a very large bowl. In a small bowl, stir together the mayonnaise, chili garlic paste, salt, and the juice from the reserved half lime. Pour the dressing over the slaw, add the cilantro, and toss everything together.

7 Cut the remaining 2 limes into wedges.

8 Serve the pork in the tortillas with a forkful of slaw and a bit of the chili garlic paste and lime wedges.

Sweet Jalapeño-Pineapple Pulled Pork

Here's another take on sweet pulled pork with a Tex-Mex flair. Pineapple and honey are such great complements to the pork and the jalapeños. If you have a lot of meat left, you can transfer it to a freezer-safe container and freeze for a later meal. (Psst—all of the shredded-meat recipes in this book are freezer-friendly!)

Prep time 20 minutes

Serves 10

4- to 5-pound (1.8 to 2.2 kg) pork roast (loin or shoulder)

1½ tablespoons (27 g) sea salt

1 tablespoon ground ginger

1 teaspoon black pepper

4 cups (660 g) chopped fresh pineapple

4 cloves garlic, smashed

2 jalapeños, seeded and diced

1 shallot, sliced

½ cup (120 ml) chicken broth

¼ cup (85 g) honey

4 limes

Squash Noodles (page 248) or Cauliflower Rice (pages 249 and 250), for serving

1 Place the pork roast on a sheet pan. Remove the excess fat, but don't remove it all.

2 Combine the salt, ginger, and pepper in a small bowl. Rub the seasonings all over the pork roast and place it in a 6-quart (5.7 liter) slow cooker.

3 Place the pineapple, garlic, jalapeños, and shallot on and around the pork. Pour the chicken broth down the side of the cooker. Drizzle the honey over everything.

4 Cover and cook on low for 6 to 7 hours for a loin roast and 7 to 8 hours for a shoulder roast. The meat should pull apart easily with a fork.

5 Remove the roast from the slow cooker and shred it.

6 Remove any unwanted bits of fat or pork from the cooking juices. Puree the juices, pineapple, jalapeño, and garlic, preferably using an immersion blender.

7 Return the shredded meat to the slow cooker and mix it with the juices. Cut one of the limes in half and squirt half of the juice over the meat. Cut the remaining limes into wedges.

8 Serve with desired side dish.

Shredded Enchilada Pork

I love this saucy, tender pile of pork. It needs no salsa or special toppings. It's good as is, over a heap of Southwest Cabbage Slaw (page 252), or wrapped with a Paleo Tortilla (page 256). You may want to serve this with a little Simple Guacamole (page 59), because everything is better with guac.

Prep time 15 minutes
Serves 8 to 10

3- to 4-pound (1.4 to 1.8 kg) pork roast (shoulder or loin)
2 teaspoons sea salt
1½ teaspoons chili powder
1½ teaspoons garlic powder
1½ teaspoons ground cumin

4 cloves garlic, sliced
1 batch of Easy Enchilada Sauce (page 292)
½ cup (120 ml) chicken broth
½ cup chopped fresh cilantro

1 Remove the excess fat from the roast, but don't remove all of it. Turn the roast fat-side up and cut several 1-inch (2.5 cm) deep slits into it.

2 In a small bowl, combine the sea salt, chili powder, garlic powder, and cumin. Mix well. Rub the spice blend over the entire roast.

3 Stick the garlic slices into the slits you cut into the roast.

4 Place the roast fat-side up into a 4- or 6-quart (3.8 or 5.7 liter) slow cooker. Pour ½ cup (133 g) of enchilada sauce over the roast and pour the chicken broth down the side of the cooker so you don't wash the sauce and spices off of the roast.

5 Cover and cook on low for 5 to 6 hours if using a loin roast. Cook for 7 to 8 hours if using a shoulder roast.

6 Remove the roast from the cooker, shred the meat, and return it to the cooker. Pour in 2 cups (530 g) of enchilada sauce and stir together with a pair of tongs. Add the remaining ½ cup (133 g) of sauce if needed.

7 Cover and let it cook for another 15 minutes.

8 Stir in the fresh cilantro and serve.

Note: You can serve this meat with Paleo Tortillas (page 256), Southwest Cabbage Slaw (page 252), Cauliflower Rice (pages 249 and 250), "Baked" Sweet Potatoes (page 253), or Squash Noodles (page 248). It's even great added to a bed of salad greens!

Pork Carnitas

One thing I love about Mexican and Tex-Mex cuisine is how most dishes basically have the same ingredients, just rearranged and proportioned differently. If you have a few basics, like some flavorful, tender meat, a couple heads of lettuce, a handful of avocados, salsa, and Paleo Tortillas (page 256), you could make tacos, taco salads, lettuce wraps, stuffed avocados, or enchiladas. This pork is lightly seasoned, so you can use it in any of those dishes or with any kind of enchilada sauce or salsa. It's a great staple to have on hand and it also freezes well.

Prep time 25 minutes
Serves 8

4- to 5-pound (1.8 to 2.2 kg) pork roast (shoulder or loin)
1½ teaspoons sea salt
1 teaspoon black pepper
1 tablespoon cumin
½ teaspoon dried oregano
6 cloves garlic, minced

2 tablespoons (29 ml) avocado oil
1 medium onion, halved and thinly sliced
Juice from 1 large orange
Juice from 1 large lime
2 dried bay leaves
Lime wedges, for serving

1 Place the roast on a large plate. Cut off the excess fat, but don't remove all of it. Rub the salt and pepper all over the roast.

2 In a small bowl, combine the cumin, oregano, garlic, and avocado oil to form a paste. Rub the paste all over the roast and place it fat-side up in a 6-quart (5.7 liter) slow cooker. Put the onions over the roast, squeeze the orange and lime juices over the top, and drop the bay leaves along the sides.

3 Cover and cook on low for 6 to 7 hours for a loin roast or 7 to 8 hours for a shoulder roast. The meat should pull apart easily with a fork.

4 Preheat the oven broiler. Transfer the roast to a sheet pan and shred it into bite-sized pieces. Spread the meat evenly on the pan. Drizzle with ⅓ cup (80 ml) of the pot juices. Broil for about 10 to 15 minutes, until the edges of the bits of meat are golden brown and crisp.

5 Remove the pan from the oven, drizzle more of the pot juices over the meat, and toss it around with a pair of tongs.

6 Serve in tacos or on a salad with a wedge of lime.

Hot and Sweet Orange Pulled Pork

This pulled pork is covered in an orangey-sweet hot sauce that reminds me of the coating on Asian orange chicken. Many cayenne pepper sauces are paleo friendly, and it's always exciting to find commercially-made condiments that are clean! It's one less thing you have to make yourself.

Prep time 20 minutes
Serves 10

1 large orange, zest and juice

½ teaspoon crushed red pepper flakes

2 teaspoons sea salt

4 cloves garlic, minced

4- to 5-pound (1.8 to 2.2 kg) pork roast (loin or shoulder)

⅔ cup (160 ml) paleo-friendly hot sauce, divided

½ cup (120 ml) coconut aminos

¼ cup (85 g) honey

3 tablespoons (45 ml) rice vinegar

1 lime

Cauliflower Rice (pages 249 and 250), Squash Noodles, or Paleo Tortillas (page 256), for serving

1 Combine the zest from the orange, the pepper flakes, sea salt, and garlic in a small bowl. Rub everything together with your fingers, then rub the mixture all over the roast.

2 Place the roast in a 6-quart (5.7 liter) slow cooker, fat-side up. Pour ⅓ cup (80 ml) hot sauce over the roast.

3 Cover and cook for 5 to 6 hours for a loin roast or 7 to 8 hours for a shoulder roast. The meat should be tender and pull apart easily.

4 While the roast is cooking, combine the juice from the orange (about ¼ cup, or 60 ml), coconut aminos, honey, and rice vinegar in a small skillet. Cook it over medium heat and let it simmer for 10 to 15 minutes, until it has reduced and thickened some. Set the glaze aside.

5 Transfer the roast to a large plate or platter, shred the meat, and return it to the cooking liquid in the slow cooker. Stir in the glaze, the remaining ⅓ cup (80 ml) hot sauce, and the juice from half of a lime. Taste, and add more lime juice or salt if necessary.

6 Serve with desired side dish.

Sweet Potato Lasagna with Kale and Pancetta

Thinly sliced sweet potatoes are a healthier alternative to lasagna noodles. If you have a mandolin slicer, slicing uniform sweet potato "noodles" is a breeze. White sweet potatoes are a bit starchier than orange sweet potatoes and hold up better during cooking. If you can't find white sweets, using orange ones is fine.

Prep time 30 minutes

Serves 6

4 ounces (115 g) diced pancetta or bacon

1 small bunch kale (5 to 8 ounces, or 140 to 225 g), leaves removed from their stems and cut into bite-sized pieces

2 large white sweet potatoes

4 tablespoons (36 g) pine nuts

4 cups (1 kg) Basic Marinara (page 283)

1 Cook the pancetta in a large skillet over medium heat until it begins to render some fat. Add the kale to the skillet and cook for 6 to 8 minutes, until kale is wilted and the pancetta is cooked through and slightly crispy. Remove the mixture from the heat and set it aside.

2 Peel sweet potatoes and slice into ¼-inch (5 mm) thick rounds.

3 Toast pine nuts by putting them in a small skillet over medium-low heat. Cook for a few minutes, shaking the pan occasionally, until the pine nuts begin to brown slightly and become fragrant. They burn easily, so keep a close eye on them!

4 Begin layering the lasagna by spreading ½ cup (125 g) of marinara in the bottom of a 4- or 6-quart (3.8 or 5.7 liter) slow cooker. Place a single layer of sweet potatoes over the sauce. Place one third of the kale-pancetta mixture over the potatoes. Sprinkle 1 tablespoon of pine nuts on top and then another ½ cup (125 g) of marinara. Repeat layering two more times (layer of potatoes, one third of the kale, 1 tablespoon of pine nuts, ½ cup [125 g] of sauce). Pour the remaining sauce on top of the lasagna.

5 Cover and cook on low for 5 to 6 hours. Lasagna is finished cooking when you can stick a butter knife into the layers of potatoes without resistance and everything is heated through.

6 Serve hot.

Note: Try using the Basic Marinara (page 283) or the Autumn Harvest Pasta Sauce (page 282).

Chorizo, Kale, and Potatoes with Garlic-Chipotle Aioli

When I was testing this recipe, my husband, Steve, sauntered over to the slow cooker, served himself a small bowl of chorizo and vegetables, and started eating. His assessment was that it was "pretty good." I urged him to top it with a drizzle of the garlic-chipotle aioli that was on the counter. He did, and his head started bobbing up and down. He went back for seconds. And thirds, I believe. Don't skip that aioli—it really elevates this simple meat and potatoes dish!

Prep time 15 minutes
Serves 6

For the chorizo:

1½ pounds (680 g) red potatoes, quartered

6 to 8 ounces (170 to 225 g) cooked chorizo links, cut into ½-inch (1 cm) rings

4 cloves garlic, minced

4 cups (268 g) bite-sized kale leaves

1½ teaspoons sea salt

2 tablespoons (29 ml) avocado oil

Crushed red pepper flakes

½ cup (120 ml) Simple Chicken Stock (page 280) or water

For the aioli:

½ cup (115 g) Paleo-Friendly Mayonnaise (page 286)

¼ cup (60 ml) unsweetened almond milk

½ teaspoon chipotle powder

½ teaspoon honey

1 teaspoon (5 ml) freshly squeezed lemon juice

1 garlic clove, minced

Pinch of sea salt

1 Put the potatoes, chorizo, garlic, and kale into a 4-quart (3.8 liter) slow cooker. Sprinkle the salt, drizzle the oil, and throw a generous pinch of pepper flakes into the cooker. Toss everything together to ensure that things are evenly coated. Add the chicken stock to the cooker along the side, so it doesn't wash the seasoning off.

2 Cover and cook for 5 to 6 hours on low (or 2 to 3 hours on high). Stir halfway through to be sure nothing sticks to the side.

3 Meanwhile, make the aioli by stirring together the mayonnaise, almond milk, chipotle powder, honey, lemon juice, garlic, and salt. Chill until ready to use.

4 Serve chorizo, kale, and potatoes with a drizzle of aioli.

Supreme Pizza Ragu

What do you get if you take away all of the non-paleo components of pizza? Meat, vegetables, and pizza sauce. So—a pretty spectacular ragu. You can substitute any of your favorite pizza toppings if you like.

Prep time 15 minutes

Serves 8

2 pounds (905 g) uncooked sweet Italian sausage

2 green bell peppers, diced

1 14.5-ounce (411 g) can crushed tomatoes

1 15-ounce (425 g) can tomato sauce

1½ cups (150 g) sliced black olives

3 tablespoons (90 g) tomato paste

2 tablespoons dried minced onion

1 tablespoon minced garlic (about 6 cloves)

1 teaspoon Italian seasoning

1 teaspoon dried oregano

⅛ teaspoon crushed red pepper flakes

4 ounces (113 g) uncured, nitrate-free pepperoni

Squash Noodles (page 248) and nutritional yeast, for serving

1 Place the sausage in a large skillet (remove it from the casings, if possible) and cook it over medium-high heat, breaking it into small pieces, until golden brown in spots.

2 Transfer the cooked sausage to the 4-quart (3.8 liter) slow cooker, along with the remaining ingredients (except the pepperoni, squash, and nutritional yeast), and give it a good stir. Cover and cook on low for 6 hours.

3 Slice the pepperoni into strips and cook in a skillet over medium heat, stirring occasionally, until the pepperoni is crisp. Transfer the crispy pepperoni to a small bowl for serving.

4 Serve the sauce over spaghetti noodles with a sprinkle of crisp pepperoni and ¼ teaspoon or so of nutritional yeast.

Note: If it's easier to find, you can use chicken sausage instead of pork.

Breakfast Sausage Hash–Stuffed Acorn Squash

We received the most delicious breakfast sausage with our pork share from a local pig farmer a while back and we were thrilled with it. Good sausage really makes the best hash, in my opinion. Preservative-free bulk sausage can be difficult to find, so you can also use precooked uncured chicken and apple sausage in a pinch. The short cooking time on these squashes makes them flexible for brunch, lunch, or dinner. They also reheat beautifully!

Prep time 20 minutes
Serves 4 generously

1 pound (455 g) bulk-style breakfast sausage
1 bell pepper, stemmed and diced
½ cup (80 g) chopped yellow onion
1 4-ounce (113 g) can diced green chillies
2 small acorn squashes
Sea salt and pepper
2 eggs
Hot sauce and diced avocado, for serving

1 Cook sausage in a medium skillet over medium-high heat until browned. Add bell pepper, onion, and chillies to the skillet. Cook for another 6 to 8 minutes, until the vegetables are softened. Remove from heat.

2 Cut the squashes in half from top to bottom, and scoop out the seeds. Sprinkle the insides with sea salt and black pepper.

3 Crack the eggs into the pan with the cooled sausage mixture and combine thoroughly. Fill the squash halves with the sausage mixture.

4 Place the sausage halves in a 6-quart (5.7 liter) slow cooker, two halves on top and two halves on the bottom, but don't nestle them.

5 Cover and cook on low for 2½ to 3 hours, until squash is fork tender.

6 Serve with hot sauce and diced avocado.

Chorizo Frittata with Roasted Chillies

I like to use a mixture of poblano and Anaheim chillies in this. Poblano peppers are rather unpredictable and can either be incredibly mild or hot like jalapeños. If your chorizo is on the spicy side, taste the peppers first! If you have trouble finding fresh peppers, you can use a couple of 4-ounce (113 g) cans of fire-roasted diced green chillies in a pinch.

Prep time 25 minutes
Serves 6

3 large chillies (poblanos, Anaheim, sweet banana peppers)

2 jalapeño peppers

¾ teaspoon sea salt

½ teaspoon cumin

½ teaspoon chili powder

½ teaspoon garlic powder

1 medium zucchini, cut into ½-inch (1 cm) circles

2 Roma tomatoes, cut into ½-inch (1 cm) slices

6 ounces (170 g) fully cooked chorizo links, diced

10 eggs

½ teaspoon onion powder

1 tablespoon nutritional yeast

Hot sauce and diced avocados, for serving

1 Preheat the oven broiler.

2 Place the peppers on a sheet pan and place them on the top oven rack. Broil them for 8 to 10 minutes, until the skins of the peppers are blackened and blistered. Turn them once or twice during roasting. Remove the pan from the oven and cover it with aluminum foil or a tea towel. Let them steam for 5 minutes. Remove most of the skins from the peppers; they should slip off fairly easily, but you don't need to pick off every piece. Pull the tops off, cut the peppers open, and rinse out the seeds. Dice the peppers.

3 Line a 4-quart (3.8 liter) slow cooker with a large piece of parchment paper. In a small bowl, combine the salt, cumin, chili powder, and garlic powder. Layer the zucchini in the bottom of the slow cooker and sprinkle them with 1 teaspoon of the spice mixture. Layer the Roma tomatoes, chorizo, and diced chillies over the zucchini.

4 In a medium bowl, whisk together the eggs, remaining spice blend, onion powder, and nutritional yeast. Pour the egg mixture over the meat and vegetables.

5 Cover and cook on low for 2½ to 3½ hours, until the center of the frittata is cooked through. Lift out the frittata using the parchment and set it on a large plate to cool.

6 Cut into wedges and serve with hot sauce and diced avocados.

Spring Frittata with Ham, Asparagus, and Fresh Herbs

This frittata makes a fabulous dinner, but honestly, I love it even more for breakfast. After my workouts, I've warmed up a slice and covered it with avocados, a spoonful of paleo Ranch Dressing, and a big squirt of hot sauce. That frittata lasted me all week.

Prep time 20 minutes

Serves 6

4 to 5 medium red potatoes, sliced ¼-inch (5 mm) thick

1 pound (455 g) asparagus, trimmed and cut into 1-inch (2.5 cm) pieces

6 ounces (170 g) uncured deli ham, chopped

10 eggs

½ cup (120 ml) unsweetened almond milk

2 tablespoons (16 g) coconut flour

1 garlic clove, minced

2 teaspoons onion powder

1 teaspoon sea salt

½ teaspoon grated lemon zest

½ cup (25 to 30 g) chopped mixed fresh herbs (parsley, dill, chives, thyme), divided

Ranch Dressing (page 285) and/or hot sauce for serving

1 Coat the interior of a 4-quart (3.8 liter) slow cooker with coconut oil nonstick spray.

2 Lay the potato slices flat in the bottom of the cooker in 3 to 4 layers. Add the asparagus and the ham on top of the potatoes.

3 Add the eggs to a large bowl and whisk them together. Whisk in the almond milk and the coconut flour until no lumps from the flour remain.

4 Add the garlic, onion powder, sea salt, and lemon zest to the egg mixture. Mix well, then pour the mixture over the vegetables and ham. Sprinkle half of the fresh herbs on top.

5 Cover and cook on low for 4 to 5 hours, until the center of the quiche is completely cooked through.

6 Remove the lid and let it cool for 10 minutes. Run a knife around the edges of the cooker, then press a rubber spatula down the sides, all the way around, to loosen the corners.

7 You may serve this by simply scooping out servings from the cooker. Or you can put a large plate upside-down on top of the cooker and flip the whole thing upside-down to remove the quiche from the cooker. (You may end up with a few potatoes at the bottom of the cooker.) Take another plate and place it upside-down on the bottom of the quiche, and flip the whole thing again to turn the quiche right-side up.

8 Slice into wedges and serve with Ranch Dressing, hot sauce, or both. Garnish with the other half of the fresh herbs.

Chorizo Shepherd's Pie with Orange-Scented Sweet Potatoes

I have never been very excited about traditional shepherd's pie, so I decided to make a spunkier version with some Spanish influence—spicy chorizo, piquillo peppers, and saffron-scented sweet potatoes with a hint of orange. It all blends together beautifully, and it makes me want to add orange and saffron to sweet potatoes for the rest of my life.

Prep time 30 minutes

Serves 6

1 pinch of saffron

3 cups (984 g) cooked, mashed sweet potatoes

½ teaspoon orange zest

½ teaspoon sea salt

12 ounces (340 g) ground pork

½ teaspoon salt

6 ounces (170 g) Spanish chorizo, diced

2 tablespoons (60 g) tomato paste

1 teaspoon paprika

2 cloves garlic, minced

1 cup (160 g) chopped yellow onion (about half a medium onion)

½ cup (75 g) chopped piquillo peppers (or regular roasted red peppers, 90 g)

2 heaping cups (60 g) chopped baby spinach

1 Put the saffron in a tablespoon (15 ml) of warm water and let it bloom for a couple of minutes.

2 Put the potatoes in a medium mixing bowl. Stir in the orange zest, salt, and the saffron with its yellow liquid. Set the potatoes aside.

3 Cook the ground pork in a large skillet over medium-high heat, breaking the meat into small bits, for 10 to 12 minutes, until fully cooked. Sprinkle with salt and add the chorizo to the skillet. Cook another 2 to 3 minutes, until the chorizo and pork have golden brown spots. Use a slotted spoon and transfer the meat to a 4-quart (3.8 liter) slow cooker. Discard the grease.

4 Stir the tomato paste, paprika, and garlic into the meat mixture. Fold in the chopped onions, peppers, and spinach. Spread the reserved potato mixture over the top.

5 Cover and cook on low for 4 to 5 hours. The sides should be bubbly, and the potatoes heated through.

6 Turn off the slow cooker, remove the lid, and let the shepherd's pie sit for 10 minutes before serving.

Garlicky Lamb Meatballs with Herb Vinaigrette

Meatballs are usually paired with a heavy sauce, but I love the addition of an herby vinaigrette to lighten the lamb's strong flavor. The lamb also holds up well to the garlic slivers scattered throughout the meatballs—my favorite parts.

Prep time 25 minutes
Makes 24 meatballs

For the meatballs:
2 pounds (905 g) ground lamb
1 shallot, minced (about ¼ cup, or 40 g)
8 cloves garlic, thinly sliced
1 tablespoon Dijon mustard
1 tablespoon fresh minced mint
2 tablespoons fresh minced flat-leaf parsley
½ teaspoon sea salt
½ teaspoon black pepper
2 tablespoons (28 g) avocado or coconut oil
½ cup (120 ml) chicken or vegetable broth

For the vinaigrette:
½ cup (120 ml) red wine vinegar
2 tablespoons fresh minced mint
2 tablespoons fresh minced flat-leaf parsley
1 teaspoon fresh minced rosemary
1 teaspoon Dijon mustard
½ teaspoon sea salt
½ cup (118 ml) extra-virgin olive oil

1 In a medium bowl, combine the lamb, shallot, garlic, mustard, mint, parsley, salt, and black pepper. Mix it gently with your hands until thoroughly combined.

2 Form the mixture tightly into 1½-inch (3.5 cm) balls and place them on a large plate. You should have about 24.

3 Heat the oil in a large nonstick skillet over medium-high heat. Sear the meatballs in batches on two sides until a golden brown crust forms. Transfer the meatballs to a 4-quart (3.8 liter) slow cooker. Pour the broth into the cooker. Cover and cook on low for 3 to 4 hours, until the meatballs are cooked through.

4 Combine the vinaigrette ingredients in a lidded container (like a pint-size [475 ml] mason jar). Close and shake well. Store chilled until ready to use.

5 Serve the meatballs with a couple of spoonfuls of vinaigrette over the top.

Note: If the taste of lamb is too gamy for you, try substituting ground beef for half of the lamb.

Shredded Lamb Korma

Lamb korma usually has chunks of meat, but this version has tender shreds of lamb. I prefer shredded meat over larger pieces, because more of it is covered in whatever sauce or gravy it's cooked in. And let's face it—the sauce is the best part. For some extra fabulous flavor, try this with some Spicy Curried Mango-Pineapple Chutney (page 38).

Prep time 25 minutes
Serves 8

1½ tablespoons dried coriander

1 tablespoon ground cumin

1 tablespoon sea salt

1½ teaspoons ground turmeric

¾ teaspoon cinnamon

½ teaspoon ground cardamom

½ teaspoon cayenne pepper

4- to 5-pound (1.8 to 2.2 kg) boneless lamb leg roast

1 large sweet onion, quartered

1 15-ounce (425 g) can diced tomatoes

6 cloves garlic

2-inch (5 cm) knob of ginger, minced

½ cup (72 g) raw cashews

1 13.5-ounce (398 ml) can full-fat coconut milk

2 teaspoons garam masala

1 lime

½ cup fresh chopped cilantro

Cauliflower Rice (pages 249 and 250) or Squash Noodles (page 248), for serving

1 Combine the coriander, cumin, salt, turmeric, cinnamon, cardamom, and cayenne in a small bowl. Rub half of the spice mixture all over the roast.

2 Place the roast in a 6-quart (5.7 liter) slow cooker.

3 In a blender, combine the onion, tomatoes, garlic, ginger, cashews, and remaining spice blend. Blend until the mixture is smooth. Pour the sauce over the roast.

4 Cover and cook on low for 6 to 8 hours, or until the meat pulls apart easily with a fork.

5 Remove the roast from the cooker, shred the meat, then put it back into the cooker. Stir in the coconut milk and garam masala. Cover and cook for another 15 minutes.

6 Squeeze the juice from half of the lime over the curry and sprinkle with fresh cilantro. Taste, and add more salt or lime juice if necessary.

7 Serve with desired side dish.

Note: If it's easier to find, you can use chicken sausage instead of pork.

6

FISH AND SEAFOOD

This chapter might seem a little unorthodox. You may be asking yourself, "Who puts fish in a slow cooker?" You'd be surprised at how well a slow cooker does with fish. Fish cooks very quickly, and it's easy to end up with a rubbery fillet, but slow cooking is much more forgiving than some other methods.

Recipes

Simple Lemon-Herb Parchment Fish and Potatoes

This is a two-part meal in one pot! Cooking the parchment-wrapped fish over a bed of potatoes makes for easy clean up, and cutting slits in the bottom of the parchment allows the herbs and juices to season the potatoes, too.

Prep time 20 minutes
Serves 6

2 pounds (905 g) red potatoes or sweet potatoes, cut into 1-inch (2.5 cm) pieces

2 tablespoons (30 ml) melted Homemade Ghee (page 287), plus more for drizzling

Sea salt

Black pepper

2 to 3 pounds (905 g to 1.4 kg) large fillets of firm white fish like cod, halibut, or rockfish

1 lemon, cut into ⅛-inch (3 mm) slices

3 cloves garlic, peeled and thinly sliced

2 sprigs fresh thyme

Chopped fresh parsley, for garnish

1 Put the potatoes in a 6-quart (5.7 liter) slow cooker. Drizzle with 2 tablespoons (30 ml) ghee and sprinkle with 1¼ teaspoons sea salt and ¼ teaspoon black pepper. Stir well. Cover and cook on low for 2½ to 3 hours until the potatoes are mostly cooked through. (Cook for 2 hours if using sweet potatoes.)

2 Lay a piece of parchment paper or aluminum foil twice the size of the fish on a flat work space. Cut a 2-inch (5 cm) slit in the center of one side. Place two of the fillets on top of the slit. Sprinkle liberally with sea salt and a few pinches of black pepper. Lay half of the lemon slices and garlic on the fillets. Place the other two fillets on top. Sprinkle those liberally with

sea salt, black pepper, and lay the other lemon slices, garlic, and thyme sprigs on top. Fold the other half of the paper over the fish and, starting on one end, fold and crimp the edges of the paper together until it forms a packet.

3 Place the packet on top of the potatoes. Turn the slow cooker on high, cover, and cook for another 45 minutes. Check the fish for doneness every 15 minutes, until the fish flakes easily with a fork.

4 Transfer the fish and potatoes (with sauces) to serving dishes and sprinkle with parsley.

Pesto Cod and Mashed Sweet Potatoes

I love getting a main dish and a side dish out of one slow cooker. The pesto you spread over the cod drips down onto the sweet potatoes and seasons them. And it's easy to make your own Paleo Pesto (page 293).

Prep time 15 minutes
Serves 6

3 pounds (1.4 kg) sweet potatoes, peeled and cut into 2-inch (5 cm) pieces

1½ teaspoon sea salt, plus more to taste

¼ teaspoon black pepper

4 tablespoons (59 ml) melted Homemade Ghee (page 287) or avocado oil, divided

3 large cod fillets (about 2 pounds, or 905 g)

1 lemon

¼ cup (65 g) Paleo Pesto (page 293)

1 Place the sweet potatoes into a 6-quart (5.7 liter) slow cooker. Sprinkle with 1 teaspoon sea salt and the black pepper. Drizzle with ghee and give the potatoes a good stir.

2 Cover and cook on low for 2 to 2½ hours until the potatoes are almost fork tender.

3 Sprinkle the cod with ½ teaspoon sea salt and the juice from half of the lemon. Rub ⅓ cup (90 g) pesto on one side of the fillets, then lay the fillets over the potatoes in a single layer, if possible. Drizzle the fish with 2 tablespoons (30 g) of ghee.

4 Cover and continue to cook for 30 to 45 minutes, or until the fish flakes easily with a fork.

5 Transfer the cod to a platter and cover to keep it warm.

6 Mash the sweet potatoes inside the cooker. Taste, and add more salt, ghee, or pesto if needed. Transfer the potatoes to a serving bowl.

7 Serve the cod with the mashed potatoes.

Jerk Salmon and Pineapple Packets

I love making jerk salmon and pineapple skewers on the grill in the summer, and wanted to make a parchment packet version. The ghee is key here. It elevates all of the flavors and makes the fish extra tender and rich.

Prep time 15 minutes
Serves 6

3 limes
½ of a fresh pineapple
6 tablespoons (90 ml) of melted Homemade Ghee (page 287) or grass-fed butter
5 teaspoons Dry Caribbean Jerk Rub (page 288)

1 teaspoon sea salt
6 4- to 6-ounce (115- to 170-gram) salmon fillets
1 red bell pepper, thinly sliced

1 Prepare 6 pieces of parchment or foil, roughly the size of a placemat. Thinly slice 2 of the limes. Cut the third lime into wedges. Set the wedges aside until you're ready to serve the salmon.

2 Cut the top, bottom, and skin off of the pineapple. Slice the pineapple in half length-wise. Wrap and chill one half for another use. Take the other half and cut it in half again length-wise. Stand each wedge on end and cut the core out. Slice those wedges into long, thin pieces, and then cut them in half width-wise so you end up with 3- to 4-inch pineapple slices.

3 Combine the ghee, jerk seasoning, and 1 teaspoon sea salt in a small bowl to form a paste.

4 Assemble the packets by placing a piece of salmon on one half of the parchment. Spread a teaspoon of the seasoning paste on the fillet and top with a couple of lime slices, then top with a few pieces of pineapple and a couple of bell pepper strips. Drizzle another 1½ teaspoons of seasoning blend over the top of the stack. Fold the parchment in half, covering the salmon. Beginning on one side, crimp and fold the edges until the packet is completely closed.

5 Layer the packets in a 6-quart (5.7 liter) slow cooker. If you have fillets of varying thickness, place the thickest ones on the bottom.

6 Cover and cook on low for an hour. Then check for doneness every 15 to 20 minutes until the fish is mostly cooked through and flakes easily. The salmon will continue to cook inside the packets for a few minutes after they are removed from the cooker, and they'll be nice and moist.

7 Serve salmon packets with lime wedges.

Whole Fish with Grapefruit and Dill

I never thought in a million years that I would put a whole fish in a slow cooker. It works surprisingly well and leaves the fish so tender it's difficult to remove it from the slow cooker in one piece. Line the cooker with parchment if getting it out in one piece is important for presentation.

Prep time 20 minutes
Serves 6

1 grapefruit

2 Meyer lemons

4 cloves garlic, minced

2 tablespoons fresh minced dill, plus 3 to 4 sprigs

1 tablespoon fresh minced flat-leaf parsley, plus 3 to 4 sprigs

3 to 3½ pounds (1.4 to 1.6 kg) fresh, whole fish, such as trout or snapper, cleaned and descaled

Sea salt

1 leek, trimmed and quartered

⅓ cup (80 ml) chicken or vegetable broth

1 teaspoon (5 ml) of melted Homemade Ghee (page 287) per fish

1 Remove the zest from the grapefruit and one lemon. Place the zest in a small bowl. Cut the grapefruit in half and squeeze the juice from one half into the bowl with the zest. Cut the other half of the grapefruit in half and slice both quarters into half-moons. Slice both of the lemons into thin rounds and set the sliced citrus aside.

2 Add the garlic, minced dill, and minced parsley to the bowl with the zest and juice. Mix well. Place half of the mixture in a separate small bowl and set aside.

3 Cut any side fins off of the fish with a pair of kitchen shears, if necessary. Use a sharp knife and cut 3 or 4 ¼-inch (5 mm) deep slits into each side of the fish. Sprinkle salt liberally into the slits and inside the cavities. In each cavity, place one slice of grapefruit, two slices of lemon, and a sprig of each herb. Spoon one of the bowls of zest-herb mixture over the fish, getting the mixture into the slits.

4 Place the sliced leeks and broth in the bottom of a 6-quart (5.7 liter) slow cooker. Lay the fish on top of the leeks, drizzling 1 teaspoon (5 ml) ghee on each fish and overlapping if necessary. Trim the tails if the fish are a bit long. Place the remaining citrus slices and any remaining herb sprigs on top of or around the fish.

5 Cover and cook on low for 2 to 2½ hours. Check for doneness after about 2 hours. The fish should flake easily with a fork.

6 Carefully remove the fish from the slow cooker with a large spatula and transfer them to a serving platter. Remove the meat from the fish, removing any bones. An easy way to do this is to take a small spatula and run it down the side of the fish, starting at the head. The fillet should come off in large sections. Pull the backbone out, and then remove any bones from the other fillet.

7 Serve immediately with reserved zest-herb mixture.

Note: If you can't find Meyer lemons, use one small lemon and one mandarin orange instead, and use the zest from half of each for the zest-herb mixture.

Salt-Baked Whole Fish

I love salt-baking things. You take an obscene amount of salt and pour it over meat or hearty root vegetables, then bake. After salt-"roasting" beets (page 239), I've moved on to fish and chicken. I was happy when I discovered that this method works just as well in the slow cooker! You would think that the fish baked in a frightening amount of salt would come out much too salty, but it doesn't. The salt makes its way through the skin and seasons the fish deeply and thoroughly—and perfectly. Use this method only with whole fish or fish with skin. The skin prevents the meat from becoming overly salty.

Prep time 15 minutes
Serves 6

2 medium whole fish (that will fit in a 6-quart [5.7 liter] slow cooker), like trout, striped bass, or snapper, cleaned and scaled
1 3-pound (1.36 kg) box of kosher salt

1 Line the slow cooker with parchment paper, pressing and creasing the paper to the edge of the pan. It won't lay completely flat at this point, so don't worry.

2 Lay the fish in a 6-quart (5.7 liter) slow cooker to size them. Trim off the tail fins if necessary.

3 Pour 1 cup (300 g) of salt in the bottom of the cooker—on top of the parchment. Lay one fish inside the cooker, and cover with 2 cups (600 g) of salt. Lay the other fish inside, over-lapping if necessary, and continue to pour salt over both of the fish until they are mostly covered. You'll probably use about half of the box.

4 Cover and cook on low for 2½ to 3 hours.

5 Carefully remove the fish from the slow cooker using the edges of the parchment, and transfer it to a large serving platter. Remove the cooked fish from the bones in pieces, and serve.

Note: Do not use this method with fillets, because they will be much too salty.

Jambalaya with Roasted Cauliflower Rice

You'll love this version of jambalaya made with cauliflower rice. There's a bit of chopping, but you can prepare everything ahead of time and then put it all into the slow cooker when you're ready.

Prep time 20 minutes
Serves 8

1 medium onion, diced (about 1½ cups, or 240 g)

1 green bell pepper, diced

2 stalks celery, diced

2 cloves garlic, minced

8 ounces (225 g) andouille sausage, chopped

3 dried bay leaves

3 sprigs of fresh thyme or ½ teaspoon dried

1 tablespoon (15 g) Homemade Ghee (page 287)

1½ tablespoons Cajun Spice Blend (page 284)

3 cups (710 ml) chicken broth

3 tablespoons (90 g) tomato paste

1 recipe Roasted Cauliflower Rice (pages 249 and 250)

1 pound (455 g) uncooked medium shrimp, tails removed

1 Place all of the ingredients except the cauliflower rice and shrimp into a 6-quart (5.7 liter) slow cooker. Give the mixture a good stir.

2 Cover and cook on low for 6 to 7 hours.

3 Stir the cauliflower rice and shrimp into the stew. Crack the lid and let it cook for another 20 to 30 minutes until the shrimp is pink and cooked through.

4 Taste, and add more salt if necessary, before serving.

Tuna "Noodle" Casserole

Out of all of the recipes in this book, I think this one surprised me the most. I had a crazy idea, threw it in a pot one day, and ate nearly half of it myself because I liked it so much! Parsnip noodles go really well with the tuna, and the creamy sauce ties everything together. So, if zucchini noodles are called zoodles, does that mean parsnip noodles are poodles?

Prep time 20 minutes
Serves 6

2 large parsnips, peeled and spiral-cut into noodles (See Squash Noodles, page 248)

7 ounces (198 g) canned tuna, drained

1¼ cups (285 g) Paleo-Friendly Mayonnaise (page 286)

4 teaspoons Dijon mustard

4 cloves garlic, minced

¼ teaspoon dried dill

1½ teaspoons dried minced onion

3 tablespoons (15 g) nutritional yeast, divided

¾ teaspoon sea salt

⅓ cup (32 g) blanched almond flour

1 tablespoon (15 ml) melted Homemade Ghee (page 287)

1 Place the parsnip noodles in a 4-quart (3.8 liter) slow cooker and sprinkle the tuna on top.

2 In a small bowl, combine the mayonnaise, mustard, garlic, dill, onion, 2 tablespoons of the nutritional yeast, and the salt. Mix well, then pour the sauce over the noodles and tuna. Using a pair of tongs or a couple of large forks, toss to coat the noodles in the sauce.

3 In another small bowl, combine the almond flour, 1 tablespoon of nutritional yeast, and the melted ghee. Stir until clumps form. Sprinkle this mixture over the noodles.

4 Cover and cook on low for 4 to 5 hours, until the noodles in the center are cooked through and the edges are golden brown.

5 Serve hot.

Note: If your spiral cutter has the option for thin or thick noodles, choose the thick noodles (about ⅛ inch [3 mm] wide). If you use thin noodles, you may need to reduce the cooking time by an hour or so.

Creamy Sole and Asparagus Packets

Asparagus cooks quickly and is the perfect vegetable to pair with fish and a creamy garlic-dill sauce. You can also prepare these several hours ahead of time and keep in them in the refrigerator until you're ready to put them in the slow cooker.

Prep time 15 minutes
Serves 6

½ cup (115 g) Paleo-Friendly Mayonnaise (page 286)

3 large cloves garlic, minced

½ teaspoon Dijon mustard

½ teaspoon nutritional yeast

1 pound (455 g) asparagus, trimmed

12 Dover or petrale sole fillets

Sea salt

3 lemons, sliced into ¼-inch (5 mm) rounds

6 sprigs fresh dill

1 Combine the mayonnaise, garlic, mustard, and nutritional yeast in a small bowl. Set aside.

2 Rip off six sheets of parchment paper or aluminum foil, each about the size of a placemat.

3 Determine how many pieces of asparagus you'll need to divide them among the six packets.

4 For each packet, place that number of asparagus spears on one half of the parchment. (If you have both thin and thick asparagus spears, group similar-size spears together within packets.) Place two sole fillets over the asparagus, overlapping a little if needed. Sprinkle each fillet with a generous pinch of salt. Spread a heaping teaspoon of garlic mayonnaise, and lay two lemon slices on each fillet. Lay a sprig of dill on top of the fish and fold the other half of the parchment on top of the stack.

5 Starting on one end of the packet, crimp and fold the edges together. Work your way around until the packet is sealed. Place the packets in a 6-quart (5.7 liter) slow cooker. Place the packets with the larger spears on the bottom. You can press them down slightly to help them fit, if needed.

6 Cook on low for 1½ to 2 hours, depending on the thickness of your asparagus. The fish should flake easily with a fork and the asparagus should be cooked through.

7 Serve hot.

Spicy Garlic Lime Salmon and Zoodles

This is a great summertime recipe for when it's too hot to grill or turn your oven on and you've got squash exploding out of your garden. Salmon also happens to be in season during the summer, when it's easier to find fresh wild-caught fillets. The spicy-citrusy fish and zoodles are light, easy, and delicious.

Prep time 15 minutes
Serves 6

6 salmon fillets, 5 to 7 ounces (140 to 200 g) each
Sea salt
3 limes, zest and juice
3 cloves garlic, minced
1 tablespoon (15 g) hot sauce
1½ teaspoons honey

2 pounds (905 g) summer squash (zucchini and yellow squash work well)
2 tablespoons (30 ml) melted Homemade Ghee (page 287)
Additional limes and hot sauce, for serving

1 Lay the salmon fillets on a rimmed baking sheet in a single layer. Sprinkle about ⅛ teaspoon salt on each fillet.

2 In a small bowl, combine the zest from one and one half of the limes and the juice from all three. Stir in the garlic, hot sauce, and honey. Pour the mixture over the salmon, covering all of them. Let the salmon rest for 10 to 15 minutes.

3 Cut the squash with a spiral cutter to make "noodles." If you don't have a spiral cutter, slice the squash lengthwise into planks and then into long ¼-inch (5 mm) "noodles." Put the squash into a 6-quart (5.7 liter) slow cooker and sprinkle them with a few pinches of salt.

4 Lay the salmon on top of the noodles. Try to lay them in a single layer, if you can, but if they don't fit, just overlap them slightly.

5 Put 1 teaspoon (5 ml) ghee on top of each salmon fillet.

6 Cover and cook on low for about 2 hours, or until all of the fillets are just barely cooked through.

7 Transfer the fillets and squash to a serving platter. Serve with lime wedges and hot sauce.

Thai Green Curry with Lobster

Thai curry paste is a great shortcut! Depending on where you live, it might be hard to find Thai ingredients like lemongrass, kefir leaves, and galangal. The store-bought paste has all of those. Just check the ingredient labels for undesirable ingredients!

Prep time 20 minutes
Serves 6

1 14-ounce (400 ml) can full-fat coconut milk

2 cups (475 ml) chicken broth

3 tablespoons Thai green curry paste

1 tablespoon tapioca flour

3 large carrots, halved lengthwise and cut into ½-inch (1 cm) pieces

2 cups trimmed green beans, cut into 1-inch (2.5 cm) pieces

1 medium sweet potato, cut into 1-inch (2.5 cm) cubes

1 medium yellow squash, halved lengthwise and cut into 1-inch (2.5 cm) pieces

1 lime

1 teaspoon fish sauce

½ teaspoon sea salt

4 to 5 uncooked 8- to 10-ounce (225 to 280 gram) lobster tails

⅓ cup fresh chopped cilantro

Additional limes, cut into wedges, for serving

Cauliflower Rice (pages 249 and 250) or Squash Noodles (page 248), for serving

1 Whisk together the coconut milk, chicken broth, curry paste, and tapioca flour in a 6-quart (5.7 liter) slow cooker.

2 Add the carrots, green beans, sweet potato, squash, juice from half the lime, fish sauce, and salt to the slow cooker. Give it a stir, then cover and cook on low for 2 to 3 hours, or until the carrots are nearly cooked through.

3 Prepare the lobster by cutting the top of each shell down the middle with a pair of sharp kitchen shears. Pull apart each shell carefully, removing any pieces of broken shell, and pull the lobster meat away from the shell and the lower membrane. It should come out in one piece.

4 Add the lobster meat to the curry, nestling it among the vegetables. Cover and cook for another 30 minutes, until the lobster is just cooked through.

5 Remove the lobster meat from the curry with a pair of tongs. Put the meat on a large cutting board and cut it into bite-sized pieces. Stir the meat back into the curry, along with the juice from the remaining lime half and the cilantro. Taste the curry, and add more lime juice or salt if necessary.

6 Serve the curry with desired side dish.

Lemon-Garlic Shrimp and Zoodles

Here's another seafood plus zoodle recipe. This one comes together quickly and would be a great lunch or light dinner option if you've got company.

Prep time 15 minutes
Serves 6

2 pounds (905 g) summer squash (zucchini, yellow squash), spiralized (See Squash Noodles, page 248)

5 cloves garlic, minced, divided

2 lemons

1¼ teaspoons sea salt, divided

1½ pounds (680 g) thawed, uncooked, shelled medium shrimp

¼ teaspoon dried thyme

2 to 3 tablespoons (30 to 45 ml) melted Homemade Ghee (page 287)

1 Place the spiralized squash in a 4-quart (3.8 liter) slow cooker. It should fill it to the top.

2 Sprinkle half of the minced garlic, ½ teaspoon lemon zest, and ¼ teaspoon salt over the squash noodles. Toss them around with a pair of tongs to spread the garlic and seasonings.

3 Cover and cook for an hour.

4 Right after you start the slow cooker and get the noodles going, put the shrimp in a large bowl. Remove the tails, if you prefer. Add the juice from one of the lemons (about ¼ cup, or 60 ml), the other half of the garlic, 1 teaspoon salt, and the dried thyme. Mix everything to coat the shrimp. Cover and refrigerate until the noodles have cooked for an hour.

5 The noodles should be softened and partially cooked. Toss them around in the cooking liquid. Add the marinated shrimp to the slow cooker, on top of the zoodles. Cover and cook for another hour or so, until the shrimp is pink and barely cooked through.

6 Transfer the shrimp and zoodles to a large serving bowl. Drizzle with 2 tablespoons (30 ml) ghee and toss to coat. Taste, and add more ghee or salt if necessary.

7 Slice the remaining lemon into wedges.

8 Serve the shrimp and zoodles with the lemon wedges.

Simple Shrimp Fajitas

Here's a fun, colorful, and incredibly easy recipe to make if you've got company. I love making a Mexican-inspired meal for guests, but I find it tedious to prepare all of the necessary components. Tossing the peppers, onions, and shrimp in the slow cooker allows you to whip up some Paleo Tortillas (page 256) or Southwest Cabbage Slaw (page 252) at a comfortable pace.

Prep time 15 minutes
Serves 8 to 10

4 bell peppers (any color), seeded and sliced into ½-inch (1 cm) strips

2 medium sweet onions, halved and thinly sliced

1 tablespoon chili powder

1½ teaspoons ground cumin

½ teaspoon dried oregano

¼ to ½ teaspoon chipotle powder, to taste

3 limes

6 cloves garlic, minced

1 teaspoon sea salt

2 pounds (905 g) uncooked medium shrimp, tails removed

Paleo Tortillas (page 256), sliced avocado, and hot sauce, for serving

1 Place the bell pepper and onion in a 6-quart (5.7 liter) slow cooker.

2 In a small bowl, combine the chili powder, cumin, oregano, chipotle powder, juice from one of the limes, garlic, and salt to form a paste. Add half of the spice paste to the vegetables and toss with a pair of tongs to coat them thoroughly. Reserve the rest of the paste for the shrimp.

3 Cover and cook on high for 2 to 2½ hours, until the peppers and onions are tender.

4 Coat the shrimp with the rest of the spice paste and place them on top of the vegetables. Cover and cook for another 15 to 20 minutes, until the shrimp are pink and just cooked through.

5 Slice the remaining limes into wedges. Serve the shrimp and vegetables in Paleo Tortillas with avocado slices, lime wedges, and hot sauce.

7

VEGETABLE SIDES

Meat is pretty much the star of the show when it comes to paleo slow cooking, but there are certain types of vegetables that can handle prolonged cooking and wind up being just as impressive as their meaty competitors.

Recipes

Chipotle Caramelized Onions and Mushrooms

This little concoction might not win any beauty contests, but it's my favorite addition to a burger and it makes me jump out of bed in the morning to eat it with fried eggs. It's spicy and mushroom-y, and our family absolutely adores it.

Prep time 15 minutes
Makes about 1 quart (946 ml)

2 medium sweet onions, halved and thinly sliced

1 pound (455 g) brown mushrooms, sliced

1 chipotle pepper, from a can of chipotles in adobo sauce, minced

½ teaspoon sea salt

1 Place all of the ingredients into a 4-quart (3.8 liter) slow cooker. Cover and cook on high for 3 to 4 hours, stirring once or twice during cooking.

2 Serve alongside burgers, eggs, or grilled meat—or even alone.

Salt-"Roasted" Beets

The amount of salt in this recipe might seem absurd, but that white sandy mountain does wonders for the beets underneath. They're seasoned right to the centers without being too salty. Being a picky beet eater, I was surprised at how irresistible they are!

Prep time 5 minutes
Serves 4 as a side

1 pound (455 g) beets, ends trimmed
3 to 4 cups (900 g to 1.2 kg) kosher salt

1 Place beets in a foil-lined 2- or 3-quart (1.9 or 2.8 liter) slow cooker. Pour enough salt on the beets to cover them. You may need more salt, depending on the size of your slow cooker.

2 Cover and cook beets on low for 8 to 9 hours. They should pierce easily with a fork when done cooking.

3 Pull the beets out of the salt and onto a paper towel. Rub the skins and any salt off of the beets—they should come off easily. Rinsing under warm water should help.

4 Slice and serve warm or cold.

Dijon-Braised Beets

One of my favorite ways to eat beets is roasted and finished with a vinaigrette. I used the components of a lemon-Dijon dressing to flavor the beets as they cooked, resulting in tangy, mustardy, tender fuchsia bites. These would make a great winter side dish, alongside some peppered pan-fried steaks or breaded chicken fillets.

Prep time 15 minutes

Serves 8 as a side

2 pounds (905 g) beets, peeled and cut into 1-inch (2.5 cm) chunks

1 shallot, peeled and diced

¼ cup (60 ml) freshly squeezed lemon juice

1 tablespoon Dijon mustard

½ teaspoon sea salt

¼ teaspoon black pepper

2 tablespoons (30 ml) extra-virgin olive oil

1 Put the beets and shallots in a 2- or 3-quart (1.9 or 2.8 liter) slow cooker.

2 Whisk together the lemon juice, mustard, salt, pepper, and olive oil. Pour the mixture over the beets.

3 Cover and cook on low for 5 to 6 hours.

4 Serve hot, warm, or cold.

Orange-Maple Carrots

Here's a side dish that would be great as a potluck offering or as part of a holiday meal in order to free up some precious stove space. These sweet carrots make great baby food, too. My youngest ate these nearly every day for a week, and I was glad to have something in the fridge already cooked and ready to feed him.

Prep time 15 minutes
Serves 6

1½ pounds (680 g) carrots, peeled and cut into 1-inch (2.5 cm) pieces
½ teaspoon grated zest and juice from 1 large orange

1 tablespoon (20 g) pure maple syrup
Pinch of crushed red pepper flakes

1 Put the carrot pieces into a 2- or 3-quart (1.9 or 2.8 liter) slow cooker. Add ½ teaspoon of the orange zest and the orange juice to the slow cooker, as well as the maple syrup and pepper flakes.

2 Cover and cook for 5 to 6 hours on low, until carrots are tender but not mushy.

Creamy Dilled Cauliflower

Here's another side dish that would be great to take to a potluck. These tender bits of cauliflower would be a creamy complement to any grilled or slow-cooked barbecue meat— like the BBQ Apple Pulled Pork (page 196) or Greek Peperoncini Beef Lettuce Wraps (page 146).

Prep time 15 minutes
Serves 6

2 large heads cauliflower, trimmed and cut into bite-sized florets

4 cloves garlic, minced

1 lemon, zested and juiced

½ teaspoon sea salt

4 green onions, thinly sliced (both white and green parts)

½ cup (120 ml) chicken or vegetable broth

½ cup (115 g) Paleo-Friendly Mayonnaise (page 286)

4 teaspoons fresh chopped dill (or ½ teaspoon dried)

1 Place the cauliflower florets in a 4-quart (3.8 liter) slow cooker. Add the garlic, 1 teaspoon grated lemon zest, salt, and half of the sliced green onions to the slow cooker. Stir to distribute the seasonings. Pour the chicken broth into the cooker, near one of the edges.

2 Cover and cook on low for 4 to 5 hours, stirring once halfway through cooking (if possible), until the cauliflower is cooked through, but not mushy. Turn the slow cooker off and keep the cauliflower warm while you make the dressing.

3 In a small bowl, combine the mayonnaise, 4 teaspoons lemon juice, dill, and half of the remaining chopped green onions. Mix well.

4 Remove the cauliflower from the slow cooker with a slotted spoon and place it in a serving bowl. Discard the cooking liquid. Pour the dressing over the cauliflower and stir gently to coat everything evenly. Taste, and add a pinch or two of salt if necessary.

5 Serve warm or at room temperature.

Rosemary-Garlic Mashed Potatoes

I'm an Idaho girl at heart, and the thought of mashed potatoes without milk, cream, or butter seemed like food I wanted nothing to do with. Luckily ghee, chicken stock, and lots of garlic and herbs came to the rescue! These spuds are packed with flavor, but you can add even more ghee if you'd like. Good fats are our friends.

Prep time 15 minutes
Serves 8 as a side

3 to 4 pounds (1.4 to 1.8 kg) red or russet potatoes, cut into large chunks

2 teaspoons chopped fresh rosemary

6 cloves garlic, smashed

1 cup (235 ml) Simple Chicken Stock (page 280)

2 teaspoons sea salt

½ teaspoon black pepper

6 tablespoons (86 g) Homemade Ghee (page 287) or grass-fed butter

1½ cups (355 ml) unsweetened almond milk

1 Place the potatoes in a 4-quart (3.8 liter) slow cooker. Add the rosemary, garlic, chicken stock, salt, and pepper.

2 Cover and cook on low for 4 to 5 hours, or until the potatoes are very tender.

3 Place the ghee and almond milk in a small saucepan. Warm gently over medium heat. Do not boil.

4 Add the ghee and almond milk to the cooker. Smash the potatoes using a potato masher or a large serving fork. Taste, and add more salt and pepper if necessary before serving.

Note: You can substitute sweet potatoes in this recipe if you'd like.

Ginger-Honey Spaghetti Squash

This is a fun little side dish that takes spaghetti squash to a sweeter place with honey, orange, and ginger. It would be the perfect cooling sidekick to a spicy Asian-style meat dish.

Prep time 15 minutes

Serves 6 as a side

1 large spaghetti squash, cut in half and seeds scooped out

Sea salt

1-inch (2.5 cm) knob of ginger, finely grated

2 tablespoons (29 ml) avocado oil

2 tablespoons (40 g) honey

½ orange

1 Sprinkle a few generous pinches of salt and grated ginger into the insides of the squash and drizzle them with the avocado oil and honey.

2 Place the squash cut-side up in a 6-quart (5.7 liter) slow cooker. You'll probably need to put one half on top of the other, but be sure that the halves aren't nested. Add ½ cup (120 ml) water to the bottom of the cooker.

3 Cover and cook on low for 2 to 2 ½ hours, until the squash flesh pulls away easily with a fork, forming spaghetti-like strands.

4 Remove the squash from the cooker and scrape out the flesh with a fork. Squeeze the juice from the orange half over the top. Taste, and add more salt if necessary before serving.

Spaghetti Squash with Warm Bacon Vinaigrette

When I realized that I could use bacon drippings as the oil in a vinaigrette, it was a game changer. My three-year-old and I ate the entire half-squash with bacon vinaigrette for lunch one day. If you have some self-restraint, it's an excellent side dish with grilled or roasted meat.

Prep time 15 minutes
Serves 6 as a side

1 large spaghetti squash
(4 to 5 pounds, or 1.8 to 2.2 kg)
1 tablespoon avocado or coconut oil
Sea salt and black pepper

4 slices thick-cut, uncured bacon
2 tablespoons (30 ml) red wine vinegar
½ teaspoon Dijon mustard

1 Carefully cut the squash in half lengthwise. Scoop out and discard the seeds and membranes. Drizzle the oil into the insides of the squash halves and generously sprinkle with salt and pepper.

2 Place both halves in a 6-quart (5.7 liter) slow cooker, overlapping them if you need to. Cover and cook on low for 2½ to 3 hours (or 1½ to 2 hours on high).

3 When the squash is nearly finished, cook the bacon in a skillet over medium heat until crispy. Remove the bacon from the pan and set aside.

4 While the bacon drippings are still hot, add the vinegar, mustard, and a pinch of salt to the pan. Stir and let it bubble for about a minute before you remove it from the heat. Set aside.

5 Remove the squash from the slow cooker and scrape out the insides with a fork forming spaghetti-like strands. (This is my favorite part.) Transfer the spaghetti squash to a serving dish. Pour vinaigrette over the squash and toss to coat. Taste, and add more salt or vinegar if necessary.

6 Crumble up the cooked bacon and sprinkle it over the squash before serving.

Squash Noodles

Spiralized squash "noodles" and zucchini "zoodles" are a versatile staple in paleo cooking. You can eat them hot or cold with any type of meat or vegetable main dish, and they absorb whatever flavors you put on them. To make your meal prep easier, you can also spiralize a big batch of these at the beginning of the week and store them raw and chilled for several days, until you're ready to cook them.

Prep time 10 minutes

Serves 6

4 to 5 medium zucchini or yellow squash

1 tablespoon avocado oil or Homemade Ghee (page 287)

Sea salt and black pepper

1 Spiralize all of the squash using a spiralizer, using the manufacturer's directions. If you don't have a spiral cutter, slice the squash lengthwise into planks and then into long ¼-inch (5 mm) "noodles."

2 Heat the oil in a large skillet over medium-high heat. Add the squash noodles and cook, tossing them around with a pair of tongs occasionally, until they're cooked, but not mushy, about 6 to 8 minutes. Sprinkle a pinch or two of salt and pepper on the squash.

3 Remove the squash noodles from the pan and transfer them to a serving dish.

Notes: If your spiral cutter has the option for thin or thick noodles, choose the thick noodles (about ⅛ inch [3 mm] wide). If you use thin noodles, you may need to reduce the cooking time by half.

You can add garlic, minced onion, or other seasonings to the skillet when you add the squash.

You can also use peeled butternut squash or sweet potatoes as noodles. They take a bit longer to cook, but they don't release as much liquid as summer squash.

Cauliflower Rice
(stovetop method)

One of the first times I made cauliflower rice, I was visiting my parents in Idaho. We sat down to eat, and my meat-and-potatoes dad asked what it was. I told him it was "special rice." He's used to the fact that I eat strange things like kale and sushi, and just gave me a skeptical look. Being a good sport, he tried some anyway—and had seconds. No one mentioned that he was actually eating cauliflower.

Total time 20 minutes

Serves 4 as a side

1 large head cauliflower

3 tablespoons (42 g) avocado or coconut oil

1 cup (160 g) chopped onion

1 clove garlic, minced

½ teaspoon sea salt

1 Remove the leaves and thick stems from the cauliflower and cut into 1- to 2-inch (2.5 to 5 cm) florets. Working in batches, pulse the florets in a food processor until they are the size of rice grains.

2 Heat the oil in a large skillet over medium-high heat. Add the onion. Cook for 3 to 4 minutes, until the onion begins to soften and turn translucent.

3 Add the minced cauliflower, garlic, and salt to the skillet. Stir the mixture to combine. Reduce the heat to medium-low and cover. Let it steam for 3 to 4 minutes. Uncover and bring the heat back up to medium-high, stirring often, until the cauliflower is fully cooked and begins to turn golden brown in spots.

4 Transfer to a serving dish and serve immediately.

Roasted Cauliflower Rice (*oven method*)

This is my favorite version of cauliflower rice. I'm a sucker for any vegetable if it's roasted. Feel free to add any spices or aromatics to this; minced onion, garlic, and ginger are excellent. I've also tried different dried herbs and spices. (Cumin is great for Mexican rice.) Just toss the add-ins with the cauliflower and oil before you roast it. If you add garlic, stir it often, so it doesn't burn, and don't roast it too long.

Prep time 15 minutes
Serves 4 as a side

1 large head cauliflower

3 tablespoons (42 g) avocado or coconut oil

¼ teaspoon sea salt

1 Preheat oven to 425°F (218°C).

2 Remove the leaves and thick stems from the cauliflower and cut into 1- to 2-inch (2.6 to 5 cm) florets. Working in batches, pulse the florets in a food processor until they are the size of rice grains.

3 Transfer minced cauliflower to a rimmed baking sheet. Drizzle with oil and salt, and using your hands, toss to ensure that the cauliflower is coated evenly, and then spread it out in an even layer on the pan.

4 Roast on a lower oven rack for 20 to 25 minutes, stirring once or twice, until the cauliflower is golden brown or as brown as you like.

5 Transfer to a serving bowl and serve immediately.

Note: This recipe can easily be doubled. Just use one head of cauliflower per baking sheet and rotate the pans halfway through roasting.

Southwest Cabbage Slaw

This is my go-to slaw for Mexican or Tex-Mex dishes. It's my default taco topping, and makes great taco salads when you're not in the mood for lettuce. It takes only a few minutes to slice the cabbage, but if you've got a food processor with a slicing blade, it comes together in a snap.

Prep time 15 minutes

Serves 6

½ large head cabbage
(green or purple), thinly sliced

3 green onions, thinly sliced

Juice from ½ lime

⅓ cup chopped fresh cilantro

1 tablespoon (15 ml) extra-virgin olive oil

A generous pinch of sea salt

1 Combine all of the ingredients into a large mixing bowl. Toss everything together with your hands until well mixed.

2 Cover the slaw and refrigerate it until ready to use. The slaw will keep in the refrigerator for 4 to 5 days.

"Baked" Sweet Potatoes

"Baking" sweet potatoes in the slow cooker is so easy! You can also use this method for regular potatoes or any other large starchy root vegetable, such as parsnips, turnips, or rutabagas.

Prep time 5 minutes
Serves 8

3 to 4 pounds (1.4 to 1.8 kg) sweet potatoes

1 If the sweet potatoes are different sizes, cut some of them in half or in thirds, so that all of the pieces are roughly the same size.

2 Place the potatoes and ⅓ cup (80 ml) water into a 4-quart (3.8 liter) slow cooker and make sure to put the lid on tight.

3 Cook on low for 5 hours, or until a butter knife inserts easily into the potatoes.

4 Turn off the slow cooker and keep the potatoes in there until you're ready to eat.

Note: For red potatoes, cook 5 pounds (2.3 kg) in a 6-quart (5.7 liter) slow cooker with ½ cup (120 ml) water for 2½ to 3 hours on high or 5 to 6 hours on low.

Zucchini "Flatbread"

This zucchini-based flatbread is an excellent breadlike accompaniment to curries, like Shredded Lamb Korma (page 216), or as a tortilla for Thai Pulled Pork Tacos (page 198). It's also great on its own as a snack!

Prep time 15 minutes
Makes 1 sheet of flatbread

1½ pounds (680 g) zucchini
¼ cup (32 g) tapioca flour
1 egg
1 egg white

1 clove garlic, minced
½ teaspoon dried diced onion
Sea salt
Black pepper

1 Preheat oven to 425°F (218°C). Line a rimmed baking sheet with parchment paper.

2 Grate the zucchini and place it in the center of a clean kitchen towel. Wrap up the zucchini and squeeze it to remove any excess water.

3 Transfer the zucchini to a large mixing bowl. Add the tapioca flour, egg, egg white, garlic clove, dried onion, and a big pinch of sea salt and pepper.

4 Spread the zucchini mixture in an even layer on the parchment.

5 Bake on a lower oven rack for 25 minutes, until the edges become golden brown. Flip the whole thing over and bake for another 5 to 8, minutes until no squishy spots remain.

6 Slice and serve warm.

Note: Spreading the zucchini in an even layer is important for even baking. If you find pockets of mushy areas, simply cut off the edges and return the under-baked sections to the oven.

Paleo Tortillas

In my hunt for a respectable grain-free tortilla, I mostly found glorified crepes and thin, flat omelets. I wanted a tortilla with a more substantial texture, one with some bite—more like a regular tortilla. After tinkering with some alternative flours and eggs, I discovered that using only egg whites creates a chewy texture similar to an actual tortilla. I am thrilled!

Prep time 20 minutes

Makes 6 to 7 tortillas

1 cup (243 g) egg whites (from about 6 or 7 eggs)
2 tablespoons (30 ml) water
1 cup (128 g) tapioca flour
2 tablespoons ground flaxseed

2 tablespoons (16 g) coconut flour
½ teaspoon sea salt
Homemade Ghee (page 287), for cooking

1 Combine all of the ingredients except the ghee in a blender, in the order listed. Blend for a minute or so, until smooth batter forms. Let it sit for 5 minutes, and then pulse to blend it again if the ingredients have settled. The batter should be thicker than pancake batter, but thinner than pudding.

2 Heat a small nonstick skillet over medium-high heat. Brush the pan with ghee. Pour a small amount of batter into the skillet (3 to 4 tablespoons), in a spiral motion. Tilt the pan to swirl the batter in an even, round layer. If it doesn't spread easily, use a rubber spatula to gently push the batter outward.

3 Cook for 2 to 3 minutes, until the sides of the tortilla become dry and curve slightly upward. Flip, and cook it for another 2 to 3 minutes on the other side. Both sides should have golden brown spots. Transfer the tortilla to a plate and cover with a paper towel. Repeat with remaining batter, brushing ghee on the pan before each new tortilla.

4 Serve the tortillas warm.

Note: For best results, you can make these up to a few hours ahead of time, but not more than that. Make sure to serve them warm.

8

SWEETS AND DESSERTS

I think slow cookers show their versatility the most when you use them for desserts. Pots of chili and pulled pork are impressive, but wait until you see your guests' eyes when you pull out a cake or a cobbler!

Recipes

Spiced Pomegranate Poached Pears

In the midst of parties and rich-dessert spreads, it's easy to overindulge during the holiday season. Making a batch of these naturally sweet poached pears when you're tempted by sugar cookies will make you feel as if you're indulging without the regret (or the lethargic, heavy feeling afterward). I especially love the spiced pomegranate juice—it's like a tart, berry-like variation of wassail.

Prep time 10 minutes

Serves 6

5 to 6 Bosc pears, nearly ripe, with no soft spots

3 cups (710 ml) unsweetened pomegranate juice

½ cup (161 g) pure maple syrup

6 cardamom pods

6 strips orange peel, removed with a vegetable peeler

2 2-inch (5 cm) cinnamon sticks

Cinnamon and Whipped Coconut Cream (page 273), for serving

1 Lay the pears in a 6-quart (5.7 liter) slow cooker, just to make sure they all fit in a single layer.

2 Peel the pears, leaving the stems intact, and place them on their sides in the slow cooker.

3 Pour the pomegranate juice and maple syrup over the pears. Add the remaining ingredients (except the coconut cream) to the liquid in the slow cooker.

4 Cover and cook on low for 3 to 4 hours, turning the pears halfway through, until the pears are tender.

5 Remove the pears from the cooker and serve them whole or sliced with a generous drizzle of spiced pomegranate juice, a dollop of Whipped Coconut Cream, and a sprinkle of cinnamon.

Ginger-Spiced Pear Sauce and Pear Butter

One summer, I bought a big box of pears and waited patiently for them to ripen. One day, I checked and they were all ripe at the same time. Not wanting to waste any, I frantically chopped a bunch and threw them into my biggest slow cooker. A few hours later, I realized how easy and delicious homemade pear sauce is! Leave the sauce in the cooker even longer and you'll end up with pear butter.

Prep time 15 minutes
Makes about 3 quarts (2.9 kg) of pear sauce or 3 cups (960 g) of pear butter

12 to 15 medium pears, enough to fill a 6-quart (5.7 liter) cooker, cored and roughly chopped (peeling isn't necessary)

1 3-inch (7.5 cm) knob of fresh ginger, sliced into rings (again, peeling isn't necessary)

4 green cardamom pods or 2 cinnamon sticks

To make pear sauce:

1 Fill a 6-quart (5.7 liter) slow cooker with the pears. Add the ginger and cardamom (or cinnamon). Pour 1 cup (235 ml) water into the cooker.

2 Cover and cook on low for 4 to 5 hours, until the pears break down and it starts to look saucy.

3 Remove the ginger and cardamom and blend the pears to reach your desired consistency, preferably with an immersion blender. If you want the sauce chunky, blend lightly.

4 Pour the pear sauce into quart-size (946 ml) mason jars. The pear sauce will keep in the refrigerator for up to two weeks.

To make pear butter:

1 Pour 2 quarts pear sauce (2 kg) into a 2- or 3-quart (1.9 or 2.8 liter) slow cooker. Add a few more slices of ginger and a couple of cardamom pods or cinnamon sticks.

2 Turn the slow cooker on high and, instead of putting the lid on, tent the cooker with aluminum foil so the steam can escape and the foil can shield splattering sauce.

3 Cook for 2 to 3 hours, stirring a few times and checking the consistency.

4 When the pear butter is as thick as you like, taste it and add more spices or sweetener if you'd like.

5 Transfer it to a jar and store, covered, in the refrigerator. It will keep for up to two weeks.

Note: If you'd like the pear sauce plain, you can omit the ginger and cardamom. You can also use this method with apples, prepping them the same way and adding an hour or two to the cooking time.

Whole Caramelized Pineapple with Sweet Ginger Sauce

The first time I made this, I couldn't help but think of the whole, cooked pineapple as a "roast" as I lifted it out of the slow cooker, laid it on a cutting board, and sliced it. It made me giggle. Those giggles turned to lip smacks after I drizzled some of the ginger-spiked pineapple syrup over the top and added some Whipped Coconut Cream (page 273). I'm a huge fan of grilled pineapple, but I must admit that this method of caramelizing a pineapple is even better.

Prep time 15 minutes
Serves 6

¼ cup (38 g) coconut sugar

2 tablespoons fresh ginger, finely grated or minced

1 whole pineapple, ends cut off and peeled

1 cup (235 ml) unsweetened pineapple juice

Whipped Coconut Cream (page 273) and toasted coconut flakes, for serving

1 Combine the coconut sugar and ginger. Rub the mixture over the entire pineapple.

2 Place the pineapple in a 4-quart (3.8 liter) slow cooker. If it will fit on its side, that is preferable.

3 Pour the pineapple juice in the bottom of the cooker.

4 Cook on low for 6 to 7 hours, turning the pineapple over halfway through cooking, until the pineapple is very tender and a medium golden brown color.

5 Remove the pineapple from the cooker and set aside to keep warm.

6 Turn the cooker up to high heat and leave the lid cracked open slightly. Cook the juices for about 30 minutes or so, until it has reduced and thickened slightly.

7 Turn the pineapple on its end and slice the fruit from the core in large strips. Cut into smaller pieces and serve with Whipped Coconut Cream, pineapple ginger sauce from the pot, and toasted coconut flakes, if desired.

Note: To toast coconut flakes, spread 2 cups (140 g) unsweetened coconut on a baking sheet and bake at 350°F (177°C) for a few minutes, until golden brown. It burns easily, so keep an eye on it!

Nutty Coconut Baked Apples with Cider Sauce

If you have a hankering for apple pie but can't seem to nail down a grain-free pie crust (I feel your pain), this is a great alternative. You have the same soft, juicy apples, but with a sweet-tart cider sauce and a chewy nut-coconut mixture for contrast. Add a dollop of Whipped Coconut Cream (page 273) and you've got the perfect bowl of autumn.

Prep time 25 minutes
Serves 6

6 medium tart baking apples (Pink Lady, Honeycrisp, or Jonagold work well)

½ lemon

¾ cup (90 g) raw, unsalted walnuts, chopped

¾ cup (60 g) unsweetened coconut flakes

6 *Medjool* dates, pitted and chopped

3 tablespoons (60 g) raw honey

¾ teaspoon cinnamon

Pinch of sea salt

Pinch of nutmeg

2 cups (475 ml) unsweetened apple cider

3 tablespoons (43 g) Homemade Ghee (page 287) or grass-fed butter

¼ cup (38 g) coconut sugar

Whipped Coconut Cream (page 273), for serving (optional)

1 Arrange the apples in a 6-quart (5.7 liter) slow cooker—just to make sure you've got room for all of them.

2 Hollow out each apple by cutting an inch or so around the stem, toward the center. Remove the top and scoop out the core and seeds with a spoon. You don't need to scrape out additional apple flesh. Squirt the insides and cut edges with the lemon juice to prevent browning.

3 In a medium bowl, combine the walnuts, coconut, and dates. Drizzle in the honey and add the cinnamon, salt, and nutmeg. Mix well.

4 Fill each apple with the nut mixture, pressing it in tightly. You may have a little bit of filling leftover.

5 Add the cider, ghee, and coconut sugar to the slow cooker. Arrange the apples in the cider, standing upright.

6 Cover and cook on low for 3 hours.

7 Remove apples carefully with tongs and transfer them to a serving platter. Pour the cider syrup into a small bowl.

8 Serve each apple with a generous drizzle of cider syrup and a dollop of Whipped Coconut Cream.

Pumpkin Spice Cake with Chocolate Pecan Streusel

Before creating this recipe, I had never baked anything in a slow cooker. I imagined overcooked edges, gooey centers, and a layer of cake left in the bottom that refused to release itself. As apprehensive and doubtful as I felt, I dived in and tried it. After a few test runs, I ended up with a legit-imate cake that tasted great! The combination of pumpkin and chocolate is one of my favorites, and I think the streusel on top really makes this cake shine.

Prep time 20 minutes
Serves 6

1 cup (96 g) almond flour
¼ cup (32 g) tapioca flour
1 tablespoon coconut flour
1½ teaspoons pumpkin pie spice
1 teaspoon baking soda
¼ teaspoon sea salt
3 eggs

⅓ cup plus 1 tablespoon (59 g) coconut sugar
½ cup (123 g) pumpkin puree
1 tablespoon (20 g) pure maple syrup
1 teaspoon (5 ml) vanilla
½ cup (55 g) pecans, chopped
¼ cup (44 g) chopped 70% cacao chocolate

1 Line a 2- or 4-quart (1.9 or 3.8 liter) slow cooker with a piece of parchment paper large enough to reach the top of the insert. Press the paper to the bottom and sides, making creases and flattening the paper as best you can. The batter does a good job of flattening it out, so don't worry too much.

2 Whisk together the flours, pie spice, baking soda, and salt in a medium bowl.

3 In a smaller bowl, combine the eggs, ⅓ cup (50 g) coconut sugar, pumpkin, maple syrup, and vanilla.

4 Add the wet mixture to the dry mixture and fold gently until no dry pockets remain.

5 Pour the batter into the parchment-lined slow cooker.

6 Combine the pecans, chocolate, and remaining 1 tablespoon of coco-nut sugar. Sprinkle the mixture over the batter.

7 Cover and cook on low for 2 to 3 hours. Check for doneness at 2 hours by sticking a toothpick into the cen-ter. It should come out clean when finished, and the cake should feel firm to the touch. If it isn't ready yet, cover and check every 20 minutes until it is ready.

8 Turn off the slow cooker and remove the lid to let it cool off for 15 minutes or so. Then, run a rubber spatula around the edges, pressing down so the spatula also scrapes along the bottom edges of the cake. Turn the cooker upside-down on a large plate or cooling rack to release the cake. Flip the cake over so that the streusel is on top.

9 Cut and serve.

Upside-Down Cranberry Gingerbread

Baking in a slow cooker might seem odd, but for grain-free recipes (which can easily turn out dry and chalky) it's the perfect, steamy cooking environment to keep cakes moist. The dense, but not too dense, pound cake–like gingerbread is studded with plump, juicy cranberries and soaked in a spiced wassail-like syrup.

Prep time 20 minutes
Serves 6

For the topping:
1 cup (100 g) fresh or frozen cranberries
½ teaspoon orange zest
½ teaspoon cinnamon
3 tablespoons (60 g) pure maple syrup
Pinch salt
Pinch ground cloves

For the cake:
1 cup (96 g) blanched almond flour
¼ cup (32 g) tapioca flour
1 tablespoon coconut flour
1 teaspoon baking soda
1 teaspoon ground ginger
½ teaspoon cinnamon
¼ teaspoon sea salt
Pinch of ground cloves
3 eggs
1 teaspoon (5 ml) vanilla extract
⅓ cup (50 g) coconut sugar
¼ cup (60 g) unsweetened applesauce
⅓ cup (113 g) molasses
2 tablespoons (28 g) melted coconut oil
Whipped Coconut Cream (page 273), for serving

1 Place the topping ingredients into a 2- or 3-quart (1.9 or 2.8 liter) slow cooker. Stir to combine.

2 In a large mixing bowl, stir together the almond, tapioca, and coconut flours, baking soda, ginger, cinnamon, salt, and cloves.

3 In a medium mixing bowl, whisk together the eggs, vanilla, coconut sugar, applesauce, molasses, and coconut oil.

4 Pour the wet mixture into the dry mixture and mix gently until the batter no longer has dry spots. Do not overmix.

5 Pour the batter over the cranberry mixture in the slow cooker. Do not mix together. Cover and cook on low for 3 to 3½ hours. The cake is finished when the center is firm and a toothpick inserted into the center comes out clean.

6 Turn the slow cooker off, remove the lid, and let the cake cool for 15 minutes. Run a knife around the outside edges of the cake. To further loosen the cake from the cooker, push a flexible rubber spatula down around the outside edges—the spatula should bend and go underneath the cake about an inch or so. Place a large plate upside-down on top of the slow cooker, and holding the plate firmly against the rim, flip the whole thing upside-down so that the cake turns cranberry-side up on the plate.

7 Cut the cake into sections and serve with Whipped Coconut Cream.

Note: Although regular, unsulfured molasses is not considered paleo, it is what gives gingerbread its dark, rich flavor. I would not recommend using blackstrap molasses here.

Blueberry Muffin Cake

The first time I tested this recipe, I used loads of fresh blueberries. When I pulled the cake out, it was lumpy, bluish-green, and seemed to be covered with a slimy substance. Time to try again. Not wanting to re-create the swamp thing, I used freeze-dried blueberries—and the new result was just what I wanted! The steamy slow-cooking environment rehydrated the dried blueberries enough so they were soft and plump but didn't explode over the whole cake. It also gave the cake a more pronounced blueberry flavor—just like a blueberry muffin.

Prep time 15 minutes
Serves 6

¾ cup (188 g) blanched almond flour
¼ cup (32 g) tapioca flour
1 tablespoon coconut flour
½ teaspoon baking soda
¼ teaspoon cinnamon
¼ teaspoon sea salt

3 eggs
½ cup (125 g) unsweetened applesauce
⅓ cup (107 g) pure maple syrup
1 teaspoon (5 ml) vanilla extract
1 cup (24 g) freeze-dried blueberries
1 tablespoon coconut sugar

1 Line a 2- or 3-quart (1.9 or 2.8 liter) slow cooker with a piece of parchment, pressing the paper to the bottom and creasing the side folds as best as you can. It doesn't have to lay flat at this point. The batter will take care of that.

2 Combine the flours, baking soda, cinnamon, and sea salt in a large mixing bowl.

3 In a medium bowl or large glass measuring cup, whisk together the eggs, unsweetened applesauce, maple syrup, and vanilla extract. Pour the wet mixture into the dry and whisk it gently to combine and remove lumps.

4 Pour the batter into the lined slow cooker. Scatter the blueberries over the top and sprinkle the coconut sugar over them.

5 Cover and cook on low for 2½ to 3½ hours. Check the cake as little as possible, to keep the heat in the slow cooker. A toothpick inserted into the center should come out clean.

6 Turn off the slow cooker and remove the lid. Let the cake rest 10 to 15 minutes and then lift the cake out, using the parchment. Place the whole thing on a cooling rack. Let it continue to cool another 5 minutes before slicing.

7 Cut into wedges and serve.

Nut-Free Fudgy Brownie Cake

Paleo baking typically relies on nut flours, and because nut allergies are becoming more common, I wanted to create a cake that was free of nuts. This chocolate dessert is like a cross between a cake and a fudgy brownie. I love how the avocado keeps it moist—an unlikely ingredient in a cake, yet it works like a charm!

Prep time 15 minutes
Serves 6

1 avocado, pitted and peeled
1 egg
½ cup (170 g) honey
1 teaspoon vanilla extract
1 cup (128 g) tapioca flour
⅓ cup (29 g) cocoa powder
¼ cup (38 g) coconut sugar

2 tablespoons (16 g) coconut flour
½ teaspoon baking soda
¼ teaspoon sea salt
2 ounces (55 g) dark 70% cacao chocolate
Whipped Coconut Cream (page 273), for serving

1 Line a 4-quart (3.8 liter) slow cooker with a piece of parchment paper large enough to reach the top of the insert. Press the paper to the bottom and sides, making creases and flattening the paper as best you can. The batter does a good job of flattening it out, so don't worry.

2 Place the avocado, egg, honey, and vanilla in a food processor or blender. Process until smooth.

3 Add the tapioca flour, cocoa powder, coconut sugar, coconut flour, baking soda, and salt. Pulse until a thick batter forms. (If you don't have a food processor or blender, smash the avocado with a fork and use a hand mixer to blend the rest.)

4 Transfer the brownie batter to the slow cooker and spread it evenly. Break up the dark chocolate and stick the pieces into the batter.

5 Cover and cook on low for 2 to 3 hours. Check the cake after 2 hours by inserting a toothpick into the center, avoiding the melted chocolate pieces. The cake is done if the toothpick comes out mostly clean in the center.

6 Serve with Whipped Coconut Cream.

Vanilla Cake with Strawberry-Balsamic Sauce

If you happened to try the Strawberry-Balsamic Chicken (page 118), this sauce should look familiar. It amuses me that you can use the same sauce over chicken or a cake and they both turn out delicious!

Prep time 20 minutes
Serves 6

For the cake:

1½ cups (144 g) blanched almond flour

¼ cup plus 2 tablespoons (48 g) tapioca flour

1 tablespoon coconut flour

1½ teaspoons baking soda

½ teaspoon salt

3 eggs

½ cup (125 g) unsweetened applesauce

½ cup (165 g) pure maple syrup or honey

1 tablespoon (15 ml) vanilla extract

For the sauce:

½ cup (120 ml) good-quality balsamic vinegar

1 pound (455 g) strawberries, trimmed and diced

2 tablespoons (40 g) honey

Whipped Coconut Cream (page 273), for serving

1 Line a 4-quart (3.8 liter) slow cooker with a piece of parchment paper large enough to reach the top of the insert. Press the paper to the bottom and sides, making creases and flattening the paper as best you can. The batter does a good job of flattening it out, so don't worry.

2 Combine the almond flour, tapioca flour, coconut flour, baking soda, and salt in a large mixing bowl.

3 In a medium bowl, combine the eggs, applesauce, maple syrup, and vanilla. Whisk well.

4 Pour the wet mixture into the dry mixture and whisk gently until no lumps remain. Pour the batter into the prepared slow cooker.

5 Cover and cook on low for 2½ to 3 hours, until a toothpick inserted into the center of the cake comes out clean.

6 Meanwhile, prepare the sauce by placing the balsamic vinegar, strawberries, and 2 tablespoons honey in a small saucepan. Bring the mixture to a boil, reduce the heat to medium-low, and let it simmer for 20 to 25 minutes, or until the mixture becomes more sweet and less vinegary. Taste, and add more honey if you'd like it sweeter.

7 When the cake is finished, gather the pieces of parchment hanging out of the top and lift the cake out, transferring it to a large plate or platter. Let it rest 10 minutes before cutting.

8 Serve the cake with the strawberry-balsamic sauce and Whipped Coconut Cream.

Whipped Coconut Cream

Although our family does splurge sometimes and use real whipped cream, it's nice to have a dairy-free option if you don't tolerate dairy well—or eat it at all. I love the coconut flavor this adds, too!

Prep time 5 minutes
Serves 6

2 to 3 13.5-ounce (398 ml) cans chilled full-fat coconut milk

1 tablespoon (20 g) of preferred sweetener (honey or pure maple syrup), or stevia, to taste

¼ teaspoon vanilla extract (optional)

1 Open the cans from the bottom and drain out the liquid. (You can save it for smoothies later.)

2 Scoop out the hardened coconut cream and place it into a medium bowl. Whip the cream using a hand-held mixer until soft and fluffy. Blend in the sweetener and vanilla extract. Taste, and adjust the sweetener if needed.

3 Chill until ready to use. If you find the mixture has hardened, rewhip it with a hand mixer.

Note: The creaminess of coconut milk varies among brands, so you may need three cans of coconut milk to collect enough coconut cream. Alternately, you can use a can of coconut cream to get an entire can of the cream. If you use liquid stevia as a sweetener, you'll only need a few drops.

Apple-Pomegranate Crumble

One aspect of a paleo lifestyle I like a lot is how fine the boundary is between a dessert and a sweet breakfast. They could almost be interchangeable. And if a doughnut can be considered a breakfast food, I'm pretty sure that this lightly sweetened crumble can join the ranks as well.

Prep time 20 minutes
Serves 6

For the cake:

1½ pounds (680 g) tart baking apples (about 3 to 4), cored and cut into ½-inch (1 cm) cubes

1 cup (174 g) pomegranate arils (from 1 small pomegranate)

2 tablespoons (16 g) tapioca flour

1 teaspoon cinnamon

2 tablespoons (40 g) honey

2 tablespoons (30 ml) freshly squeezed lemon juice

For the topping:

1 cup (96 g) blanched almond flour

½ cup (43 g) unsweetened coconut flakes

½ cup (60 g) chopped raw walnuts or pecans

¼ teaspoon ground ginger

¼ teaspoon ground nutmeg

1 tablespoon coconut sugar

3 tablespoons (45 ml) melted Homemade Ghee (page 287) or coconut oil

Pinch of sea salt

Whipped Coconut Cream (page 273), for serving

1 Place the diced apple and pomegranate arils in a 2- or 3-quart (1.9 or 2.8 liter) slow cooker. Add the tapioca flour and cinnamon, and mix well. Stir in the honey and lemon juice.

2 In a medium mixing bowl, combine the almond flour, coconut, nuts, ginger, nutmeg, and coconut sugar. Drizzle the ghee over the top and stir until the mixture begins to resemble wet sand. Sprinkle a pinch of salt over the top.

3 Pour the crumble mixture on top of the apples and arils. Spread evenly.

4 Cover and cook on low for 3½ to 4 hours, until the apples are tender, but not mushy.

5 Serve warm with a dollop of Whipped Coconut Cream.

A Big Chocolate Chip Cookie

This is just what the title says—a big chocolate chip cookie. It began as a fun experiment, but after three or four tries, it became a contest of me vs. the cookie. After six tries, I finally had something I was excited about. You could also use this dough (or even double the recipe) in the oven to bake regular cookies. If you want to do that, spoon dough onto a coconut oil-greased baking sheet and bake for 8 to 10 minutes at 350°F (177°C).

Prep time 15 minutes
Serves 6

½ cup (103 g) palm shortening
¼ cup (64 g) unsweetened almond butter
¼ cup (85 g) honey
2 tablespoons (28 g) coconut oil
1 egg white
1 teaspoon (5 ml) vanilla extract
10 drops vanilla stevia

¾ cup (96 g) tapioca flour
¾ cup (188 g) blanched almond flour
½ teaspoon sea salt
¼ teaspoon baking soda
½ cup (87 g) dark chocolate chips or chopped 70% cacao chocolate
Sliced strawberries and Whipped Coconut Cream (page 273), for serving

1 Combine the shortening, almond butter, honey, and coconut oil in the work bowl of a stand mixer or a large food processor. Beat well until no lumps remain.

2 Add the egg white, vanilla extract, and vanilla stevia. Blend until smooth.

3 Add the tapioca flour, almond flour, sea salt, and baking soda. Beat until combined. Stir in the chocolate chips.

4 Lay a piece of parchment paper on a flat surface (about the size of your 6-quart [5.7 liter] slow cooker). Spoon the dough onto the parchment. Shape the dough into an oval (smaller than the bottom of your slow cooker), making the sides about two or three times thicker than the center.

5 Lower the parchment with the dough into the bottom of the slow cooker. Press the parchment to the sides of the cooker—it does not need to be completely smooth.

6 Cover and cook on low for 60 to 90 minutes. If possible, check the cookie through the lid instead of opening it. The sides should be a dark golden brown and the center should look slightly undercooked.

7 Turn off the slow cooker and re-move the lid. Let the cookie sit for 5 minutes. Lift the cookie out, using the parchment edges, and set it onto a cooling rack. Let the cookie cool for at least 15 minutes before slicing.

8 Cut the cookie into squares or wedges and serve with some straw-berries and a dollop of Whipped Coconut Cream.

Notes: Palm shortening is vegetable shortening made from palm oil. Be sure to find a brand that is 100 percent palm oil and not a blend of two oils.

If you have some paleo-friendly ice cream, you could put a few scoops in the center of the cookie, pass out some forks, and eat it right off the parchment.

Chocolate Berry Cobbler

This is one of my favorite recipes in this chapter. I love the variation on a cobbler, using a chocolate cakelike topping over saucy cooked berries. It's heavenly. And don't forget about the Whipped Coconut Cream (page 273).

Prep time 20 minutes
Serves 6

1½ pounds (680 g) frozen mixed berries
⅔ cup (100 g) coconut sugar, divided
½ cup (64 g) plus 1 tablespoon tapioca flour, divided
¼ teaspoon cinnamon
1 cup (96 g) blanched almond flour
¼ cup (23 g) unsweetened cocoa powder
1 teaspoon baking soda
¼ teaspoon sea salt
½ cup (103 g) palm shortening
1 egg
2 tablespoons sliced or slivered almonds
2 tablespoons (19 g) chopped dark 70% cacao chocolate
Whipped Coconut Cream (page 273), for serving

1 Place the frozen berries in a 4-quart (3.8 liter) slow cooker. If there are large strawberries in the mixture, cut them in half or in quarters. Sprinkle the berries with ⅓ cup (50 g) of the coconut sugar, 1 tablespoon tapioca flour, and the cinnamon. Give it a stir to coat the berries well.

2 In the work bowl of a food processor, combine the other ⅓ cup (50 g) coconut sugar, ½ cup (64 g) tapioca flour, almond flour, cocoa powder, baking soda, and salt. Pulse several times to mix well. Add the shortening and pulse until the mixture resembles wet sand. Add the egg, and pulse until a dough forms and wedges itself onto one side of the bowl.

3 Carefully remove the dough from the work bowl, avoiding the mixing blade. Break the dough into 1-inch (2.5 cm) pieces and scatter them over the berries in the slow cooker. Sprinkle the almonds and the chopped chocolate on top.

4 Cover and cook on high for 3 to 3½ hours. The dough on top of the cobbler should be fairly firm around the edges and slightly soft in the center, and the berries should be hot and bubbling around the edges of the cooker.

5 Turn off the cooker, remove the lid, and let the cobbler sit and cool for 15 minutes, to allow the juices to settle and thicken.

6 Serve with Whipped Coconut Cream.

SLOW COOKER PANTRY BASICS

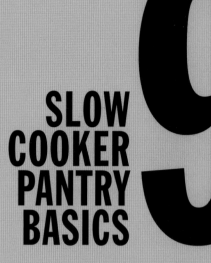

Warning: Making your own pantry basics from scratch may result in healthier, better-tasting ingredients, but once you get used to them, you may find yourself unable to tolerate store-bought versions.

Recipes

Simple
Chicken Stock

I started making my own stock around the time my husband and I became more conscientious about the meat we eat. He was in chiropractic school at the time, so eating higher-quality meat meant we didn't eat it often. After paying premium prices for whole chickens, I wanted to get everything I could out of them. Stashing the bones in the freezer makes it easy to find time to "stock up" later.

Prep time 10 minutes
Makes 3 to 3½ quarts (2.8 to 3.3 liters)

1 meaty carcass from a 3- to 5-pound (1.4 to 2.3 kg) whole chicken (or the equivalent in miscellaneous chicken bones)
1 large onion, quartered
2 to 3 stalks celery, cut into large pieces
2 to 3 carrots, cut into large pieces
A large handful of fresh herbs (like thyme, sage, parsley, or rosemary)
1 tablespoon whole black peppercorns
2 bay leaves
2 garlic cloves, peeled

1 Place all of the ingredients into a 6- or 7-quart (5.7 or 6.6 liter) slow cooker. Fill the cooker with water about an inch or two from the top.

2 Cover and cook on low for 18 hours.

3 Remove the bones and large vegetable pieces with tongs and discard them. Pour the rest of the stock through a large fine-mesh strainer. Let the stock cool until it reaches room temperature.

4 If you aren't using the stock right away, transfer it to containers for chilled storage. For freezing, I like to use quart-size (946 ml) plastic containers. You can also use mason jars, leaving a couple inches of head space, or zip-top freezer bags.

Homemade Beef Stock

Over the past several years, my husband and I have purchased beef shares from a local grass-fed beef ranch. In every share, we get packages of soup bones, which I love. They make the best-tasting bone broth—and all of those minerals and collagen from the bones are really good for you!

Prep time 10 minutes
Makes 3 to 3½ quarts (2.8 to 3.3 liters)

3 to 5 pounds (1.4 to 2.3 kg) beef bones
1 large onion, quartered
2 to 3 stalks celery, cut into large pieces
2 to 3 carrots, cut into large pieces

A large handful of fresh herbs (like thyme, sage, parsley, or rosemary)
1 tablespoon whole black peppercorns
2 bay leaves
2 cloves garlic, peeled

1 Place all of the ingredients into a 6- or 7-quart (5.7 or 6.6 liter) slow cooker. Fill the cooker with water about an inch or two from the top.

2 Cover and cook on low for 36 hours.

3 Remove the bones and large vegetable pieces with tongs, and discard them. Pour the rest of the stock through a large fine-mesh strainer. Let the stock cool until it reaches room temperature.

4 If you aren't using the stock right away, transfer it to containers for chilled storage. For freezing, I like to use quart-size (946 ml) plastic containers. You can also use mason jars, leaving a couple inches of head space, or zip-top freezer bags.

"Roasted" Garlic

Roasting garlic in the oven is easy, but using a slow cooker is good for large batches if you don't have the time to "babysit" it. Also, it's much more forgiving and won't burn as easily as it does in the oven. Roasted garlic is such a versatile, flavor-boosting condiment. You can add it to soups, stews, vegetable side dishes, sauces, or even a simple baked potato.

Prep time 20 minutes
Makes ½ to 1 cup (75 to 150 g) smashed, roasted garlic

3–5 bulbs of garlic
1 tablespoon avocado oil
Sea salt

1 Line a 2- or 3-quart (1.9 or 2.8 liter) slow cooker with aluminum foil.

2 Slice an inch off the tops of the garlic bulbs, so that the cloves are exposed. Place them in the foil-lined cooker. Drizzle with oil and sprinkle with salt.

3 Cover and cook on low for 5 to 6 hours, or until cloves are very tender.

4 Remove cloves from bulbs and smash them. Store in an airtight container, chilled, until ready to use—within a couple of weeks.

Autumn Harvest Pasta Sauce

I noticed an autumn-inspired pasta sauce during one of my shopping trips to Trader Joe's, and snagged a jar to try at home. Wow. I loved that the tomato base takes a back seat to the squash and pumpkin flavors. I was determined to create a version of my own, and love the way this turned out.

Prep time 20 minutes
Makes about 1½ quarts (1.5 kilograms)

⅓ cup (90 g) tomato paste
1 cup (245 g) pumpkin puree
1½ cups (210 g) cubed butternut squash
½ cup (120 ml) coconut milk
2 medium carrots, peeled and cut into 1-inch (2.5 cm) chunks
⅓ cup (82 g) unsweetened applesauce
1 tablespoon (20 g) pure maple syrup
1 teaspoon sea salt
½ teaspoon onion powder

1 small garlic clove, quartered
1 tablespoon (15 ml) lemon juice
¼ teaspoon black pepper
¼ teaspoon ground sage
⅛ teaspoon cayenne pepper
1 2-inch (5 cm) sprig fresh rosemary or ¼ teaspoon dried
2 tablespoons (30 g) Homemade Ghee (page 287)

1 Whisk the tomato paste with 2 cups (475 ml) of water. Pour it into a 4-quart (3.8 liter) slow cooker.

2 Add the remaining ingredients to the slow cooker, except the ghee. Stir to combine.

3 Cook on low for 5 to 6 hours.

4 Use an immersion blender (or regular blender) to blend the sauce until smooth. Stir in the ghee. Taste, and add more salt if necessary.

5 Store in a large airtight container, chilled, for up to 10 days. Or freeze the sauce for up to 3 months.

Basic Marinara

I love this "dump and walk away" marinara sauce—it's versatile enough to use on anything from zoodles to eggs to paleo pizza. If tomatoes are in season, try using 3 to 4 pounds (1.4 to 1.8 kg) of fresh, ripe ones instead.

Prep time 15 minutes

Makes about 1½ to 2 quarts
(1½ to 2 kilograms)

2 28-ounce (794 g) cans of whole San Marzano tomatoes

4 tablespoons (60 g) Homemade Ghee (page 287)

4 tablespoons (60 ml) extra-virgin olive oil

4 garlic cloves, chopped

1 medium carrot, diced

⅓ cup (55 g) chopped onion

2 tablespoons (30 ml) coconut aminos

1 teaspoon sea salt

½ teaspoon dried basil

1 tablespoon (15 ml) balsamic vinegar

½ bunch fresh basil

1 Place all the ingredients except for the basil and vinegar into a 4-quart (3.8 liter) slow cooker.

2 Cover and cook on low for 5 to 6 hours.

3 Blend, preferably with an immersion blender. Taste, and adjust salt if necessary.

4 Add the balsamic vinegar and basil leaves, and blend lightly, leaving bits of basil throughout.

Cajun Spice Blend

I like making my own Cajun seasoning, because sometimes the prepared kind is too spicy for my kids. Or it isn't spicy enough for my husband and me. I like this version because it has a bit of heat, but not too much. And I have all of these seasonings in my cupboard, so it's easy to whip up another batch when I run out.

Prep time 10 minutes
Makes about ½ cup (50 g)

2 tablespoons paprika

4 teaspoons onion powder

4 teaspoons garlic powder

2 teaspoons celery seed

2 teaspoons dried thyme

2 teaspoons dried basil

2 teaspoons sea salt

2 teaspoons black pepper

½ teaspoon cayenne pepper

¼ teaspoon crushed red pepper flakes

Shake ingredients together in an airtight container. Store at room temperature.

Homemade Taco Seasoning

When I realized that taco-seasoning packets were simply a mix of things I probably already had in my kitchen, it was a revelation. And that discovery ultimately resulted in the best homemade taco seasoning I've ever had. Cocoa might seem like an odd addition, but it gives the blend a deep, rich flavor.

Prep time 10 minutes
Makes about ¾ cup (75 g)

¼ cup (30 g) chili powder

2 tablespoons (16 g) tapioca flour (optional, see note)

4 teaspoons ground cumin

4 teaspoons dried oregano

4 teaspoons unsweetened cocoa powder

4 teaspoons (24 g) sea salt

2 teaspoons granulated garlic

2 teaspoons onion powder

2 teaspoons freshly ground black pepper

½ teaspoon cayenne pepper

½ teaspoon ground coriander

Combine all of the ingredients in a lidded container. Shake well and store at room temperature.

Note: The tapioca flour allows the seasoning to form a bit of a sauce when added to ground beef with a small amount of water. If you prefer to leave it out, that's fine. This taco seasoning is a bit more concentrated than the packets you buy in the store, so keep that in mind when you use it.

Dry Ranch Seasoning Mix

This is one of the first seasonings I started making from scratch. I was trying to wean myself off of those little green packets, and although it doesn't taste exactly the same (it's hard to compete with MSG), it still hits the spot and adds that familiar creamy, herby flavor.

Prep time 10 minutes
Makes about ½ cup (50 g)

1 tablespoon dried parsley

2 teaspoons freeze dried chives

1½ teaspoons dried dill

1 teaspoon dry mustard

½ teaspoon paprika

½ teaspoon dried onion

½ teaspoon garlic powder

½ teaspoon onion powder

½ teaspoon sea salt

Freshly ground black pepper

Shake ingredients together in an airtight container. Store at room temperature.

Note: To make Ranch Dressing, combine 1 cup (225 g) Paleo-Friendly Mayonnaise (page 286), 1 to 2 tablespoons Dry Ranch Seasoning Mix, a squeeze of fresh lemon, a pinch of salt, and enough almond milk to reach the desired consistency.

Thai Spice Blend

I bought a Thai spice blend once and was hooked! It was a rather expensive blend, so I decided to re-create it at home, and I love the way it turned out.

Prep time 10 minutes
Makes about ½ cup (50 g)

2 tablespoons (14 g) paprika

1 tablespoon turmeric

1 tablespoon coarsely ground black pepper

1 tablespoon ground coriander

1 tablespoon ground fenugreek

1½ teaspoons dry mustard

1½ teaspoons ground cumin

1½ teaspoons ground ginger

½ to ¾ teaspoon cayenne powder (to taste)

Shake ingredients together in an airtight container. Store at room temperature.

Paleo-Friendly Mayonnaise

Homemade mayonnaise is a game changer for me. I was never a fan of commercial mayo, and the homemade kind has a mild flavor that's perfect for making aioli and also adds a creaminess to many recipes.

Prep time 10 minutes
Makes about 1 cup (225 g)

2 egg yolks (from fresh eggs, preferably pasture-raised)

3 tablespoons (45 ml) freshly squeezed lemon juice (about ½ large lemon)

½ teaspoon dry mustard

¾ teaspoon sea salt

½ clove garlic (optional)

1 cup (236 ml) avocado or light olive oil

1 Place the yolks, lemon juice, dry mustard, salt, and garlic in a food processor. Blend until smooth.

2 While the machine is running, slowly drizzle the oil into the machine. The mixture should thicken quite a bit. Do not continue blending after you finish drizzling the oil.

3 Transfer the mayonnaise to an airtight container. Taste, and add more salt or lemon juice if needed. Store chilled for up to a week.

Notes: I like to put a little garlic in my mayonnaise, because it gives it more flavor. It's fine to leave it out.
I like mayo thick, which is why I use two egg yolks. To make a looser mayonnaise, use just one egg yolk.

Homemade Ghee

Ghee, or clarified butter, is butter that has had the milk solids removed. This allows you to heat the oil that is left over to higher temperatures without burning it. Ghee is one of my favorite cooking fats—it has a nutty, buttery flavor, and is great for sautéing, roasting, or drizzling as a finishing oil. You can purchase ghee in some stores or online, but making it is incredibly easy and less expensive if you find high-quality, grass-fed butter on sale.

Cooking time 15 to 20 minutes
Makes about 3½ cups (773 g)

2 pounds (905 g) grass-fed butter (organic, if possible)

1 Cut the butter into large pieces and put it into a medium saucepan.

2 Cook the butter over medium-low heat until it is all melted.

3 Continue to cook the butter over medium-low heat. The butter will bubble and simmer for several minutes and get very foamy at the top. Then the foam will subside, and the top will be relatively clear. After a few more minutes, it will get foamy again, with smaller bubbles. At this point, remove the pan from the heat and use a spoon to skim the foam from the top. Do not scrape the residue from the bottom of the pot.

4 Pour the clear ghee into a lidded glass container for storage. Allow the ghee to cool completely, and store, covered, at room temperature for a few days or chilled for a few weeks.

Dry Caribbean Jerk Rub

Jerk seasoning often comes in paste form, but if you're looking for a dry version, you probably have all of these spices in your cabinet, just waiting to be mixed. This blend is rather spicy, so reduce the amount of cayenne pepper if you'd like.

Prep time 10 minutes
Makes about ½ cup (50 g)

4 tablespoons (24 g) dried minced onion
2 tablespoons paprika
4 teaspoons dried thyme
4 teaspoons garlic powder
2 teaspoons black pepper

2 teaspoons ground allspice
1 teaspoon cayenne pepper
½ teaspoon cinnamon
½ teaspoon ground nutmeg
¼ teaspoon ground cloves

Combine all the ingredients in an airtight container. Shake well and store at room temperature.

BBQ Dry-Rub Seasoning

This dry rub is a great all-purpose seasoning for grilling. It's smoky, peppery, and has just the right amount of heat. Add more cayenne and chipotle powder if you like your seasoning extra hot!

Prep time 10 minutes
Makes about ½ cup (50 g)

2 tablespoons (15 g) chili powder
1 tablespoon black pepper
1 tablespoon ground cumin
1 tablespoon (18 g) sea salt
1 tablespoon coconut sugar (optional)
1 teaspoon onion powder

1 teaspoon garlic powder
1 teaspoon dried thyme
1 teaspoon chipotle powder
1 teaspoon smoked paprika
½ teaspoon cayenne pepper

Combine all the ingredients in an airtight container. Shake well and store at room temperature.

Cider BBQ Sauce

This sauce is especially good in pork and chicken dishes. It has just the right amount of sweetness, tanginess, and a hint of apple.

Prep time 10 minutes
Makes about 3 cups (750 g)

¾ cup (180 ml) unfiltered, unsweetened apple cider

¾ cup (180 ml) apple cider vinegar

1⅓ cup (327 g) tomato sauce

1 tablespoon plus 1 teaspoon (15 g) Dijon mustard

1 tablespoon plus 1 teaspoon (27 g) pure maple syrup

3 tablespoons (60 g) honey

1 clove garlic, minced

¾ teaspoon chili powder

¼ teaspoon cinnamon

¼ teaspoon salt

1 Whisk all ingredients together in a small saucepan and simmer for 30 minutes.

2 Store the sauce chilled in an airtight container for up to a month.

Balsamic BBQ Sauce

I found my favorite barbeque sauce recipe in an unlikely place—a cookbook by the famous Italian chef, Giada De Laurentiis. If you've watched even an hour of the Food Network, you've probably seen her face pop up. She's one of my favorites, and I adapted this recipe from her book, Giada's Kitchen, *and made it paleo by swapping out a few ingredients. It's still my favorite BBQ sauce!*

Prep time 10 minutes

Makes about 2 cups (500 g)

1 cup (235 ml) balsamic vinegar
1 8-ounce (227 g) can tomato sauce
3 tablespoons (60 g) honey
1 clove garlic, minced

2 tablespoons (30 ml) coconut aminos
1 tablespoon Dijon mustard
½ teaspoon sea salt
½ teaspoon freshly ground black pepper

1 Combine all of the ingredients in a small saucepan. Bring to a boil.

2 Reduce heat and simmer on medium-low for about 20 minutes, or until the sauce has thickened slightly and will coat the back of a spoon.

3 Remove the sauce from the heat and let it cool. Taste, and add more honey if you'd like it sweeter.

4 Store in an airtight container for up to a month.

Blackberry-Chipotle BBQ Sauce

I had intended to make a raspberry-chipotle barbecue sauce, but noticed the blackberries in the fridge. I made a sauce base, split it in two, and put one type of berry in each saucepan for a side-by-side test. After a blind testing, the whole family agreed that we all preferred the sauce with the blackberries. If you happen to have an allergy to blackberries or simply prefer the taste of raspberries, just swap the berries in the recipe. The raspberry sauce is also good!

Prep time 15 minutes
Makes about 3 cups (750 g)

1 15-ounce (425 g) can tomato sauce
⅓ cup (115 g) honey
½ cup (120 ml) red wine vinegar
¼ cup (60 ml) balsamic vinegar
2 cloves garlic, minced
2 tablespoons (40 g) pure maple syrup

1 teaspoon sea salt
½ teaspoon Applewood-flavored liquid smoke
2 ½ cups (225 g) fresh or frozen blackberries
1 chipotle pepper, from a can of chipotles in adobo sauce

1 In a medium saucepan, whisk together the tomato sauce, honey, vinegars, garlic, maple syrup, salt, and liquid smoke. Add the blackberries.

2 If you wish to take some heat out of the chipotle pepper, split it in half and scrape out most of the seeds. Mince the pepper and add it to the saucepan.

3 Bring the sauce to a boil, then reduce the heat and simmer for 20 minutes, stirring once or twice, until slightly thickened and reduced by about a third. If the berries haven't cooked down, smash them with a spoon or blend the sauce, preferably with an immersion blender. (You can also strain the seeds at this point, if you wish.)

4 Transfer to an airtight container (it fits perfectly in a pint-size mason jar), and chill until ready to use. The sauce should keep for about a month.

Easy Enchilada Sauce

It's fairly difficult to find store-bought enchilada sauce that doesn't have vegetable oil, sugar, or other undesirables. Luckily, making your own is incredibly easy—and it also freezes well.

Prep time 20 minutes
Makes about 2½ cups (665 g)

3 tablespoons (44 ml) avocado oil

¼ cup (30 g) chili powder

2 cups (475 ml) Simple Chicken Stock (page 280)

1 6-ounce (170-gram) can tomato paste

1 tablespoon tapioca flour

1 tablespoon (20 g) honey

1 teaspoon ground cumin

1 teaspoon dried oregano

¼ teaspoon sea salt

1 In a medium saucepan, heat the oil over medium-high heat. Add the chili powder and cook for 30 seconds.

2 Whisk in the remaining ingredients and bring to a boil. Reduce the heat to medium-low and simmer for about 15 minutes. The sauce should be smooth and slightly thickened.

3 Taste, and adjust the seasonings if necessary. If it seems too acidic to your taste, add another teaspoon or so of honey.

4 Use the sauce right away or transfer it to an airtight container and chill until ready to use.

Paleo Pesto

Paleo pesto is simply regular pesto without Parmesan cheese. I like adding some lemon juice to brighten the flavor, and it also keeps the pesto from browning for a few days. You can even freeze it in an ice-cube tray and have perfect-size portions to add to sauces or soups.

Prep time 15 minutes
Makes about ⅔ cup (173 g)

2 packed cups (172 g) fresh basil leaves (1 large or two small bunches)

⅓ cup (45 g) pine nuts

2 tablespoons (30 ml) freshly squeezed lemon juice

½ clove garlic, smashed

½ teaspoon sea salt

¼ teaspoon black pepper

⅓ cup (79 ml) extra-virgin olive oil

1 Place all of the ingredients except the oil into a food processor. Pulse until everything is minced well and combined.

2 While the machine is running, drizzle in the olive oil. Let it run for another 10 seconds or so, until it is thoroughly blended. Scrape down the sides and pulse it a few more times if necessary.

3 Transfer to an airtight container and use right away or cover and chill. It should keep for about 4 to 5 days.

ACKNOWLEDGMENTS

Thank you to the lovely folks at Harvard Common Press and Quarto for helping me make the jump from blogger to author, and for the beautiful job you did of organizing my recipes and scattered thoughts.

To my small army of recipe testers, thank you for your honesty, your critiques, your enthusiasm, and for helping me weed out the "iffy" recipes. And Lora, I'm pretty sure you've already eaten a third of what's in this book. Bless you, friend.

To my dear friends and readers at Perry's Plate: *You* are the reason I was able to have this opportunity. All those years of honing my recipe developing and photography techniques on my blog would not have been nearly as productive without your encouragement and comments. Blogging would surely be a lonely place without a community of food-loving friends. Thank you for being mine.

To my dear Peacock, to whom I send 1,000 texts per month and with whom I fall down every rabbit hole: Thank you for your faith in me and for reminding me to occasionally give my tiger a rest. You're the best.

To my amazing family: Thank you for teaching me to love good food and for instilling in me the importance of food traditions and memories—even if we sometimes eat fish tacos on Christmas (sorry, Grandma). There are some things I will eat for the rest of my life that will always remind of me of the tastes and smells from my childhood. Thank you for that long-lasting gift. And thank you to my in-laws, who raised an honest son who has such a discerning taste. I can always count on him for a good critique.

Oh, my sweet girls: You were my toughest critics, you know. I know you would have liked to have bacon and potatoes in every recipe, but we'll save that idea for another time. Thank you for letting me surprise you with something new every day and thank you for (sometimes) eating it a couple more times. Nothing gave me a boost of encouragement like six thumbs up from you while your baby brother enthusiastically shoved fistfuls of food in his mouth. I love you little people so much.

And Steve. I could not have done this without you. Thank you for encouraging me to chase this dream of mine and for always gently encouraging me (sometimes kicking and screaming) to be the healthiest, best version of myself. I'm a much better person because of you. And I still can't believe you washed all of those slow cookers every night. You're a keeper. Love you.

ABOUT THE AUTHOR

Natalie Perry is the cook, writer, and photographer behind the gluten free and paleo blog Perry's Plate, which she founded in 2008. Perry has been and remains a regular contributor to Ree Drummond's websites, first at the Tasty Kitchen Blog and now at Pioneer Woman: Food & Friends. Her work has also been featured online at Bon Appetit, Glamour, HuffPost Food, LDS Living, Gourmet Live, and The Kitchn, and in print in *Clean Eating* magazine. She lives with her chiropractor husband and four children in northern Nevada.

INDEX